# 50 SIMPLE WAYS
## TO S
## YOUR

D1404491

OTHER BOOKS BY BRUCE JOHNSON

*Knock On Wood*

*Tips for Refinishers*

*How to Make $20,000 a Year in Antiques & Collectibles*
*(Without Leaving Your Job)*

*The Official Identification and Price Guide*
*to the Arts and Crafts Movement*

*The Weekend Refinisher*

*The Wood Finisher*

# 50 SIMPLE WAYS TO SAVE YOUR HOUSE

## Bruce Johnson

**Ballantine Books** • **New York**

Sale of this book without a front cover may be unauthorized. If this book is coverless, it may have been reported to the publisher as "unsold or destroyed" and neither the author nor the publisher may have received payment for it.

NOTICE

The author and editors have worked to provide you with the most accurate and reliable information available. Nevertheless, each home is unique, and the problems you encounter may not always be resolved by the suggestions offered in this book. When in doubt, seek the advice of a qualified professional. Before undertaking any work, become familiar with your local building codes and related regulations. Brand names mentioned in this book are not necessarily endorsed by the author or publisher, nor does the omission of a similar product imply a criticism of any kind.

Copyright © 1995 by Bruce E. Johnson
Illustrations copyright © 1995 by Judith Cummins

All rights reserved under International and Pan-American Copyright Conventions. Published in the United States by Ballantine Books, a division of Random House, Inc., New York, and simultaneously in Canada by Random House of Canada Limited, Toronto.

Library of Congress Catalog Card Number: 94-94565

ISBN: 0-345-38504-7

Cover design by Judy Herbstman
Cover photo by George Kerrigan

Book design by Alex Jay/Studio J

Manufactured in the United States of America

First Edition: April 1995

10  9  8  7  6  5  4  3

To my mother and father,
whose lessons in self-reliance
will never be forgotten.

# CONTENTS

# 50 SIMPLE WAYS TO SAVE YOUR HOUSE

# INTRODUCTION

I'm not quite sure how it compares to the national average, but I took a moment one day to tally the number of different houses I have lived in over the course of my 44 years. As you might imagine, this didn't exactly amount to a major revelation, but I had never thought about them as a list. Instead, each one had always existed individually, with little or no relationship to the others. But when I wrote down each house and its construction date, I was amazed at the variety:

- two-story wooden foursquare (1911)
- one-story nondescript farmhouse (1928)
- series of brick apartment buildings (c. 1970)
- one-story wood ranch house (1976)
- two-story rehabilitated brick carriage house (1890)
- one-story wooden bungalow (1929)
- three-story brick Georgian (1914)

What each had in common, beginning with my parents' foursquare in Illinois and ending with the brick Georgian where I now live in North Carolina, is that I was involved in their repair and restoration, albeit sometimes against my wishes and my better judgment. You see, I was born to parents who are die-hard do-it-yourselfers. The idea of calling in a professional plumber, carpenter, electrician, or painter would have been as alien to my father as calling in the local sheriff to settle a dispute between my younger brother and me. In our family, if you couldn't do it yourself, it didn't need to be done.

Naturally, our reasoning was a bit flawed. My father eventually did relent, after much persuasion, and hired professional roofers to tear off and replace the shingles on our house. Today, my wife, Lydia, has convinced me that the built-in gutters on the roof are going to rot and fall off before I ever get them patched. I've also relented; after all, it is more than 30 feet up to some of those gutters. And if there is one thing I dislike more than hiring others to do something I know in my heart I could do myself, it's falling off a ladder. I did that once when I was working my way through college as a roofer, and it's something I've never quite managed to forget.

During the many years I have been responsible for the houses I have lived in, I have accumulated a number of helpful books on home repair and improvement. One thing do-it-yourselfers don't mind is learning from someone else's mistakes. It saves time and money, not to mention a few bumps and bruises to the ego, as well as the body. The problem I found with all the books I bought was that the authors were better at explaining how to repair something than they were at explaining how I could have avoided making that repair in the first place. Personally, I didn't want to jack up my house and rebuild the foundation on Saturday morning. What I wanted to know was what could have been done to prevent the foundation from deteriorating. If past owners had been told that gutters and downspouts were designed to save foundations, not roofs, they might have avoided a good deal of trouble.

With 44 years and seven houses behind me, I decided that the how-to manual I was looking for didn't exist. That's how this book came to be. With all the different styles of houses in this country and the hundreds of different problems lurking in each of them, I started and finished this book knowing that it could not solve every problem for every house and every homeowner. But it can help solve a few minor problems before they grow into major ones.

*Fifty Simple Ways to Save Your House* starts you off with how to conduct a home inspection and how to assemble your own inspection kit of common household tools you probably already own. An inspection gives you a clear picture of the condition of your home—what preventive measures and repairs are necessary.

Maintaining your home and avoiding costly repair bills require only a small investment in knowledge, time, and supplies. Here, I provide you with the knowledge. Each Home-Saving Guideline includes warning signs of typical, yet often overlooked, problems a homeowner can encounter; do's and don'ts that can help you avoid costly mistakes; and, of course, step-by-step instructions to repairs and maintenance.

Remember this: What distinguishes a do-it-yourselfer from a professional isn't the size of the tool belt, it's the size of the problem. Take care of a small problem today and you won't have to pay someone else to mend a big one tomorrow.

Good luck!

Bruce Johnson

# GETTING STARTED

The toughest part of any project is getting started. Fortunately for you, that hurdle has already been surmounted when you flipped open this book and started reading. You've already taken the first step toward saving your house.

Saving it from what?

- Wood rot
- Decay
- Fungi
- Termites
- Water damage

- A buckled foundation
- Cracked plaster
- Sagging floors
- Leaky roofs

And the list goes on. As you can see, the variety of invaders that can ruin your home's beauty and undermine its structure can be overwhelming for anyone to tackle. But I'm going to show you simple preventive measures that can save you money and add years to your home's life.

No house lasts forever, but some come a lot closer than others. The difference between Thomas Jefferson's Monticello and the thousands of houses that were also built in 1770 but didn't survive isn't how much it cost to build them, but how well they were maintained. That is, how well problems were *prevented*.

If you anticipate problems before they happen, or spot and correct them when they are still a minor inconvenience or annoyance, you need only a small investment in time and materials, simple, straightforward instructions, and the basic tools. You probably already own most of the tools, and those you don't can be bought, borrowed, or rented.

This chapter gets you started with Home-Saving Guidelines 1 through 5.

# #1
# Assemble a basic home inspection and repair kit.

Most of us have more tools than we realize. The problem is, our tools are never where we are, at least not when we need them. Not long ago, I needed my utility knife to trim a section of plastic drainage pipe I was installing along the east side of our house. We had been having problems with rainwater running down the steps leading to the basement sliding glass doors, and I decided to divert the water before it reached the first step. The 20-foot section of perforated pipe was longer than I needed, but the utility knife I try to keep in the toolbox on my basement workbench wasn't there.

By the time I found the knife, my five-year-old son and our Gordon setter had discovered the drainage pipe coiled in the yard. The snakelike pipe kept them—and me—entertained for about 30 minutes, which is better than I can do by myself with either one of them. Nevertheless, my one-hour project was quickly escalating into an all-afternoon project. While the two of them played with the drainage pipe, I tracked down my tape measure, a hammer, some wooden stakes, a screwdriver, and the spade.

While I was locating my tools, I realized that very few of my home repair projects ever take place in my workshop. Those that do generally require very specialized tools, such as varnish and stain brushes, no. 0000 steel wool, a soldering gun, the drill press, or an orbital sander. Most of my projects take place somewhere in or around the house, but most of my tools are generally scattered about my workbench or hanging on the pegboard above it. In those rare instances when I can immediately find the tools I need, I invariably end up making a dozen trips to the basement to pluck yet another tool from the wall. As proud as I am of my neat display of tools, it just doesn't make much sense for home repairs.

What does make sense is a basic home inspection and repair tool kit. It needn't be elaborate or fancy, nor does it have to hold every tool you own. If it just contains basic tools, then it wouldn't be necessary to make several trips back and forth between project and workshop. Keep the tool kit in the workshop, and you won't have the opposite problem when you're at the workbench regluing a chair rung or rewiring a table lamp.

When I began assembling my basic home inspection and repair kit, I discovered that I had more tools than I thought. I found tools in the trunk of my car, on a shelf in the garage, scattered about the basement, even in a desk drawer. After I determined which tools I needed in my kit, I still had plenty to fill up my pegboard.

No two home inspection and repair tool kits are identical. The contents of your own kit are determined by your skill level, your personal interests, and the typical problems you encounter. The toolbox itself can range from a sturdy cardboard box to a handcrafted oak tool chest. Plastic dishpans may not have a handle, but they are waterproof, which makes them ideal for plumbing projects and for holding cans of varnish or stain; they also don't scratch hardwood floors. Rubber and plastic tool caddies are inexpensive and popular. They have all of the advantages of a plastic dishpan, along with compartments for tools and a convenient handle. Traditional metal toolboxes seem to be declining in popularity, because they are susceptible to rust and can scratch a floor or counter. In addition, the closed-lid style is designed for smaller, flat tools and won't hold a portable drill or a bulky extension cord.

Regardless of your choice of a toolbox, your basic home inspection and repair kit should include the following:

| | |
|---|---|
| __ Flashlight | __ Pliers |
| __ Cloth or leather gloves | __ Crescent wrench |
| __ Safety glasses | __ Assortment of screws and nails |
| __ Claw hammer | __ Utility knife |
| __ Nail punch | __ Woodworker's glue |
| __ Tape measure | __ Vise grips |
| __ Regular screwdrivers | __ Putty knife |
|    (small and medium tips) | __ Circuit tester |
| __ Phillips screwdrivers | __ Flat pry bar |
|    (small and medium tips) | __ File |

Nearby, but not necessarily in your tool kit, you should have:

| | |
|---|---|
| __ Rechargeable drill | __ Toilet plunger |
| __ Assorted bits | __ Wood rasp |

__ Hacksaw
__ Handsaw
__ Pipe wrench
__ Wire brush
__ Assorted clamps
__ Crowbar
__ Paint scraper
__ Level

__ Assortment of paintbrushes
__ Assortment of sandpaper
__ Stepladder
__ First-aid kit
__ Trowel
__ Caulking gun and assortment
of caulking tubes
__ Long rope

TIP: The most annoying problem associated with a stepladder is where to put your tools while you are perched on one. The top step (which isn't safe to balance on) isn't designed to hold *anything*, unless you make a few modifications. Here are three inexpensive options for making your stepladder more user-friendly:

1. Cut the strings off a cloth nail apron and tack the apron to the edge of the top step. The cloth pockets can hold screws, nails, a tape measure, and small tools.
2. Drill a few 1/2-inch holes in the top step to hold your screwdrivers and pliers. But don't forget, too many holes will weaken the board.
3. Screw a plastic or metal pan, such as an old cake pan, to the top step. Besides providing a handy place for your tools and parts, it reminds you not to use the top of the ladder as a step.

## Why Not Rent It?

With the growing popularity of tool rental centers, homeowners should consider alternatives to purchasing any major tool. Well-stocked rental centers are as apt to carry 40-foot extension ladders as they are floor buffers, power sanders, and circular saws. Consider, for a moment, some of the advantages rental centers offer.

First, rental centers carry professional equipment. Most homeowners buy only medium-quality tools, destined to quit when the going gets tough. Second, rental centers service their equipment and shoulder the cost of any repairs. Most homeowners don't know how to maintain, let alone repair, major equipment, and they discover too late that it costs more to repair an inexpensive belt sander than to buy a new one. Third, rental centers have storage space. Most homeowners are short on space, especially a dry, safe storage area.

Finally, most homeowners don't use major tools, such as table saws, floor buffers, and hammer drills, enough to justify the purchase price.

Besides, if you did, your neighbors would all borrow them.

# #2
# Conduct your first home inspection.

Most of us can rattle off important dates and information regarding our lives just as easily as we can name the days of the week: what year we were born, the make of our first car, when we graduated from high school, what year we were married, the names and ages of our children, perhaps even which month our dog gets its annual checkup.

But what if someone asks you some important details about your home, such as the year it was built, the age of the wiring and plumbing systems, the year the roof was installed, or the last time the heating system was inspected?

Each and every home, from a double-wide trailer in Montana to the White House, has a history that very definitely is affecting its present and its future. Unfortunately, most of us never take the time to learn our home's history, even though it can save us money, time, and grief. And, on a lighter note, it can help us appreciate the most important structure in our lives.

Begin collecting, organizing, and documenting the history of your home in a three-ring notebook. Label separate pages for each room of the house: kitchen, dining room, living room, downstairs bathroom, basement, master bedroom, and so on. In addition, assign pages to plumbing, heating, and electrical systems, as well as to the roof, the exterior, the yard, attic, garage, porch, and major appliances. The categories should be custom-tailored to your home's specifications. Unlike a bound spiral notebook, a three-ring binder lets you add more pages and move sections around.

Your notebook should contain as much information as is available under each category. Begin by writing down all you know about each room in your house, from the color of the paint on the walls to the age of the carpet. Sketch a drawing of the room, noting important measurements. How many electrical outlets are there? Do they all work? In what condition is the finish around the windows? Do the windows work properly? Are there any cracks in the walls? Any stains on the ceiling? Is there a fireplace? If so, when was the last time it was cleaned and inspected? Leave nothing out, including questions to which you don't know the answers. In some categories, such as major appliances, all that matters is the most recent installation, but in other categories, such as your roof, knowing what type of roofing had originally been applied or how many layers of shingles are on your house right now will help you make future decisions.

Your notebook should also contain items you want to change, from the 14-year-old wallpaper to the window that is painted shut to the antiquated two-prong electrical outlet behind the couch. Later, the book will serve as a repository for estimates, lists of building supplies, names of craftspersons, sources for materials, contacts, deadlines, brand names, and code numbers. Remember: Yesterday's project is today's history. Write it down so you won't forget it.

### Inspection Checkpoints

Additional questions will become apparent as you read through the various sections of this book, but to get started, consider these:

| Section | Checkpoint Questions |
|---|---|
| Roof | What type of roofing material was used? |
| | When was it installed? |
| | What condition is the roof in? |
| | Is the chimney in good repair? |
| | Is the flashing around the chimney and vent pipes intact? |
| | Do the gutters leak? |
| Exterior | What type of siding is on the house? |
| | Is it original? |
| | When was the siding installed? |
| | What condition is it in? |
| | Any signs of paint failure? |
| | Any loose, split, or missing boards or trim? |

Any gaps between windows or doors and the siding?

What type of foundation does the house have?

What condition is the mortar in?

Any signs of termite activity around the foundation?

**Basement**

Any cracks in the basement walls?

Are there signs of moisture on the walls or floor?

Do you smell mold?

Do any of the floor joists sag?

Is there any indication of insect damage?

When was the house last treated for termites?

**Decks and Porches**

How old is the deck or porch?

Are there any signs of sagging or cracked floorboards?

Is the paint peeling?

Does the water bead on the deck or porch after a rainstorm?

Do any of the wood supports come in contact with the ground?

Is the crawl space well ventilated?

**Heating System**

What type of heating system does your home have?

When was it installed?

When was it last inspected?

Has it ever failed? If so, how often and under what conditions?

**Plumbing**

Are the pipes in good condition?

Are there signs of leakage around or under any of the joints?

Are there any slow-moving drains?

| *Section* | *Checkpoint Questions* |
|---|---|
| Electrical | When was the electrical system installed or upgraded?<br>Do fuses blow or circuit breakers trip easily?<br>Is the wiring neat and organized?<br>Any stripped insulation on the wires?<br>Are there any bare or exposed wires?<br>Are there any dead outlets throughout the house? |
| Interior<br>(complete on a<br>room-by-room basis) | |
| Paint and/or<br>Wallpaper | How old is the most recent coat?<br>Is it peeling in places?<br>Has it faded?<br>Has it discolored?<br>Are there any water stains? |
| Plaster and<br>Plasterboard | Is it the original plaster or plasterboard?<br>Is it cracked?<br>Are the seams of the plasterboard visible?<br>Are there any water stains?<br>Has either the plaster or the plasterboard been heavily patched?<br>Are any pieces missing? |
| Floors: Wood | What type of wood is the floor?<br>Is the finish still intact?<br>Is the finish badly scratched?<br>Has the finish worn off the boards in traffic lanes?<br>Has the color of the wood faded?<br>Are any of the boards warped or water-stained?<br>Do they squeak when you walk across them?<br>Have any been poorly repaired or replaced? |

Floors: Vinyl

Is the floor covering badly worn?
Is there evidence of chipping at the
    doorways?
Are there any humps in the vinyl?
Can you detect any soft spots in the
    floor beneath the covering?
Has it been poorly repaired?
Are there water stains in the floor
    covering?

Floors: Tile

Is the glaze on the tiles scratched or
    chipped?
Is the grout between the tiles cracked?
Has it begun to crumble?
Are any tiles loose or missing?
Have any been replaced?

Floors: Concrete

Has the concrete begun to crumble in
    places?
Is it badly cracked?
Are there water stains in the concrete?
Has the concrete been patched?
Is there a gap between the concrete and
    the wall?

Electrical Outlets

Does each outlet have a cover?
Are there any outlets that do not work?
Are there any loose outlets?
Is there any sign of scorching on the
    outlet cover?
Are any of the outlets the older, non-
    grounded (two-prong) variety?

Windows

Does each window work properly?
Are any windows painted shut?
Does each window have a working latch?
Are any panes of glass cracked?
Is the caulking intact around each pane
    of glass?
Has condensation or rain made the
    wood sill soft and weak?

| *Section* | *Checkpoint Questions* |
| --- | --- |
| Stairs | Are any of the treads cracked? |
| | Does any stair sag as you step on it? |
| | Are any spindles loose or missing? |
| | Are the treads slippery from too much wax? |
| | Is the carpet loose and dangerous? |
| | Are there any protruding nail heads? |

TIP: Be sure to document any major changes you make to your home with photographs. Photos can help a sales- or craftsperson visualize what you are working on and how you hope to improve it. Photographs can also be used to document any loss covered by your insurance company.

## Do You Live in a Historic House?

Living in a house built before 1939 or in one of any age that is unique, was designed by an important architect, or was previously occupied by a historic figure brings with it added responsibilities. Renovations and other improvements must be considered with the structure's original appearance in mind if you hope to preserve the structural integrity of the building, as well as its increased value, which often accompanies well-maintained and properly restored historic homes. Hastily conceived additions and demolitions can permanently alter a historic house in such a way as to lessen its resale value and its aesthetic beauty.

Before undertaking any significant alterations to a structure, you should first study the home's history thoroughly. Begin in the county courthouse, hall of records, or government agency where deeds are recorded and stored. The deeds contain the names of previous owners as far back as the year your home was constructed. Records of building permits can also help date any changes to the structure. With a list of owners and sales dates, you can further research your home and its previous occupants at the public library, where you can find annual directories, newspaper articles, and detailed insurance maps.

Among the most important sources of information are the descendants of the original owners. I spent nearly a year casually flipping through stacks of postcards in local antiques shops hoping to find a vintage photograph of our 1914 home. Then, one of the dealers casually asked me if I had met Marjorie Chipman yet.

"Who?" I asked.

"Marjorie Chipman, the daughter of Herbert Miles, the man who built your house. She grew up in it, you know."

I didn't know, but less than a mile from our home there lived the 92-year-old woman who had been raised and married in our house. Over the course of the next few weeks, we became good friends. For the first time in more than four decades she visited our home, along with her 87-year-old brother, and together they pointed out changes that had been made and details that had survived since 1914. In a few weeks, they had gathered for us a collection of more than 40 photographs spanning the first 30 years of our home's history. Their family photographs enabled us to duplicate missing railings on the porch, identify trim that had been removed from the living room, spot interior French doors that had been removed, and undertake a proper and accurate restoration. Without the photographs, our home could never have been restored to its original appearance.

# #3
# Run a safety inspection.

Before you become too deeply involved in the intricacies of peeling paint, damp basements, or worn-out flashing, you must make sure that your home is a safe, secure structure. Not only does this dramatically reduce the odds that your home will be damaged or destroyed by fire, for instance, but it also ensures the safety of your family and guests.

The checklist below has been organized by different rooms or sections of a house, but bear in mind that many of these tips apply to several of, if not all, the rooms in your home.

| *Section* | *Checkpoints* |
| --- | --- |
| Basement | __ Smoke detector installed in critical areas. |
| | __ Any used rags spread out to dry. |
| | __ All electrical outlets covered. |
| | __ Circuit breaker box well marked. |
| | __ No old cans of paint or wood-finishing products being stored. |
| | __ No flammable liquids stored in the same area as the furnace or hot water heater. |
| | __ No gasoline stored in the basement. |
| | __ Lumber stored above the ground or concrete floor. |
| | __ No trash accumulated. |
| | __ Trash cans conveniently located. |
| | __ Any windows and outside doors secured against break-ins. |
| | __ Fire extinguisher located at bottom of the stairs. |
| | __ Cabinets containing toxic chemicals are locked. |

Kitchen

___ Fire extinguisher nearby.
___ All dangerous cleansers and chemicals stored in locked cabinets.
___ No paper products stored near the
stove.
___ No cookies or children's snacks
stored near the stove.
___ Smoke detector installed.
___ No overloaded receptacles.
___ Cabinet doors and drawers containing knives, cleaning supplies, and
plastic trash bags secured with
childproof latches.

Bedrooms

___ Telephone located next to bed,
with emergency numbers written
down or stored on automatic dial
memory.
___ No frayed or overloaded extension
cords.
___ No smoking permitted in bed.
___ Flashlight in nightstand.

Attic

___ No accumulations of trash.
___ No evidence of faulty wiring.
___ No boxes stored over old wiring.
___ Chimney bricks and mortar in good
condition. No odor of smoke during
heating season.
___ No signs of rodent activity.
___ Smoke detector installed.
___ No evidence of water damage.

Living Quarters

___ No nonfunctional outlets.
___ No overloaded extension cords.
___ Smoke detectors installed.
___ Adequate space between the back of
television or stereo and the wall.
___ Fireplace screen and damper in
place.
___ All door and window locks func-
tioning properly.

# #4
# Recognize the hazards of lead-based paint.

In recent years, health officials have determined that lead, once standard in gasoline, plumbing fixtures, furniture finishes, pottery glazes, and house paints, can cause permanent brain damage, especially in young children. If your home was built before 1978, there is a distinct possibility that it may contain paint with highly poisonous lead pigments or driers. If it was built before 1950, that possibility becomes a likely probability.

Lead-based paint is suspected of being the prime cause of lead poisoning, but not necessarily in the way that you might imagine. Contrary to popular belief, the majority of young children suffering from lead poisoning did not eat paint chips. Instead, they inhaled dust caused by the improper removal of lead-based paint. In many instances, homeowners have actually taken a small problem and, through improper removal of old paint, created a dangerous situation.

Young children are extremely susceptible to even small amounts of lead. When exposed, children under the age of six, including fetuses, can suffer permanent brain damage, loss of intelligence, reduced attention span, degenerated hearing and speaking, learning disabilities, and stunted growth.

Adults are also susceptible. Among the symptoms associated with lead poisoning in adults are chronic irritability, high blood pressure, nerve damage, kidney failure, and deteriorated muscle control. Lead poisoning can also be fatal.

Many times it is not easy to identify lead-based paint. Most older homes that were originally finished with such paint have since been repainted. If your home was built before 1950, chances are it originally was painted with lead-based products, which are probably still there. Fortunately, lead-based paint does not spontaneously produce fumes that can seep through subsequent layers of latex or oil-based paint. Since the lead does not readily break down, however, it remains hidden under the more recent layers. When the paint is scraped or sanded, or when it begins to peel, the lead is released into the air. If you live in a house built before 1978, carefully check for the following:

- exposed old paint
- peeling paint of any age
- fine paint dust in windows
- old paint that is "chalking," or turning into dust
- evidence that lead-based paint has been scraped or sanded by a previous owner

Do-it-yourself lead test kits are available, but they are not as reliable as professional or laboratory tests. Most companies, in fact, advise homeowners to use the services of a licensed lead-based paint inspector. One brand, Lead Check, relies on a lead-reactive dye applied through a porous tip. When the dye comes in contact with lead, it immediately turns a pinkish red color. Critics of do-it-yourself tests question the kits' ability to detect small amounts of lead, but most agree that the higher-quality kits are effective tools for identifying dangerous levels of lead.

Unfortunately, there is no safe and easy way to remove lead-based paint, especially for the do-it-yourselfer. Improper methods only magnify the problem, releasing microscopic particles of lead dust or lead fumes into the air, where they float—odorless, tasteless, and invisible—waiting to be inhaled. The particles do not dissolve, but settle in carpets, on clothes, or in food. Large paint removal projects should be turned over to licensed professionals who are well recommended. Even then, it's a good idea to plan your family vacation while the workers are in your home. It is possible to undertake a small paint removal project, such as removing peeling paint from a window frame, provided you are willing to follow *every* safety precaution recommended here and by professionals in the field. Failure to do so can mean that your entire home could be contaminated with lead dust, placing your family in a dangerous situation that will not disappear over time.

If you suspect that you or your child has been exposed to lead dust or fumes during a recent remodeling or restoration project, contact your family physician or local health department immediately to inquire about a blood test.

## Lead Poisoning Warning Signs

### In Children

- loss of appetite
- stomach pains
- reduced energy level
- insomnia
- constipation
- reduced attention span

### In Adults

- headaches
- dizziness
- irritability
- loss of weight
- numbness
- nausea

### In Household Pets

- vomiting
- drowsiness
- unexplained death

## Lead-based Paint Do's and Don'ts

### Do

- have your pre–1978 home tested for lead-based paint before beginning any remodeling project. The Yellow Pages or your local health department should be able to provide the names of qualified testing firms and laboratories.
- remove any older painted doors or woodwork and have them stripped by a professional paint-removing company.
- dampen any suspected lead paint chips or dust with a fine mist of water, being careful not to stir up any more dust. Wear a respirator and rubber gloves while you wipe up the chips and dust using a damp rag. Place the chips, dust, and rag in a plastic garbage bag, then seal and place the first bag inside a second for additional protection against tearing. Contact your local sanitation department for proper disposal.

• use professionals for large lead-based paint removal projects.

## Don't

• use sanders, scrapers, sandblasters, or heat guns to remove even small amounts of lead-based paint, since they can release highly toxic lead dust or lead fumes into the air.
• sweep or vacuum suspected dust. This will only spread the finer particles throughout your house.
• track lead-based paint dust into other areas of your home.
• rely totally on do-it-yourself lead checks. Some brands do not detect small, but potentially hazardous, levels of lead. When in doubt, get a second opinion.

## How to Remove Lead-based Paint (Small Projects Only!)

| *Steps* | *Tools and Materials* |
|---|---|
| 1. Work outdoors or in a well-ventilated room. Tape furnace filters over the fan to capture any lead-based paint dust that might be produced. | fans<br>furnace filters<br>duct tape |
| 2. Allow no children, pregnant women, or women who are nursing in the area until after the final cleanup is completed. | |
| 3. Wear a certified respirator guaranteed to filter out dangerous fumes. | respirator |
| 4. Wear eye protection, heavy-duty rubber gloves, and old clothes that you can throw away if necessary. | goggles<br>rubber gloves<br>old clothes |
| 5. Completely seal off the room from the rest of the house. Cover any furniture, fixtures, and carpets. | plastic sheets<br>tape |
| 6. Apply a non-methylene chloride paint and varnish remover according to the manufacturer's instructions. When the paint is soft, carefully scrape off using a putty knife. Use steel wool where a putty knife cannot reach. Wipe dry. | paint and varnish<br>   remover<br>(non-methylene<br>   chloride)<br>putty knife<br>rags<br>coarse steel wool |
| 7. Strip the wood a second time to avoid | |

*Steps*                                                    *Tools and Materials*

sanding any remaining paint. *Never* sand lead-based paint or strip with a heat gun. Strip as many times as necessary to remove all of the paint from the wood while the paint is wet (to avoid creating any dust).

8. After the wood has dried, sand lightly by hand, while wearing a respirator, rubber gloves, and safety glasses.

sandpaper
respirator
rubber gloves
safety glasses

9. Dampen the wood dust and wipe up with a damp rag. Dispose of the rags in a plastic garbage bag. Call your local sanitation department for specific disposal instructions.

water mister
damp rags
garbage bag

10. Do not eat, drink, or smoke in the work area. Do not allow other persons to enter the work area.

11. Do not walk through the rest of your house wearing work clothes or shoes. Wash items thoroughly at the end of each day. (TIP: Wear disposable coveralls.)

12. Clean up the entire room using damp rags.

bucket
water
rags or mop
phosphate
    detergent

13. Collect all loosened paint in a plastic garbage bag. Include gloves, dried rags, plastic sheets, and work clothes. Take care to roll up the plastic sheets to avoid losing any paint dust or chips.

plastic garbage
    bag

14. Afterward, seal, label, and dispose of the bag according to local regulations.

tape
label

15. Remop the floor 24 hours later to remove any dust that may have settled.

mop
bucket
water
phosphate
    detergent

TIP: Painting over lead paint is *not* considered a solution to this problem. It may, in fact, give the next owners a false sense of security, misleading them into scraping, sanding, or stripping both layers of paint, thereby exposing themselves to the dangers of lead poisoning.

## Lead in Your Water?

Old paint is not the only source of lead. Once researchers concluded that lead poisoning causes learning disorders and behavioral problems in small children, the search for other sources of lead began in earnest. As a result, scientists now agree that approximately 20 percent of our combined lead intake comes from drinking water.

While, in recent years, the amount of lead present in our environment has steadily declined as stricter regulations have taken effect, additional research has revealed that even a microscopic amount of lead in the bloodstream can diminish a child's IQ. Pregnant women are also at risk, for even though adults have a higher resistance to lead poisoning than children, the passage of blood from the mother to the fetus can cause lead poisoning in the unborn child.

Tests have demonstrated that nearly all rainwater, well water, and water leaving a water treatment plant is virtually lead-free. Yet the tap water in a significant number of homes has been found to contain high levels of the toxic metal. Further investigation has revealed that lead can enter the water supply in three ways: (1) from lead water supply pipes leading from the service main to individual residences, (2) from lead solder used to connect copper water pipes inside the home, and (3) from brass water faucets containing as much as 8 percent lead (by weight).

The lead in the pipes, solder, and faucets enters the water through a process called leaching. The amount of lead which leaches into the water is determined by several complex factors, including the length of time the water stands in the pipes as well as the chemicals and minerals present in the water. Homeowners who are burdened with "hard" water with a high mineral content are often saved the worry of lead contamination, for the minerals in the water can coat the insides of the pipes and form a barrier between the water and the toxic lead. Acidic water that is also "soft" or low in minerals is more likely to attract lead from pipes, soldered joints, and brass faucets.

Only a certified testing agency can determine how much, if any, lead is present in your water. Every home should be tested, especially if there are small children or pregnant women present. Call your water utility, for some cities offer a free water testing service. If not, the staff should have the names of firms that they recommend. The cost is often less than twenty dollars.

If your water does contain lead, immediately have any child under the age of six tested for lead poisoning by your physician. Depending on the amount of lead in your water system, the testing agency may make several recommendations, including:

- running your drinking and cooking water for one to two minutes if it has been standing undisturbed in the pipes for more than six hours
- using bottled water for cooking and drinking
- hiring a plumber to resolder the lead solder joints in your home supply system with nonlead solder
- meeting with the water utility to determine if the service lines are lead and at whose cost they could be replaced
- installing a lead removal system in your home (for additional information on lead removal systems, see *Consumer Reports*, February 1993)

Owners of newer homes should not be lulled into believing that lead poisoning is a problem only old house owners have to deal with. Lead solder was not outlawed until 1987 and some plumbers may have continued to use their supply of lead solder after that date. In the city of Chicago, lead water service pipes were *required* by the city building code as recently as 1985. Many large, older cities, including Chicago, New York, Boston, and Washington, are plagued with lead water pipes still in active service. And while, statistically, lead-tainted water is not considered a widespread national problem, for those individuals whose children have been poisoned, the problem is serious.

# #5
# Fight fungi with simple, proven methods.

One of the greatest enemies of the wood in our homes is decay caused by fungi. And while there are various forms of fungi, nearly all begin as airborne spores that land where they find their three basic requirements of life: oxygen, moisture, and food. Without all three, the fungi simply cannot take root and spread.

Oxygen is the easiest for the fungi to obtain. Food is readily available as well; the fungi can feed upon the cell walls of either living or deceased trees or even kiln-dried lumber. Whether the fungi feed upon a log lying in the forest or the siding attached to your house is determined by the availability of moisture. Without it, the fungi simply cannot survive.

Moisture literally surrounds your home, but if you can control and channel it, the wood that gives your home its strength will not be exposed to decay-causing fungi. Moisture, however, does not simply disappear without some careful planning, from the gutters along your roof to the exhaust fan in your bathroom to the ventilation windows under your porch.

The best thing you can do to prevent the growth of fungi is to first study the means by which moisture is diverted away from your home. Begin at the roof, where the shingles, flashing, and gutters work together to direct rainwater toward the downspouts. Inspect the siding, especially directly underneath the eaves and gutters, around downspouts, and over windows and doors. And make sure that rainwater does not simply fall next to the foundation. It should be piped several feet away. Check, too, if rainwater is splashing against the foundation and the siding, a sure sign that either gutters are needed or those you have are plugged with debris.

Remember: If you keep the wood dry, the fungi that cause it to decay will never be a problem.

## Fungi Warning Signs

- water stains on siding or beams
- peeling or blistered paint
- soft, spongy wood
- moss, mold, or mildew growing on wood siding or trim

## Do's and Don'ts to Fighting Fungi

### Do

- realize moisture is the cause of numerous major house problems. Don't take it lightly.
- frequently check areas that are never in the sun.
- install vents in soffits that remain damp for months at a time.
- use mildew-resistant paint in troublesome areas.
- keep vegetation trimmed back to increase the air circulation necessary to dry out the wood.
- learn to recognize wood's unprotected end grain, which is highly vulnerable to moisture and fungi.

### Don't

- forget that moisture can penetrate an exterior wall from the inside, especially from high-humidity rooms, such as bathrooms and laundry rooms. Provide ventilation inside these rooms if unexplained warning signs are appearing on the exterior.
- assume that water repellents prevent fungi from growing in wood that is continually damp. Eliminate the source of the moisture and only use a water repellent as an insurance policy.
- let wood remain in contact with the ground; it can soak up moisture like a dry sponge.

## Steps to Eliminating Fungi and Decay

*Steps*                                    *Tools and Materials*

1.  Take a walk around your house, looking for warning signs of moisture and potential fungi growth.

*Steps*                                    *Tools and Materials*

2. Determine the source of moisture that
   has caused the warning signs you find.

3. Probe the wood to determine the          screwdriver, awl,
   extent of the damage.                        or long nail

4. If necessary, repair or replace the wood.

5. Apply a water repellent to any           commercial water
   exposed end grain, gapped joints, or         repellent or a
   bare wood.                                   homemade
                                                formula
                                                (see sidebar)
                                             brush
                                             rubber gloves
                                             eye protection

6. Repeat as necessary.

---

TIP: Check the ingredients in any water repellent you use.
Those chemicals with the prefix *penta* are highly toxic and
should be handled only by trained professionals.

---

### But What About Mold and Mildew?

Mold and mildew should not be confused with decay-
causing fungi, for unlike fungi, mold and mildew do not
actually feed upon wood cells. They do, however, thrive
in the same environment and can be warning signs of the
potential for fungi.

   Left unchecked, mold and mildew can leave semi-
permanent stains on wood, release a musty odor into the
air, and destroy such items as fabric and paper. A mild
case of mildew generally can be eradicated with a solution of trisodium phosphate dissolved in warm water.
One cup per gallon of water is a standard formula, but
don't hesitate to adjust it to fit your particular situation.
If trisodium phosphate isn't available, you can substitute
a strong detergent, such as Spic & Span or Borax.

   For more severe cases, including stains left by the
mold or mildew, mix a solution of household bleach and
clean, warm water. Since household bleach is already

heavily diluted, a ratio of one quart per gallon is not too strong. Nevertheless, you do need to protect shrubs, as well as your skin and eyes, from the mold-killing solution. After scrubbing a section of wood, rinse it thoroughly with clean water to prevent the bleach from leaving streaks on the paint.

But will the mold or mildew return? Yes, if you treat only the symptoms and not the problem. Once the bleach residue evaporates, the mold and mildew will return, provided they still find moisture, warm temperatures, shade, and food.

If you want to avoid biannual scrubbings with bleach and trisodium phosphate, change the environment where you find the mold and mildew growing. Eliminate the moisture, increase the air circulation, and let in the sunlight.

## The Do-It-Yourself Water Repellent

You can buy water repellents at most hardware, paint, and home maintenance stores—or you can mix your own. I have done both and, to be perfectly honest, I can't tell the difference between the wood I treated with the commercial blend and that which I treated with my own mix.

A water repellent is simply a penetrating sealer that prevents the pores of the wood from absorbing excessive amounts of water. Unlike a surface finish that dries on top of the wood, a water repellent is absorbed into the wood's pores, leaving few resins on the surface. That explains, in part, why commercial water repellents are so thin.

There are several formula variations of do-it-yourself water repellents, most of which are very similar, if not superior, to some of the commercial products. Since it would make little sense to treat lumber with a water-based water repellent, most formulas rely on mineral spirits (paint thinner) or turpentine as the solvent.

Here, then, are three basic formulas for you to consider. Adjust the units of measure to fit the size of your project.

Note: "Boiled linseed oil" is a product, not a process. You should never attempt to boil raw linseed oil to make boiled linseed oil, for doing so may result in a fire. Instead, purchase boiled linseed oil in a ready-to-use can.

*Formula A*

   1 quart boiled linseed oil
   2 quarts turpentine

*Formula B*

   1 quart boiled linseed oil
   1 quart mineral spirits

*Formula C*

   2 quarts mineral spirits
   2 cups spar varnish

Although you can save any leftover water repellent, why take the chance that someone is going to knock it over or mistake it for something else? Play it safe by using it up. A quick inspection of your property is sure to reveal some wood in need of extra protection.

Afterward, immediately clean your brush with mineral spirits and place any rags in a container of water until you have the opportunity to spread them out in the sun (away from children and pets) to completely dry, cure, and harden before you dispose of them in a metal trash can away from any structures.

# FROM THE TOP

Your roof is the umbrella that protects everything and everyone in your home. While it might not be as obvious as the missing spindle in the staircase or the crack in the dining room wall, your roof must always be a top priority in any home improvement plans. Ignore it, and you will awake some dark and stormy night to the sound of dripping water. Pretend it doesn't need any special attention, and you will come home to find the floor covered with what used to be the kitchen ceiling.

The purpose of the Home-Saving Guidelines in this section is to keep the ceiling where it belongs and to prevent all of the serious problems associated with roofs of every style, type, and material. A leaky roof causes more trouble than most homeowners can even imagine: failed exterior paint, peeling interior paint, decayed rafters, warped floors, ruined plaster, even a wet basement or a buckled foundation.

So this is where you start—at the top!

This chapter includes Home-Saving Guidelines 6 through 12.

# #6
# Clean your gutters and downspouts twice a year.

Most of the tens of thousands of gallons of water that fall on your roof during the course of a year are guided safely away from your house through a system of gutters and downspouts. Gutters generally are attached to the edge of the roof or built into the roof itself. Built-in gutters are more often found on older homes, while hung gutters, either steel, aluminum, copper, or plastic, encircle most twentieth-century houses. Either style can provide an effective means of guiding the water safely away from your house, provided, of course, that (1) the gutters do not leak and (2) the gutters and downspouts are not plugged.

What many homeowners do not realize is that a plugged or leaky gutter or downspout can be worse than none at all. Some homes, in fact, can survive without gutters. To do so, the ground beneath the gutterless roof must slope away from the house so that the water does not have a chance to seep through the foundation and into the basement. A plugged gutter or downspout, however, blocks the flow of water, forcing it against the soffit, roof sheathing, rafter ends, and exterior wall siding. Since these boards often never have a chance to dry out, they soon begin to rot, leading to an expensive and time-consuming repair.

The best way to avoid a costly repair bill is to check and clean your gutters and downspouts twice a year. If you have large trees hanging over any portion of your roof, you will need to clean your gutters more often, especially in the fall, when wet leaves are more apt to plug your system. A spring cleaning is also in order, since dead twigs, seed pods, bird nests, and shingle granules can also accumulate and cause problems.

Most gutter-cleaning projects begin with a ladder. It is never advisable to attempt to clean a gutter while perched precariously on the roof. With all your weight leaning forward, it takes but a small gust of wind or a slippery shingle to send you over the edge. If you are unsteady on a ladder, then this is a job you should supervise from the ground rather than attempt yourself. Regardless who is on it, be careful when positioning a ladder. Finding a proper resting place for the top of the ladder may prove difficult, as you can damage a hung gutter by placing your weight and that of the ladder against it. Ladder ends can also damage your home's siding. Stabilizer bars, purchased or rented, attached to the top of the ladder protect your home's siding and provide you with a safe ladder angle for reaching the gutters.

Cleaning out the debris from a gutter doesn't require specialized equipment. In fact, chisels, scrapers, or putty knives can puncture or damage a gutter. The best tool for the job is your hand, but since gutters can be loaded with thorns, old roofing nails, sharp granules, and exposed metal seams, you must wear gloves. Regular garden gloves are fine for dry debris, but heavy-duty rubber gloves are more comfortable when working with wet leaves and mud. If you have to remove a good deal of water, mud, or wet leaves, you may want to make a gutter scoop. To make a handy scoop, cut the bottom out of a narrow plastic jug, preferably one with a handle, that will fit snugly inside your gutter. You will find that it is a faster, safer, and neater means of transferring wet leaves and mud from the gutter to a bucket. Use a garden hose for the final rinse and to check for leaks in the gutters and blockages in the downspouts.

## Warning Signs of Blocked Gutters

- water and dirt stains below the gutter or beside a downspout
- peeling or blistered paint adjacent to a gutter or downspout
- tree limbs hanging over your roof
- water puddles next to your foundation after a rain
- sagging gutters
- loose gutter nails or straps
- mud splashed against the foundation
- gutter nails on the ground near the foundation

## Do's and Don'ts to Keeping the Gutters Clean

*Do*

- trim back overhanging tree limbs.
- wear heavy work gloves to avoid cuts.
- install leaf guard screens over gutters beneath large trees.

- insert leaf strainers into the downspouts where they join the gutters.
- repair any holes or separated seams immediately.
- use a hand-powered auger, or "snake," to unplug clogged downspouts.
- correct sagging gutters; standing water speeds the deterioration of the gutter.
- make sure the gutters are sloped properly ($1/8$-inch drop per foot) to provide good drainage.

### Don't

- attempt to clean the gutters while crouched on the roof. Always work from a secured ladder.
- work while standing on the top of a regular stepladder. The feet are apt to suddenly sink in the soft ground next to the foundation and dump you off your perch.
- throw away the soggy leaves. They make good compost.
- nail gutter brackets through the top of a shingle. Carefully raise the shingle and attach the bracket beneath it.
- force leaves into the downspout, where they can clog the length of pipe.

## How to Clean and Maintain Gutters and Downspouts

| *Steps* | *Tools and Materials* |
|---|---|
| 1. Use a safe ladder of adequate length. | extension ladder |
| 2. Install the ladder in a safe, level position and secure the top rung to the gutter or house. Have someone on the ground steady the ladder. | rope or wire<br>assistant |
| 3. Scoop out the debris with your gloved hand and deposit in a bucket attached to the ladder or gutter. | heavy-duty gloves<br>bucket and wire |
| 4. Clean out any stubborn deposits with a wire brush. | wire brush |
| 5. Rinse thoroughly and check for leaks. | garden hose |
| 6. If you discover a leak, wipe off any trace of water and let dry. | rags |
| 7. Trowel on a thin layer of roof cement around the leak, extending 3 inches on all sides. | trowel<br>roof cement |

*Steps*                              *Tools and Materials*

8. Trim a piece of asphalt roofing mesh      asphalt mesh
   to extend 2 inches from all sides of      scissors
   leak.
9. Press the mesh into the roofing
   cement with your trowel. Smooth
   out any air bubbles.
10. Cover the mesh with another layer of
    roofing cement. Feather the edges to
    let the water pass over rather than
    under the patch.

TIP: If gutter cleaning is a regular chore for you, customize a plastic bucket just for this task. Cut the wire handle in half, then bend the two pieces into hooks that you can slip over the edge of the gutter. If the wire handle is too weak, replace it with stiffer wire. Then, as you clean the gutters, simply slide this customized bucket along an edge, filling it with leaves and debris as you go.

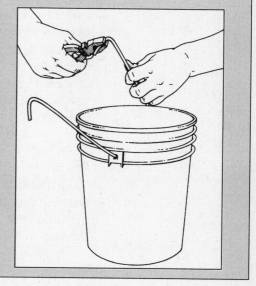

### How Not to Patch a Leaky Gutter

I knew when we bought our house that we were buying some serious gutter problems. To begin with, the gutters are built into the roof, so replacing them was out of the question. Or at least out of our budget. To make matters worse, the paint was peeling in four places on the fascia board beneath the gutter. Sure signs of leaks, I muttered to myself, as the real estate agent hustled us indoors.

Several of the gutters on our hillside home are located about 30 feet above the ground—20 feet above my personal limit for comfortable ladder work. My wife, Lydia, convinced me this was a project for a professional, but finding someone we could trust turned out to be a problem. Our first crew of professional gutter repairmen arrived in a coughing, wheezing pickup truck with a couple of ladders shooting out over the top of the cab. They quickly peeled off their shirts, passed around a fresh plug of Red Man, and scrambled up the ladders. Buckets of leaves were exchanged for buckets of roof coating and in less than an hour they were gone, along with about $200 of our money.

It didn't rain for two weeks, but when it did, three of the five spots that they had patched continued to leak. I spent the next two weeks trying to contact them. I later learned that the workers had gone to Florida to "clean up" after the hurricane. I'm sure they were laughing all the way to Miami.

It took another year for me to work up the nerve to take care of the leaking gutters myself. A college student and I set up the ladder, secured it to the roof, and began cleaning out the debris and peeling off the old roof tar. We traced the leaks to a joint in the metal gutters, wiped them clean and dry, then patched them with roofing cement and an asphalt-impregnated membrane used by roofers to repair flashing. Small cracks were patched with a special exterior caulk. I did these repairs knowing that they would probably last only a year or so, for the proper means of repairing a built-in gutter involves tearing back the first two rows of shingles and relining the gutters with new metal. Eventually we will have to do just that, but I decided that until the time comes when we have to replace the shingles on the roof, temporary patches will have to do.

# #7
# Patch or replace damaged shingles on your roof.

The roof of your house protects your family, your furnishings, and your house itself from the elements. Since the wood sheathing that gives a roof its shape cannot withstand long-term exposure to moisture, it traditionally has been covered, depending on the climate of the region and the style of architecture, with asphalt, slate, or wood shingles, copper or tin sheets, rolled asphalt roofing, or clay or metal tile. The life expectancy of these materials varies considerably, from 100 years or more for the finest slate shingles in a moderate climate to less than 20 years for asphalt shingles in a region with long, hot summers.

Asphalt shingles cover approximately three-fourths of all of the homes in this country. Ironically, water has little effect on the life expectancy of asphalt shingles, in part because the shingles are wet only a small percentage of time each year. People who walk on roofs—antenna installers, painters, carpenters, chimney masons, sunbathers, and backyard baseball players—can cause more damage to shingles than water does. Cold, brittle shingles are apt to break under the pressure applied by a misplaced foot, just as hot, soft shingles are apt to tear in the same situation. You can extend the life of your asphalt shingle roof simply by keeping people off it. When that is impossible, dictate the time of day people will be walking on the shingles to ensure that your roof will not be damaged when the shingles are either brittle or soft. If you are painting your house and must stand on the shingles, protect them with a heavy drop cloth or old blanket, provided, of course, this does not promote a slippery, dangerous situation.

The greatest enemy of asphalt shingles, though, is the sun, because ultraviolet rays eventually break down the chemical composition of the asphalt. Manufacturers of asphalt shingles slow the process by impregnating the exposed surface of each shingle with colored granules. Once the granules have eroded, however, the exposed asphalt deteriorates rapidly. The final factor in the life expectancy of the roof is the thickness of the shingle. As you might expect, thinner shingles deteriorate faster than thicker shingles.

Most roofing materials rely on an overlapping installation pattern to shed water. Nails are hidden from view and shielded from rain and snow by the overlapping material. Like the weak link in a strong chain, once any shingle, tile, or piece of metal comes loose, water can work its way under the next row. Once it does, it can travel for several feet between the roofing material and the sheathing before it emerges inside the house. If the leak goes undetected, the wood sheathing and supporting rafters can deteriorate to the point where they can no longer support the weight of the roofing material.

Whether you make the repair yourself or hire a professional, it is imperative that you (1) check your roof casually on a monthly basis, (2) inspect it closely twice a year, and (3) make sure that any damage is repaired immediately. If you have never had the experience, you will be amazed at how little water it takes to stain, even ruin, a plaster ceiling.

## Warning Signs of Roof Problems

- broken or missing shingles
- shingles whose corners are curling up
- granules completely worn off in places
- large accumulation of granules in the gutters
- protruding nail heads
- corners of shingles found in the yard after a storm
- fresh water stains on an interior ceiling
- water stains on attic rafters
- old patches of roofing tar on shingles

## Do's and Don'ts to Repairing Shingles

*Do*

- check in the basement, garage, or attic for extra shingles saved for patching purposes by the previous owner. They may match the color of the present shingles better than new shingles.
- take every safety precaution when working on a roof or from a ladder.
- trim back any tree limbs that are overhanging the roof or

encouraging moss and mildew to form on the roofing material.

- find and patch any holes left by lightning rods, weather vanes, finials, antennas, gutters, or decorative metalwork.

## Don't

- walk on an asphalt shingle roof on a hot, sunny day. The soft shingles can be damaged, and they are dangerously slippery. Select a mild, overcast day for roofing inspection and repairs.
- rush into selecting a new roofing material or color until you have considered the original color and style of roofing material.
- nail gutter straps, weather vanes, or anything else on top of the shingles. The nails eventually work loose and let in water.
- hesitate to hire a professional if you are the least bit unsteady on a ladder. It's more important that you know what needs to be done (and that it gets done!) than it is to do it yourself.

## How to Replace a Damaged Roof Shingle

| *Steps* | *Tools and Materials* |
|---|---|
| 1. Identify the broken or missing shingle. | |
| 2. If necessary, buy a replacement shingle from a lumberyard or roofing company. | shingle |
| 3. Safely secure your ladder to the gutter, chimney, or suitable stable protrusion. | ladder<br>rope or wire |
| 4. If the repair is beyond the reach of your ladder, secure a safety rope on the other side or a higher portion of your house. When you are in position to make the repair, tie the rope around your waist. | long rope |

TIP: Select roofing shoes carefully, avoiding those with hard, slick, or worn soles. Work boots with soft rubber soles or high-top athletic shoes with plenty of tread are the safest.

| *Steps* | *Tools and Materials* |
|---|---|
| 5. Carefully raise each good shingle a few inches directly above the damaged one. | |
| 6. Slide the flat pry bar between the two shingles and carefully lift the nails holding the damaged shingle in place. | flat pry bar |
| 7. Pull out the damaged shingle and clean out any loose granules, debris, or moisture. | rag or gloves |
| 8. Slide the new shingle into place to ensure a proper fit. Trim if necessary. | utility knife |
| 9. Pull out the shingle, then trowel on a $3/8$-inch layer of roof patching material over the nail holes. | trowel<br>asphalt roofing cement |
| 10. Slide the shingle back into place on the roofing cement and attach with roofing nails placed next to, but not directly over, the original holes. | hammer<br>roofing nails |
| 11. Apply roofing cement between any shingles that were disturbed and over any nails that were loosened. Press the shingles firmly into the roofing cement. | trowel<br>asphalt roofing cement |

TIP: To disguise a small patch of roof cement or caulk over a nail hole in a shingle, scoop up some clean shingle granules from the gutter and press them into the sticky patching material.

# #8
# Inspect your roof flashing every spring and fall.

Roof flashing can be metal, asphalt, rubber, fiberglass, or any suitable material that prevents water from seeping underneath your roofing around chimneys, vent pipes, dormers, or skylights. Different situations call for different types of flashing. Modern vent pipes are often flashed with one-piece neoprene or galvanized collars; older vents may have been repaired with an asphalt-coated membrane and roofing cement. Most professional roofers prefer overlapping pieces of copper around masonry chimneys and alongside dormers. Regardless of the material, flashing can develop leaks. When it does, rainwater and melting snow have a direct route through the wood sheathing to the plaster walls and ceilings below.

Flashing fails for three reasons. First, it can be installed incorrectly, even by professional roofers. A shingle nail placed too close to the chimney or dormer may actually direct rainwater through the roof. Second, the flashing can work loose from the chimney, dormer, or skylight. Roof flashing has the difficult task of remaining attached to two different types of surfaces that expand and contract, vibrate, or shift at different rates. A brick or stone chimney, for instance, has its own foundation separate from that of the house, so it may shift or settle at a rate different from the roof around it. A glass skylight expands and contracts at a rate different from asphalt roofing material; thus the flashing has to remain somewhat flexible, yet intact. Finally, inexperienced roofers and do-it-yourselfers often damage the flashing by assuming they can walk on it just as they would any other part of the roof.

Ironically, roofers often cause more problems with flashing than they solve. Many roofers opt not to replace the original flashing when they are installing the shingles, especially if they are being paid by the number of shingles they lay rather than by the hour. In the process of removing the old shingles or applying the new, they can damage the original flashing or reattach it or the shingles around it incorrectly. Instead of shedding water, the flashing in this case may actually direct the water under the new shingles.

The best time to install new flashing is when new roofing material is being applied. Attempting to work on—and under—brittle shingles can cause additional damage. By the time you are finished, the flashing may be watertight, but the shingles around it won't be.

Until you are ready to replace both the shingles and the metal flashing, the temporary cure for a minor flashing leak is roofing cement. Not to be confused with the much thinner roof coating, roofing cement—also known as plastic asphalt cement or "black-jack"—is a petroleum-based patching material that is applied with a small masonry trowel or a putty knife. It is sold in 1- and 5-gallon pails at most lumberyards and home improvement centers. Roofing cement is not considered a permanent replacement for flashing, but it is a practical patching material until you are ready for new shingles and flashing.

You can extend the life of the patch if you always use an asphalt membrane with it. This asphalt-coated netting does for roofing cement what reinforcing rods do for slabs of concrete. The membrane, which is sold in rolls of various widths, can be cut with a utility knife or scissors, then pressed into the first layer of roofing cement with the edge of a trowel. A top layer of cement bonds with the lower layer through the netting and increases the resistance to expansion and contraction, freezing and soaring temperatures, and, of course, water. Without it, the roofing cement is more apt to crack as it goes through the freeze-thaw cycles.

## Warning Signs of Flashing Problems

Carefully inspect your flashing for these telltale warning signs:

- old flashing pulled away from chimney, dormer, or other features
- metal flashing nailed on top of shingles
- excessive corrosion on metal flashing
- excessive, sloppily applied roofing cement
- holes, cracks, or breaks in flashing
- exposed asphalt membrane

- stains on the ceiling or walls beneath the chimney, dormer, skylight, or vent pipes

## Do's and Don'ts to Repairing Flashing

### Do

- make sure you are physically and mentally able to climb a ladder, walk on the roof, and perch there safely while balancing a bucket of roofing cement and your tools. If you aren't, call a professional—and volunteer to be the ground supervisor.
- keep a caulking gun within reach as you work on the roof, watching for nails, brackets, eyelets, and holes left by antenna wires, raised nail heads, curled shingles, or cracked flashing. The time to fix a hole is when you find it, because you may not be able to locate it later.
- pick a cool, overcast day for walking on your roof.

### Don't

- ever stand, walk, or place any weight within 12 inches of a flashing.
- walk directly in the middle of the "valley," where two sections of roof meet; your weight will tear the flashing under the valley covering.
- nail flashing on top of shingles.
- create asphalt dams that can trap water behind a chimney or skylight.

## How to Patch Flashing

| *Steps* | *Tools and Materials* |
|---|---|
| 1. Safely secure your ladder to the gutter, chimney, or suitable stable protrusion. | ladder<br>rope or wire |
| 2. If the repair is beyond the reach of the ladder, secure a safety rope on the other side or a higher portion of your house. When you are in position to make the repair, tie the safety rope around your waist. | long rope |
| 3. Clean out any debris and water from the break in the flashing. | old brush<br>rag |

| *Steps* | *Tools and Materials* |
|---|---|
| 4. Remove any old flashing that has peeled back, worn out, or loosened. | putty knife<br>utility knife<br>trash bucket |
| 5. Allow the area to dry completely. | rag<br>sunshine<br>hair dryer or<br>  heat gun |
| 6. Spread a ³⁄₈-inch layer of roofing cement over the break, extending it 1 to 3 inches beyond the actual opening. Press the cement firmly into the break and surrounding area. | roofing cement<br>trowel or<br>  putty knife |
| 7. Cut a membrane patch the same dimensions as your first layer of roofing cement. | asphalt-coated<br>  membrane<br>utility knife |
| 8. Press the membrane firmly and smoothly into the roofing cement. | trowel |
| 9. Cover the membrane with a second ³⁄₈-inch layer of roofing cement. | roofing cement<br>trowel |
| 10. Feather the edges of the roofing cement to discourage water from accumulating behind it. Leave the patch slightly mounded to shed water. | trowel |

TIP: Use a pair of binoculars, a telescope, or your neighbor's bedroom window to inspect the flashing on the inaccessible parts of your roof.

### Frank's Roof

My neighbor and good friend Frank called me a few weeks ago to report that he and his wife, JoAnn, had discovered a fresh water stain in their dining room ceiling. Armed with a flashlight, we ventured into their cluttered attic but could find no sign of any incoming water above the stain in the dining room. The rafters and wood sheathing were dry, with no water marks to indicate that they might have been wet earlier in the week. At one end of the attic, however, Frank and JoAnn have a small balcony. The balcony is protected by the sloping, shingled roof, which gives them a pleasant place to watch the sun set over the distant mountains.

The flat asphalt roof had originally been covered by the roofers with a half-inch layer of pea gravel to protect it from the sun. I had learned years ago to be suspicious of any roofs or balconies frequented by humans, for most people think that walking on an asphalt roof is no different from walking on the street. The fact is, flashing, which connects the flat roof to the vertical wall or parapet, is generally just rolled roofing covered with asphalt and gravel. Since the stiff roofing cannot conform to the rigid 90-degree angle formed by the roof and wall, there invariably is a hollow space behind the flashing.

Using an old broom to clear away the pea gravel, we quickly found the cause of the leak. Someone had made the predictable mistake of walking next to the parapet, denting the flashing with the toe of their shoe. The flashing eventually tore, providing the next wind-driven rain with an access to the roof sheathing and rafters beneath the balcony floor. Fortunately, Frank had some roofing cement and a trowel on hand, but we didn't have any patching membrane to span the 6-inch tear in the flashing. Since it was getting late in the evening, we decided to improvise. Frank found a section of old screen wire, which we trimmed to cover the generous layer of roofing tar I had troweled over and around the tear. I pressed the screen wire into the roofing cement, then spread another layer over the top of it, forcing the cement through the mesh so the two layers would bond together. We finished by feathering out the edges of our new patch so that water could not seep under it, then swept the gravel over the patch to help protect it from the sun.

After we completed our improvised repair, we realized that we would have to check the flashing and our patch often, but we climbed down knowing that the stain in the ceiling was not going to get any worse.

# #9
# Install a drip edge under the last row of shingles.

Most water damage on a roof occurs beneath the flashing or in the cornice, the boxlike structure supporting the overhanging roof. The cornice consists of two major elements: the fascia, which is the horizontal board directly beneath the bottom row of shingles, and the soffit, which is the underside of the overhang. When the shingles and the rain gutters are properly installed, the fascia and soffit only get wet during a driving rain. But if the gutters become clogged or the shingles fail to direct the water away from the cornice, then the fascia and soffit are subject to excess water and eventual deterioration.

When properly installed, the bottom row of shingles should extend 1 inch beyond the fascia to direct water away from the cornice. If the roofers failed to do so, or if the shingles have begun to droop, thousands of gallons of rainwater can run across the fascia and into the cornice. With no direct sunlight to dry out the boards, the combination of moisture, shade, and food provides an ideal home for decay-causing fungi. By the time you notice the paint peeling from the soffit, the decay may have spread so far that you will have to replace the soffit rather than just repaint it.

The best way to avoid the problem is to supplement and support the bottom row of shingles with a metal drip edge. Generally sold in 8-foot or longer lengths, the L-shaped metal drip edge slips beneath the bottom row of shingles and directs the water away from the fascia. The ideal time to install a drip edge is when the shingles are being replaced; but if you don't intend to replace the shingles in the near future, don't hold off on the drip edge. Although the job is a little cumbersome and is made easier with an assistant, installing a drip edge under the existing shingles is not difficult. Pick a day when the shingles are warm and flexible, and plan to work from two ladders or, better yet, a portable scaffold.

If multiple layers of shingles prevent you from being able to lift up the shingles to nail the drip edge to the roof, your next best alternative is to nail it directly to the fascia. Make sure, however, that you use aluminum nails to avoid unsightly rust spots.

## Warning Signs of an Exposed Cornice

- broken or jagged edge along the bottom row of shingles
- exposed wood beneath the edge of the shingles
- peeling paint on the cornice
- shingles laid flush with the edge of the roof

## Do's and Don'ts to Installing a Drip Edge

### Do

- work with a partner, if at all possible.
- use a sturdy scaffold.
- wear work gloves when handling metal drip edge.
- use only aluminum nails.

### Don't

- damage the gutters with your ladder.
- apply the drip edge from your roof; always work from a ladder or scaffold to avoid falling.
- overbend shingles; loosen the nails with a flat pry bar to avoid breaking shingles.

## How to Install a Drip Edge

| *Steps* | *Tools and Materials* |
|---|---|
| 1. Estimate the amount of drip edge your roof will require. Measurements can be made on the ground beneath each section of roof overhang. | tape measure notebook pencil |
| 2. Select a style of drip edge that will accommodate your roofing material and roof design. When in doubt, buy a small sample and test to make sure it will work on your roof. | |

*Steps*                                    *Tools and Materials*

3.  Provided you will not be walking on
    the roof, select a warm, sunny day;
    the heat of the sun will make the
    shingles more flexible.

4.  Position and secure your ladder.          ladder
                                              rope or wire

5.  Starting at one end of the cornice,       flat pry bar or
    carefully lift the bottoms of the shingles    putty knife
    and slide a length of drip edge into place.

6.  Slide the drip edge under any gutter       tin snips
    straps, notching the drip edge slightly,
    if necessary.

7.  Nail the drip edge, making sure all nail   roofing nails
    heads are under the shingles. If that is   hammer
    impossible, nail the drip edge to the      aluminum nails
    fascia every 24 inches.

8.  Cover each nail head under the shingles    asphalt roofing
    with roofing cement.                           cement
                                               trowel or
                                                   caulking gun

9. Repeat with the next length of drip edge, overlapping each piece by 1 inch, then press the shingles back in place. Use roofing cement as needed to hold down shingles.

asphalt roofing cement
trowel or caulking gun

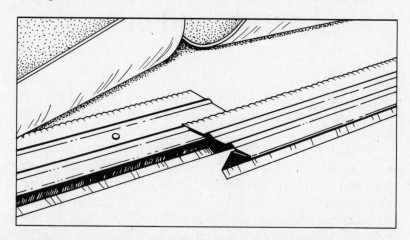

TIP: For added protection, cover each exposed aluminum nail with a dab of exterior white caulking.

# #10
# Keep the chimney intact inside and out.

Anyone who has seen houses destroyed by fire, earthquake, or simply age may have noticed one thing: the chimneys remain intact.

While it is obvious that chimneys are built to resist heat, there is yet another reason for their stubborn endurance. Most brick and stone chimneys are built on their own foundations separate from that of the rest of the house. In one sense, each chimney exists as a separate structure rising from the basement up through the house and the roof to a total height of 40 feet or more. What you see protruding from the roof is but the tip of a masonry iceberg. Fortunately, from a structural point of view, it is generally only the tip that needs our attention, since the remainder of the chimney is often encased and protected by the walls of the house.

Because it stands on its own foundation, the chimney may settle, expand, and contract at a rate different from that of the roof around it. For that reason, the flashing around the chimney that prevents water from running into the house must be checked regularly; once it becomes old and brittle, it may not adjust to the stress it must endure. (See #8, "Inspect your roof flashing every spring and fall," on page 43.) The area behind the chimney must also be checked for standing water, which speeds the deterioration of the flashing, especially when temperatures dip below the freezing point.

A chimney does more than simply direct smoke out of the house. It has to contain heat, toxic gases, even flames, and it must repel rainwater and melting snow. Effective and safe chimney operation depends on two key elements: the exterior masonry and the clay, metal, or concrete liner within the chimney.

Before this century, liners were not mandatory in chimneys, but we have since realized the dangers associated with unlined chimneys. The toxic gases produced by the flames in the fireplace or furnace will erode the interior mortar in an unlined chimney, causing it to crumble. In a matter of time, the gases can seep into your home, endangering the lives of your family. For that reason, tight, efficient liners are essential in a working chimney. Unfortunately, it is difficult for a homeowner to inspect a chimney liner. Using a strong flashlight, you may be able to peer down into your chimney, but this won't qualify as a professional inspection. If you have any suspicions regarding the liner, have it inspected and, if necessary, repaired or replaced by a qualified professional.

The exterior masonry on a chimney must be maintained for obvious reasons. First, rainwater and melting snow can make their way through a deteriorating chimney to damage plaster ceilings and walls. Second, crumbling mortar will lead to loose flashing. Third, unchecked deterioration will spread below the roofline, making repairs extremely expensive. Finally, falling bricks can break slate, damage asphalt shingles, puncture roof flashing, and possibly injure bystanders below.

Starting from the top, then, every chimney should have a cap to prevent rainwater from running down the interior of the chimney; water, especially freezing water, can damage the interior mortar and the liner. If enough of the mortar crumbles away, the chimney can actually begin to tilt slightly. Given enough time and neglect, the mortar can deteriorate to the point where bricks can actually fall out. Loose and crumbling mortar on the exterior should be scraped out and the bricks tuck-pointed with fresh masonry mix. The liner should be inspected and cleaned annually, and the flashing should be checked each spring and fall.

The greatest obstacle to chimney inspection and repair is accessibility. Owners of large older houses can be intimidated by steep roofs and chimneys that tower above the treetops. Two of the most dangerous mistakes you can make are to work from a ladder that is too short and to work while clinging to a steep roof or with one foot pressing on a gutter. In situations such as these, chimney work is extremely dangerous. As critical as chimney maintenance is to the safety of your home and family, don't take unnecessary and potentially fatal risks. Do as much as you can do safely, then call in the professionals.

## Warning Signs of Chimney Problems

- a slightly tilting chimney
- soft, deteriorating mortar
- missing or incomplete liner

- missing or ineffective chimney cap
- soot on the outside of the mortar
- excessive amount of mortar or broken liner collected in the ash pit
- snap-in pie plate covers over interior wall openings leading into the chimney
- water rings in the flashing behind the chimney
- worn or deteriorated flashing
- pieces of masonry in the gutter or on the ground below a chimney

## Do's and Don'ts to Chimney Repairs

### *Do*

- have any inactive chimney inspected by a professional before using it.
- have all chimneys inspected annually to prevent a catastrophic fire.
- take all safety precautions when working from a ladder or roof.
- remove any television antenna attached to your chimney to eliminate stress on the masonry.
- locate the ash and soot clean-out door in the basement section of your chimney. Empty the chamber yearly.
- inspect the flashing closely to make sure water is not seeping into the attic.

### *Don't*

- wait until early winter to inspect, clean, and repair your chimney. Spring is the best time to remove creosote, which otherwise could continue to harden over the summer.
- rely on a pie plate cover to prevent toxic gases from seeping into your home. Remove the cover and patch the hole with the appropriate wall material.
- assume that a chimney attached to a nonfunctioning fireplace isn't being utilized. Previous owners may have routed gases from a hot water heater or furnace without first checking to see if the chimney was safe.
- use any chimney that does not have a complete, safe liner. The gases produced in the combustion process combine with moisture to create sulfuric acid, which attacks the lime

in the mortar. In as little as two years, an unlined chimney can disintegrate from the inside, while looking perfectly safe on the outside.

- cover an ash and soot clean-out door during a basement remodeling.
- step on the flashing around the base of the chimney.

## How to Give Your Chimney a Checkup

| *Steps* | *Tools and Materials* |
| --- | --- |
| 1. Starting at the top, check the entire chimney for deteriorated mortar and brick damage. Tuck-point where necessary. (See #18, "Tuck-point brick walls to keep them sound and attractive," on page 92.) | trowel mortar bucket wire brush ladder |
| 2. Inspect the liner wherever you can gain visible access (fireplace, pie plate covers, or chimney cap). Consult with a professional on repairs and/or replacement. | flashlight |
| 3. Locate the clean-out door at the base of the chimney. Remove any debris and make sure the door seals tightly when closed. | gloves garden trowel bucket |
| 4. Clean the chimney liner once a year to remove built-up creosote, which can cause a chimney fire. | (recommend either a professional or additional research into proper cleaning methods) |

TIP: Avoid burning softwoods, such as pine, in the fireplace. They deposit more creosote on the liner than do dry hardwoods.

# #11
# Don't let pigeons become windowsill pets.

While pigeons may seem harmless to anyone whose contact with them has been restricted to city sidewalks, their excrement is not. Pigeon dung accumulates rapidly and can provide a breeding ground for various fungi that cause respiratory and nervous system disorders in humans. The spores of the fungi are airborne, posing a serious threat to individuals (especially those with a respiratory condition) residing in the same house wherein pigeon excrement has accumulated in the attic or along a windowsill.

An accumulation of pigeon nests, excrement, feathers, and dirt can also cause permanent stains on wood and masonry. Worse yet, it is not unusual for a nest to remain wet for days after a rain, especially in a shaded nook or cranny. The paint under the nest and dung eventually peels, leaving the wood exposed. The combination of water and excrement also spawns certain fungi, which, in turn, feed on the wood. In just a few seasons, the wood can deteriorate to the point where the shelter-seeking pigeons can work their way behind the soffit or the clapboards, or even into the attic. There the problem intensifies, as the dung, water, fungi, and decay accumulate.

Pigeons are a nuisance, but most people agree that they don't deserve the death penalty. They just need to find a less troublesome place to live. And while pigeons have never been known for their intelligence, they are stubborn and will continue to return to a popular roost so long as there is no real threat to their existence. Solutions to this problem have been creative, to say the least. Rubber snakes, fiberglass owls, and wildly swinging pie tins and plastic cups only seem to convince the pigeons to take a short vacation rather than move to new quarters. As soon as they realize that the snakes and owls don't move and the cups and tins don't bite, they settle back in. One frustrated homeowner considered buying a trained falcon, until he discovered that when it tires of eating pigeons, a falcon will just as gladly dine on an innocent rabbit or the neighbor's cat. Old-fashioned rural pigeon shoots were effective means of letting people vent their frustrations, but not of ridding the area of pigeons. Their effectiveness lasted for about six hours or until the shotgun shells ran out, at which time everyone, including the pigeons, returned home.

The most natural means of persuading pigeons to move to new quarters is to eliminate their food supply. As long as pigeons can feast beneath your bird feeder, beside your garbage cans, or from the cat's food dish, most methods will be ineffective. Clean up excess birdseed, and cover your garbage cans. Unfortunately, the feeding range of a pigeon is not limited to one yard. You will have to enlist the help of your neighborhood in eliminating the pigeons' food source, but, chances are, your neighbors are as irked with the pigeons as you are. If casual conversations and phone calls aren't enough, distribute a flyer to your neighbors with hints for convincing the pigeons to leave home.

Since most people can recognize the signs of a roosting pigeon, let's discuss the advantages and disadvantages of the various solutions that have been proposed. One disadvantage to nearly every possible solution is that it generally will require an extension ladder to reach the problem area. If you are not comfortable working from a ladder, this may be a job you should supervise from the ground or an upstairs window. Selecting which means will work best for your situation will depend, for the most part, on where the pigeons have decided to roost. The following suggestions are listed in no particular order:

## Galvanized Screen Wire

*advantages*          inexpensive
                      effective in corners
                      can easily be cut and bent to fit into corners
                      can be installed with a staple gun
                      can last several years
                      does not leave rust stains

*disadvantages*       requires working from an extension ladder
                      unattractive

## Plastic Netting

*advantages*          inexpensive
                      effective in corners
                      easy to cut

can be installed with a staple gun
less noticeable than screen wire
can be stretched over windows

*disadvantages*     disintegrates sooner than galvanized wire
still somewhat visible
not self-supporting like wire

### Swinging Plastic Cups or Pie Tins

*advantages*     inexpensive
easy to install

*disadvantages*     unattractive
eventually ineffective

### Electric Wire

*advantages*     effective

*disadvantages*     moderately expensive
difficult to install
increased potential for accidents

### Barbed or "Porcupine" Wire

*advantages*     effective along narrow ledges and ridges
long-lasting
less unsightly than netting
easy to install

*disadvantages*     expensive
less effective in open areas

### Spiked Boards

*advantages*     effective along narrow ledges and ridges
long-lasting
easy to install
can make yourself, using galvanized nails and
    treated wood
can be cut and painted to match your house

*disadvantages*     less effective in open areas
can be unattractive if done poorly

### Ultrasound Devices

*advantages*     effective in attics

easy to install

*disadvantages*    less effective outside

drives away songbirds

moderately expensive

## Gel Repellents

*advantages*    inexpensive

easy to install

nearly invisible

*disadvantages*    must be replenished each year

some brands can stain wood or masonry

attracts dirt

effectiveness varies by brand

## Mothballs (in a bag or sock)

*advantages*    inexpensive

easy to install

*disadvantages*    must first clean area with ammonia

must replenish mothballs regularly

unattractive

> TIP: To make annual cleanup of a sticky gel repellent easier, tape or staple a piece of stiff plastic onto the wood, then apply the repellent to the plastic. Next year, simply pull up the plastic and dispose of all the mess.

# #12
# Prevent leaks in your flat roof.

A large number of shingled houses also have a small section of flat roof over a porch or dormer. Many Victorian houses still feature a flat "widow's walk," where, according to popular legend, wives would stand atop their homes and anxiously watch for the return of their seafaring husbands. Most of these small sections of flat roof are covered with asphalt, but you don't have to call in a crew of professional roofers to maintain or repair it.

These small sections of asphalt-covered roofs were often built with little or no pitch, or slope. Some roofs will have lost all or part of their pitch as the rafters sagged or through an improper reroofing. Since standing water always seems to find a crack in the asphalt roofing, you actually need to pay more attention to your flat roof than you do to your steeply pitched shingles. Even though you can't patch or maintain a flat roof during a rainstorm, you should study it either during or immediately after such a storm. If the sky is clear and you are anxious to check your roof, a garden hose will provide a substitute shower. Inspect these areas in particular: (1) any seams in the rolled roofing; (2) any low spots that hold water; and (3) the flashing where the roofing material meets a dissimilar material, such as wood siding or a brick chimney. (See #8, "Inspect your roof flashing every spring and fall," on page 43.)

Ideally, a flat roof should have no visual seams, because standing or slow-moving water can work its way into one. If the surface has been covered with overlapping rolled roofing material, inspect the seams carefully for any separations. Patch any you find with roofing cement and asphalt-coated membrane (also called roofing fabric), a black mesh that bridges splits and holes in the roofing material. Trowel a ³⁄₈-inch layer of roofing cement between the two layers of roofing material, then press in place.

Cover the area over and around the separation with additional roofing cement, a layer of membrane, and a final layer of roofing cement.

Once they are dry, low spots in the roof can be built up with alternate layers of either roofing fabric or rolled roofing material and roofing cement until they shed, rather than hold, water. Always feather the edge of the roofing cement so water slides over it rather than catches behind it. As you inspect the roof, watch for air pockets under the roofing material. These require close inspection before deciding what course to take. If the bubble is intact and shows no sign of bursting, you can simply leave it alone, making sure that neither you nor anyone else steps on it (if necessary, mark it with chalk or spray paint).

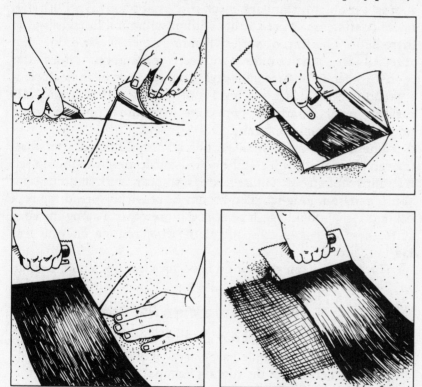

But if the bubble has burst or is about to, you should slice it from end to end with the point of a trowel or utility knife. Peel the roofing material back far enough for any moisture to evaporate. Once dry, coat the exposed area with roofing cement, then press the flaps of asphalt back into place. Cover the incision and the surrounding area with additional roofing cement, then press a piece of roofing fabric over the critical area. Complete the patch by covering the fabric with yet another layer of roofing cement, making sure to feather the edges where the cement joins the old roof. The resulting hump in the roof ensures that water won't stand over the patched area.

Depending on the amount of damage the sun does to the asphalt, a flat roof should be protected with a thin layer of liquid roof coating once every two or three years. Roof coating is available in two different colors, silver and black. Silver is generally more expensive, but it reflects more sunlight than does the black. Unless heat buildup in the room directly beneath the flat roof is a problem, standard black roof coating is fine. Both colors of coating are offered either with or without a fiberglass-type ingredient. The fibered variety is more expensive and does not spread as far as the thinner, nonfibered coating, but it does offer more protection and lasts longer. If the roof has been neglected, I would suggest using a fibered roof coating this year and, depending on its condition two years from now, possibly use a nonfibered coating next time.

Whether it is black or silver, fibered or nonfibered, roof coating can be applied with a stiff-bristled brush similar to those used by wallpaper hangers. On large areas, you can work standing up if you purchase a long-handled broom or brush to spread the roof coating. A handheld brush gives you more control along the edge of the roof and is less apt to splatter roof coating on your car, kids, or yard.

Have some paint thinner on hand for cleanup. You'll need it.

### Warning Signs of a Worn Flat Roof

- puddles of standing water after a rainstorm
- curling seams on rolled asphalt roofing
- air pockets under the roofing material
- exposed rolled roofing
- cracked coating
- fresh water stains in the attic or the ceiling beneath the flat roof
- water oozing out of the roofing when you step on it

## Do's and Don'ts to Working on a Flat Roof

*Do*

- work on a warm, but not hot, day.
- take all safety precautions when working on a roof.
- wear old athletic shoes and jeans, which you can assign to yard duty after this project.
- press gently on bubbles and splits to check for water under the roofing.
- use fibered roof coating for longer protection.

*Don't*

- attempt to patch or coat a wet surface.
- attempt to patch or coat a dusty surface.
- try to carry too much material or too many tools up a ladder at one time.
- apply so much coating along the edge that it runs down the side of your house.
- leave roofing materials or tools on the roof "for next time." They can blow or roll off during a storm, causing damage or injury.

## How to Seal a Flat Roof

| *Steps* | *Tools and Materials* |
|---|---|
| 1. Watch what happens to the water on your roof during a rainstorm. | |
| 2. Afterward, inspect your roof closely, marking any problem areas. | chalk or spray paint |
| 3. Sweep up any debris. | broom |
| | dustpan |
| | empty bucket |
| 4. Cut and peel back any fragile air pockets or splits with water in them. | utility knife |
| | gloves |
| 5. Wipe out any water and dirt and allow to dry. | rag |
| | dry paintbrush |
| 6. Patch this and any other breaks, holes, splits, or separations. (See "How to Patch Flashing," on page 45, for steps | trowel |
| | roofing cement |
| | roofing fabric |

*Steps*                                            *Tools and Materials*

on patching.) Give the roofing
cement time to form a dried "skin"
before applying a roof coating.

7. Carefully brush the roof coating          4-inch paintbrush
   along the edges of the roof and over      roof coating
   any flashing.                             gloves

8. Beginning at the point farthest from      long-handled
   your ladder, begin applying the roof          brush
   coating to the entire roof. Work the      roof coating
   coating into the roofing material with    gloves
   vigorous but controlled strokes.

9. At the end, pour enough coating on
   the roof to finish, then carry your
   bucket to the ground. Bring a large,
   clean plastic garbage bag to the top
   of the ladder with you.

10. Finish spreading the last of the
    coating while standing on the ladder.

11. Open the garbage bag completely          plastic garbage
    and carefully place the end of the long-     bag
    handled brush in the bag. Close
    tightly and carry it down to the
    ground. Do not throw the brush from
    the roof; the roof coating will stick to
    the grass, sidewalk, or house.

> TIP: Rather than making several trips up and down a lad-
> der, raise and lower any tools and materials using an
> empty bucket and a length of rope.

# THE EXTERIOR

The exterior of your home serves two basic purposes: it provides protection for the framework and interior features, and it serves as a palette for architectural details and paint colors. While it is always tempting to spend more time on the details and colors than on the less romantic aspects of protection, your next paint job is not going to last long if you don't first make sure that the exterior is in good condition.

Trimming back tree limbs, repairing cracked clapboards, caulking open joints, and learning how to spot and deter damaging termites are crucial to saving your home. If you take a few minutes to inspect the critical areas that have been identified in this section, you can avoid costly repairs. Regular maintenance is always easier, cheaper, and more rewarding than extensive repair or replacement. And most important, taking care of the exterior is, in the long run, taking care of the interior.

This chapter includes Home-Saving Guidelines 13 through 20.

# #13
# Trim bushes and tree limbs away from your house.

Like so many things in our lives, trees and shrubbery grown in moderation seem to cause fewer problems than those allowed uncontrolled growth. But for whatever reason, many homeowners seem perfectly content to bring nature as close as possible to their lives, including the trees and bushes planted next to their houses' foundations. And while no one seems averse to cutting the lawn on a weekly basis, few seem willing to take the pruning shears to the greenery leaning heavily on the side of the house.

Heavy, dense vegetation can damage the materials that were used to build your home. I've been on roofs where tree limbs actually rubbed the granules off the shingles, exposing nail heads and enabling water to drip into the attic. Even more common are homes where branches have actually sanded the paint off the siding as they swept back and forth in the breeze. Invariably, these homes experience more than the average number of problems with gutters and downspouts, which can quickly fill with leaves, needles, and twigs.

More subtle problems also develop with trees and shrubs that have been allowed to grow uncontrolled alongside the exterior walls. Branches and leaves can block out light completely and shade the wood the entire day. They also reduce air circulation, causing moisture to remain on the wood for days at a time.

Without the aid of the sun and air, the wood never completely dries out. These dark, damp surfaces then provide an ideal environment for airborne spores, which land and spawn decay-causing fungi. To take root and spread, a fungus requires three elements: food, oxygen, and moisture. The destructive fungi actually feed on the wood, literally sucking the strength out of the cells. Depending on the type of fungus, the wood gradually turns brown or bleached white and eventually crumbles when touched. In its final stages of rot, the wood appears dry; hence the misnomer "dry rot." Wood that is dry won't rot. Although it may be dry in the final stage,

moisture was without a doubt the cause of the decay. If you eliminate the moisture from the wood, you will prevent rot. But if the
wood does not have an opportunity to dry out, it is simply a matter of time before fungi takes root.

Yet as every homeowner knows, mature trees and shrubbery
are valuable visual elements of a home, so they should not be
pruned recklessly or haphazardly. While the siding might benefit
from any pruning, regardless how badly it is done, it is possible to
save both the exterior walls and the treasured greenery at the
same time. My grandfather was fond of saying, "Measure twice,
cut once." Had we been pruning trees together rather than patching up the family horse barn in Illinois, he probably would have
said, "Think twice, cut once." A basic requirement of proper
pruning is careful consideration of the placement of each cut.

Before you cut off a branch, think of it as a part of the tree's
plumbing system. The liquid nutrients traveling toward the end
of the branch are going to be diverted depending on where you
make the cut. Determine how much of the branch needs to be removed, then look for the nearest buds. Select a bud on the side of
a branch where new growth won't eventually cause a problem for
your house, then make a clean cut through the branch ¼ inch
above the bud. From that time on, the nutrients traveling along
the branch will be diverted to that bud, and the new growth will
point in the same direction.

While you're pruning, be sure to remove any dead or dying
branches. These can only harbor insects and decay, which can
then spread to adjacent healthy parts of the tree. Improper pruning can also cause decay and disease. If a cut is made several
inches above the nearest leaf or bud, that section will eventually
die. Before it does, however, it may attract insects that can spawn
and spread disease throughout the rest of the tree. Always make
clean, angled cuts using sharp tools. Clean cuts heal faster than
ragged ones. And don't worry about sealing the ends of the
freshly cut branches. The U.S. Forestry Service has concluded
that wound dressings and tree paints can actually do more harm
than good. To speed the healing process, make a small, clean
wound using a sharp pruning saw or shears, then let nature take
over.

When is the best time of year to prune? Ideally, at the close of
the dormant season, just before the advent of new growth. But if
you have a severe problem with limbs causing damage to your
roof or siding, the best time may be right now.

## Warning Signs of Greenery Damage

- branches and limbs rubbing against your house
- excessive leaves, needles, and twigs in the gutters
- damp, musty, heavily shaded areas between the shrubs and the house
- mold, mildew, or moss on the roof or walls
- dark stains on the exterior walls
- peeling or blistered paint on siding and eaves behind or beneath the limbs
- soft, spongy wood behind or beneath the limbs and shrubs

## Greenery Do's and Don'ts

### Do

- trim back weeds, limbs, and bushes 18 inches from the side of your house.
- inspect the siding as you mow around it.
- look for other potential sources of moisture, such as plugged downspouts, the laundry room, or a bathroom.
- remove broken or dead branches, which could foster infection in the rest of the tree or shrub.
- leave a clean, slightly angled cut.
- use sharp tools for clean cuts that will heal fast.

### Don't

- just treat the symptoms without attacking the source. Scrub off the moss, but also trim back the branches that helped it get started.
- create leafless stubs that will eventually rot.
- treat tree cuts with wound dressing or tree paint.

## How to Stop Mold and Mildew

| *Steps* | *Tools and Materials* |
| --- | --- |
| 1. Trim back foliage 18 inches from the house. | pruning shears |
| 2. Scrub off any mold, mildew, or moss with solution and scrub brush or rags. | bucket<br>solution of: |

| *Steps* | *Tools and Materials* |
|---|---|
| Protect plants and the ground with plastic drop cloths. | 2 quarts warm water<br>1 quart house-hold bleach<br>1 cup laundry detergent<br>1 cup trisodium phosphate (TSP)<br>scrub brush or rags<br>ladder<br>rubber gloves<br>protective glasses<br>plastic drop cloths |
| 3. Allow the solution to remain on any stained areas for several minutes or until the stain disappears. | |
| 4. Rinse thoroughly and let dry before repairing or repainting damaged boards. | garden hose |

TIP: To dislodge mold and mildew from hard-to-reach corners, use an old broom dipped in the cleaning solution.

## "I Think that I Shall Never See..."

I formerly served on the Historic Resources Commission for the city of Asheville, North Carolina, where the commissioners are charged with protecting the integrity of our three historic districts in the face of inappropriate signs, structures, demolitions, and remodelings. Not long ago, we were faced with a perplexing problem that illustrated the conflicts that so quickly arise.

In an effort to preserve, maintain, and encourage an abundance of trees in Asheville, the city council passed an ordinance requiring that all new construction and major remodeling of existing structures provide a minimum of one tree for every 40 feet of property line. The owners of a circa-1898 inn, which was being converted into luxury apartments, had already demonstrated their eagerness to restore the exterior of the structure and the grounds to their original appearance. But when faced with the tree ordinance, they brought up an interesting question. What if a tree every 40 feet was not the intention of the architect in 1898? Historically speaking, aren't too many trees as inappropriate as not enough?

To support their question, they presented photographs taken during the early years of the inn. Nowhere along the front border of the property could a tree be seen. Instead, a long grassy bank offered a beautiful, unobstructed view of the structure. While a tree every 40 feet might not seem a major obstruction, nevertheless, the point was well presented. Should one of the city's "green" ordinances be imposed on a property where, historically, it would be considered inappropriate?

The issue was sidestepped, at least momentarily, when someone pointed out that the ordinance read one tree "for every 40 feet," not "at every 40 feet." A property line 240 feet in length would require a total of six trees, but not necessarily one every 40 feet. The original photographs also revealed several trees clumped at either end of the property line. All of the parties involved then agreed that if the number of trees at either end of the 240-foot boundary totaled six or more, the owners had complied with the requirements of the ordinance.

# #14
# Repair any cracked or damaged clapboards.

Clapboards, those beveled, overlapping boards you can find on hundreds of thousands of homes across the country, are the skin of a house. Often referred to as wood lap siding or weather boards, clapboards work like a roof's shingles by shedding water as it runs down the side of the house and preventing cold air from penetrating to the framework.

Clapboards have been utilized for centuries, and they remain one of the most popular, attractive, and effective means of covering the exterior of a structure. The type of wood often varies from region to region, but the most common species include cedar, pine, and redwood. Thick, heavy siding, often referred to as novelty siding, is applied directly to the studs. But the more common wood lap siding, a thinner board, is applied to wood sheathing—individually nailed boards, plywood, or particleboard—covering the studs. Regardless of age, finish, or type of wood, when one of the clapboards is split or badly damaged, cold air, moisture, and insects can penetrate to the more vulnerable parts of your home's construction. Once they reach unpainted sheathing and studs, decay can grow and spread rapidly—out of sight and out of reach.

Replacing badly damaged clapboards is a tricky project. Begin by making vertical cuts with a backsaw to isolate the damaged section. Then, use a chisel to break the board into small pieces. This leaves the nails exposed so you can remove them with a claw hammer. Hidden nails can be cut off with a hacksaw blade slid

behind the upper clapboard. Cut a new piece of clapboard to fit. Before installing it, treat the exposed end grain with primer or a water-resistant sealer. Predrill the nail holes to eliminate splitting (see sidebar), and use galvanized nails to avoid rust stains.

You can avoid the tedious task of replacing sections of clapboards by simply inspecting and maintaining the present siding. With little more than a few simple tools and a ladder, you can repair damaged clapboards. It is important to check the siding often and make repairs while they are still simple. Look for and repair cracks, holes, and gouges, and secure popped nails.

Holes or gouges in clapboards can be patched. Enlarge the gouge using a standard drill bit, then insert a plug. You can purchase one at your local hardware store, or cut one yourself with a plug-cutter attachment on an electric drill or drill press. Line up the grain of the plug with that of the clapboard, then glue it in place. After it dries, prime and paint it.

## Warning Signs of Clapboard Problems

- protruding nail heads
- splits running along the grain
- knots that have popped out
- boards that have slipped out of line
- gouges or decayed areas
- peeling paint (indicating moisture behind the clapboard)

## Clapboard Do's and Don'ts

### Do

- tap raised nails flush with surface.
- predrill new nail holes to prevent splitting.
- use ring-shanked galvanized or aluminum nails to prevent rusting.
- follow the existing nailing pattern to avoid splitting boards (see sidebar).

### Don't

- use nonflexible caulk between joints.
- apply too much pressure when inserting clapboards.

- tear off several good boards to replace one damaged board.
- settle for replacement boards that don't match the originals.
- leave new boards unprimed and unpainted.
- caulk the underside of the clapboard (this would trap moisture behind the board).

## How to Mend a Cracked Clapboard

| *Steps* | *Tools and Materials* |
|---|---|
| 1. Pry open the crack just enough to clean out any dirt and debris with a stiff paintbrush.<br>2. Make sure the wood is dry. | screwdriver or chisel<br>stiff paintbrush<br>sunshine, hair dryer, or heat gun (low setting) |
| 3. Squeeze glue into crack.<br>4. Spread the glue evenly inside the crack. | waterproof glue<br>cotton swab, wood sliver, or thin screwdriver blade |

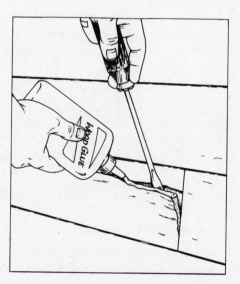

*Steps*                                                    *Tools and Materials*

5.  Press the split closed and secure un-       long board
    der pressure.                                      (jammed into
                                                                   the ground) or
                                                                   temporary nail
                                                                   below the split
                                                                   board

6.  Wipe off excess glue and allow 24            rag
    hours for drying.

7.  Use exterior wood filler and putty           exterior wood
    knife to patch gaps in the dried joint.           filler
                                                                   putty knife
                                                                   sandpaper
8.  Let dry, then sand, prime, and paint.        primer and paint
                                                                   brushes

TIP: Use a hacksaw blade, without the saw frame, to cut off nails holding a badly damaged clapboard in place. Wrap one end of the blade with electrical tape to form a handle. The thin blade will slip between the clapboards without causing any damage.

## The Great Nailing Controversy

It isn't often that you'll find two carpenters engaged in a heated debate, but bring up the subject of the proper way to nail overlapping clapboards and you just might witness one.

At the heart of the problem of where to nail clap-boards is the fact that the thin, beveled boards are prone to both cupping and splitting. Clapboards generally overlap one another approximately 1 inch. Since each board is beveled, the thicker portion of the top board overlaps the thinner portion of the clapboard beneath it.

One party in this controversy will claim that the nail should pass through both boards, pinning them securely to the sheathing.

The other party, however, will insist that any nail that close to the edge of either clapboard is going to split the wood, especially the thinner clapboard beneath the thicker one. Instead, he will argue, the nail should be positioned approximately 1½ inches from the bottom of the overlapping clapboard so that there is no chance of splitting the lower board. And since the lower board is not nailed at the top, it is free to expand and contract without splitting around a confining nail.

But wait a minute, the other side counters. If you nail above the lower board, you'll pull the upper board into the void directly above the top of the lower board. If you hit the nail once too often, the clapboard will split instantly. And even if you don't split it, the clapboard is more apt to cup in a matter of months since the nail is located so far from the bottom of the board.

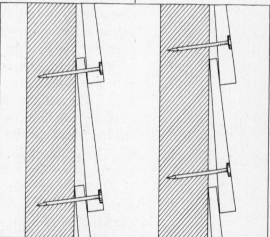

So what's the answer?

Above the overlap? Or through the overlap?

If you are simply replacing or repairing a few clapboards, I suggest you nail through the overlap, but only after you have predrilled the holes to avoid splitting either board. Obviously, professionals are not going to be satisfied with this solution for a complete project; it would be impractical to predrill all the holes if you were installing new siding over the entire house.

Personally, if I were having my house re-sided, I would insist that the nails pass through the overlap, but you and your carpenter may differ. Before you take sides, I suggest you inspect a few homes that have been newly sided, and let the condition of the clapboards illustrate which method is best.

# #15
# Buy a gun—a caulking gun—
# and use it.

The only safe gun you can keep in your house is a caulking gun, and every home should have at least one. Filling exterior gaps with caulking serves several purposes: it improves the appearance of your home; it reduces infiltration by cold air in the winter and hot air in the summer; and it discourages decay-causing penetration by insects, moisture, and fungi. If you think a small separation just isn't worth the effort, imagine if all the minor cracks in a typical older home were combined. They would form an opening the size of an average window!

Caulking guns and tubes of caulking are inexpensive. Together they represent one of the fastest paybacks in home maintenance. Caulking is so important and so easy that it pays to keep a caulking gun in more than one strategic location: in the garage, in the basement, or above your workbench.

The same advice applies to tubes of caulking. Keep a stock of cartridges readily available and try to finish each tube you open, since stored caulking can harden and become unusable. It only takes a moment to find another nearby seam that needs a bead of caulking to seal out moisture and cold air. But if you still can't finish the tube, keep the caulking from drying out by inserting a 6d or 8d nail, or a sliver of wood, in the tube's nozzle.

Caulking will last longer when it has contact with three surfaces: two sides and a bottom. Caulking that is suspended between two sides will soon tear or be punctured. If the gap you need to fill is deeper than 1/2 inch, press in a foam backer rod first so the bead of caulking will have a solid foundation.

Maintaining a continuous bead will create a more attractive job and a more effective barrier. Before you start a long run, make sure there are no obstacles in your path. Begin with a fresh, full tube, and anticipate your handle squeezes so that the gun does not travel faster than the bead forms. You will find it easier to create a neat, even bead if you keep the gun nozzle clean. Use a rag to clean off any accumulated caulking around the tip. The sign of a competent caulker is a clean index finger: only impatient caulkers have to repair their beads with a wet fingertip.

## Warning Signs of Needed Caulking

- cold air coming through electrical outlets
- drafts around baseboards or window and door casings
- peeling paint around seams and joints
- gaps between wood siding and windows, doors, chimneys, and exterior detailing

## Caulking Do's and Don'ts

### Do

- pay special attention to areas where dissimilar materials meet, such as where wood siding meets a brick chimney.
- check places where the wood changes direction, such as where horizontal wood siding meets a vertical window, or a miter joint.
- inspect openings cut for pipes and vents.
- keep different types of caulking on hand for spur-of-the-moment repairs.
- cut the tip so that it produces a bead slightly smaller than the gap you wish to fill. This will enable you to force caulking into the seam.
- steady the gun at the proper angle for a smooth, professional-looking bead.

### Don't

- caulk the lower edge of each row of wooden siding. Air circulation behind each overlapping board is necessary to avoid dry rot caused by trapped moisture.
- buy the cheapest caulking. The few cents you might save are outweighed by the time it will take next year to dig out the old caulking before you replace it with new.
- caulk when the temperature is below 55 degrees. But if you must, keep each tube indoors and warm until you are ready to use it. Even so, the caulking may not adhere to the cold boards.

## How to Caulk a Joint the Right Way

| *Steps* | *Tools and Materials* |
|---|---|
| 1. Select the type of caulking appropriate for your project. | caulking gun tubes of interior or exterior caulk |
| 2. Clean out the joint, removing old caulking, dirt, and loose paint. | screwdriver dry paintbrush |

TIP: A heat gun may soften old, stubborn caulking.

| | |
|---|---|
| 3. Pack joints deeper than ¹/₂ inch with filler material. | weather stripping foam, plastic rods, or oakum |
| 4. Cut the nozzle at a 45-degree angle, making the opening slightly smaller than the seam or crack. | utility knife |
| 5. Pierce the internal seal. | long nail, coat hanger, or stiff wire |
| 6. Starting at one end, apply a continuous bead of caulking, maintaining constant pressure by using the trigger to move the notched rod. | |
| 7. A few inches from the end, release the pressure on the caulking in the tube by turning the notches on the rod away from the trigger. | |
| 8. Wipe off any excess caulking on the nozzle. | rag |

TIP: Extend the tip of the caulking gun nozzle with a length of flexible tubing for hard-to-reach areas.

| | |
|---|---|
| 9. If necessary, smooth the bead of caulking with your finger or a spoon dipped in water. Wipe off any excess caulking. | water spoon rag |

*Steps*                                    *Tools and Materials*

10. Check for any gaps in the caulking,
    then allow to dry the recommended
    time before painting.

TIP: Fashion a wire holster on your ladder, then keep a
caulking gun loaded with an unopened tube there all the
time. The best time to caulk a crack or open seam is when
you find it.

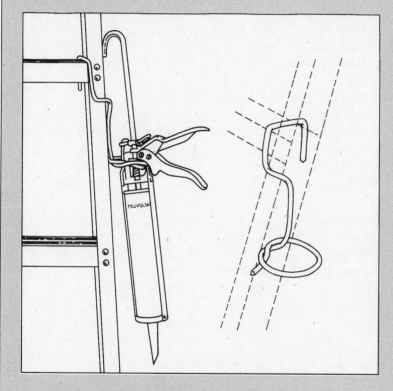

## *Which Caulking Product Is Best?*

The selection of caulking materials in a well-stocked
home improvement center can be mind-boggling. There
are concrete caulks, tile and tub caulks, silicone caulks,
acrylic caulks, butyl-rubber caulks, and others, including,
just to complicate matters, combinations of these.

The hardest part of a caulking project may be deciding which product is the best.

Among the three most popular types are silicone, butyl-rubber, and acrylic-latex. Here's a breakdown of what each has to offer and their limitations:

| | *Silicone* | *Acrylic-Latex* | *Butyl-Rubber* |
|---|---|---|---|
| **Well suited for:** | | | |
| metal | x | | x |
| wood | | x | |
| brick | | | x |
| masonry | | | x |
| flashing | | | x |
| tile | x | | |
| glass | x | | |
| interior | | x | |
| Life expectancy | 20–30 yrs. | 5–25 yrs.* | 10–20 yrs. |
| Flexibility | excellent | good | good |
| Shrinkage | little | little | moderate |
| High moisture areas | fair | poor | excellent |
| Paintable | no | yes | yes |
| Tinted | no | yes | yes |
| Cleanup | water | water | paint thinner |
| Curing time** | moderate | rapid | slow |
| Flow | smooth | smooth | coarse |
| Odor | irritable | low | low |
| Cost | $4–$5 | $2–$4 | $3–$4 |

*Varies according to quality, reflected by price.
**Slowed by low temperatures and/or high humidity.

# #16
# Give your house a bath.

Or a shower, actually.

We all like to make sure that our cars, decks and porches, and outdoor furniture get washed on occasion, but we tend to forget that the same dirt and grit accumulates on our houses. This fine layer of grime isn't as destructive as termites or wood rot, but it does obscure the original color and can encourage moss and mildew to take root. If you think your house needs painting, you might discover that the paint hasn't faded, it's just become obscured under a layer of dirt and grime.

The solution is a power washer. The water is supplied to the pump through an ordinary garden hose, then pressurized by a small gasoline-fueled engine and forced through a special hose to a wand similar to that found in many do-it-yourself car wash stalls. The wand generally comes with two or three different nozzles and spray patterns. Unlike a garden hose, which produces only about 50 pounds per square inch (psi) of water pressure, power washers can generate up to 4,000 psi. Used properly, water pressurized up to 3,000 psi won't harm intact paint, but will blast away moss, mildew, dirt, insect nests, loose or blistered paint, and years and years of tough, dirty grime.

Power washers are readily available through well-stocked rental centers. Most firms prefer to rent the washers either by the day or by four-hour periods. Rates can range from $50 to $75 a day or more, depending on the size of the power washer and the demand for it in your area. During the peak season, expect to have to reserve a power washer several days in advance for weekend use.

Portable power washers generally are built into a wheeled framework to make them easy to move. Even so, have a second person help you lift it in or out of your vehicle and move it up or down a stairs or steep embankment. The washer may or may not come with a garden hose to be attached to a standard threaded outdoor spigot, so be sure to inquire at the rental shop.

Also ask how many gallons of water the pressure washer

sprays per minute through the special 50-foot hose. This is critical. You don't want to find out too late that your water system won't operate the pressure washer you just rented. You can conduct a simple test to determine the velocity of your water supply. Hold an empty gallon plastic jug under the spigot you plan to use, then time how quickly you can fill it with water. If the power washer requires a minimum of 6 gallons of water per minute, then you must be able to fill the 1-gallon jug in 10 seconds. If it takes longer, the machine may not function.

If you rely on a private well for your water supply, you must consider an additional problem: a large washing project could run a rural well dry. Be sure to discuss this with the rental firm, as well as with someone familiar with your well's capacity.

One major concern with power washing is the potential damage to plants and shrubs around the foundation. Unprotected plants can absorb water through their leaves and their root systems. Obviously, a direct blast of water from the water wand is going to shred any foliage, but even more dangerous is the potentially fatal effect a powerful cleanser could have on each plant's root system. Cleansers are often used in power washers to remove stubborn dirt and oil from concrete driveways, but some people also prefer to use cleansers to wash their houses. Cleansers are helpful, but they also pose a danger to plants, grass, trees, and shrubs. Drop cloths can protect the leaves from the water, but it is virtually impossible to prevent the roots from absorbing the water runoff. The only truly safe cleanser is no cleanser at all. In most cases, clear water alone will adequately clean your home's siding. It is the pressure, not the cleaning agent, that does most of the work. If you have to use a cleaning agent to remove stubborn mildew or chalking, make sure that (1) the manufacturer clearly states that it will not harm plants, (2) you do not exceed the recommended dosage, and (3) to be safe, most of the water runoff is directed away from the plants using plastic drop cloths around the foundation.

If your house will require a considerable amount of preparation prior to starting the power wash, delay renting the unit until the preparation work has been completed. If the job goes quickly and you still have time, use the power washer to clean your deck, concrete patio, driveway, or garage floor, your outdoor furniture, or even your garbage cans.

## Warning Signs of a Needed Power Wash

- moss or mildew attached to the aluminum, vinyl, or wood siding
- paint that has begun to look and feel "chalky" from oxidation
- dull, lifeless paint color
- unpleasant accumulations of insect cocoons, cobwebs, pigeon dung, and dirt

## Power Wash Do's and Don'ts

### Do

- rent rather than buy a portable power washer.
- be careful not to spray power lines and other sources of electricity—fatal jolts can race through a stream of water in a split second.
- wrap all exterior lights with garbage bags, food storage bags, or plastic.
- use duct tape to cover exterior electrical outlets.
- close all windows.
- wear safety glasses.
- cover all plants with protective drop cloths.
- keep the nozzle approximately 12 inches from the surface.
- use a soft scrub brush on stubborn spots.
- wash from the bottom up; rinse from the top down.
- do be cautious when working from a ladder. The water runoff can cause the soft soil to suddenly sink under the weight of the ladder, pitching you to the ground.

### Don't

- rely on your garden hose for tough jobs.
- spray on a windy day.
- spray directly on windows; the pressure can shatter them.
- spray under overlapping boards or directly into joints, especially where the water could gain access to the interior of your house.
- use cleanser in water that will run around plants and shrubs. It could kill them.

- learn how to handle the pressure wand while standing on a ladder. Practice with both feet firmly planted on the ground.
- place your hand in the spray. The high pressure can burn your skin.

## How to Power Wash Your Home

| *Steps* | *Tools and Materials* |
|---|---|
| 1. Cover all electrical outlets and lights with plastic and duct tape. | plastic bags or wrap<br>duct tape |
| 2. Close all windows and doors. | |
| 3. Protect nearby shrubs and plants. | drop cloths |
| 4. Organize the hoses to avoid tangling as you move around your house. | |
| 5. Mentally divide your house into vertical sections, working on one at a time. | |
| 6. Hold the wand 12 inches away from the surface. | |
| 7. To avoid streaks, wash each section starting at the bottom and working toward the top. | |
| 8. Use a soft scrub brush on any stubborn spots. | scrub brush |

> TIP: Do not leave plastic drop cloths over plants or shrubs any longer than necessary, especially if they are in direct sun. The heat generated beneath the plastic can wilt a healthy plant in a matter of minutes.

9. Rinse each section starting at the top and working toward the bottom.

# #17
# Give your house
# the Paint Test.

It is important to inspect your home's paint for the inevitable
signs of failure. Letting the surface deteriorate before repainting
only gives water more time to penetrate deep into the pores of the
wood. As it does, it loosens even more paint and provides a safe
haven for decay-causing fungi. What could have been a simple
painting project can turn into an expensive, time-consuming replacement of wood siding, trim, casings, and windowsills.

On the other hand, painting your house only for the simple
pleasure of painting, to change the color every two years, or when
it becomes dirty is also going to get you in trouble. Too much
paint is almost as bad as too little. Multiple layers of paint prevent
the wood from breathing, which it must do to survive. Water vapors must be able to pass through the paint if the wood is to remain dry, stable, and strong. The moisture vapors can come from
inside the wall, in the wood itself, or from a hard, driving rain that
forces water behind the siding. If the board has too many layers of
paint, especially oil-based paint, the water vapors are going to be
trapped inside the wood, where decay will start.

Paint fails for a number of reasons:

- improper application
- improper preparation
- excessive interior moisture
- the wrong type of paint
- inferior paint
- applying old paint
- too many layers of paint
- waiting too long to paint
- incompatible types of paint
- failure to follow the manufacturer's instructions
- painting when it was either too hot or too cold

To determine the condition of the paint, give your house the Paint Test. Administering the test is easy. Simply take a walk around your house and answer the following questions.

## The Paint Test

### Has your paint begun to exhibit hundreds of tiny surface cracks, a condition called "crazing" or "checking"?

This is the first sign of paint failure. The appearance of hundreds of shallow cracks on the surface is indicative of paint that has lost its ability to expand and contract with the wood. Simply stated, crazing is a sign of old age, rather than an internal problem. If caught at this stage, serious damage can be averted with a fresh coat of paint.

### Have cracks begun to appear in the paint?

This is the second stage of paint failure. Once the hairline crazing has developed into wider cracks, moisture can penetrate to the wood. This allows for additional moisture, and additional damage. Each crack will have to be primed before painting, but removal should not be required.

### Has the checking and cracking developed into "alligatoring," or hundreds of cracks extending completely through the surface of the paint?

At this, the third stage in paint failure, the cracks have widened, deepened, and multiplied to cover a significant area. In advanced cases, the wood can be seen through the cracks. Water has easy access to the wood, causing flecks of paint to begin to separate and curl. The paint takes on an appearance similar to the skin of an alligator; hence its name. The only cure is to scrape away any alligatored paint before repainting.

### Are there blisters in the paint?

Blistering is an advanced stage of paint failure that may occur without first exhibiting the characteristics of old paint. In fact, paint can blister within weeks of being applied. It is a sign that the paint has not adhered to previous layers or to the wood. More often than not, blisters are caused by moisture in the wood. The moisture may have entered the board from inside your house, through a nearby spot where the paint had already peeled, or through a separated joint or exposed end grain.

It is fruitless to paint over a blister, even if the blister appears to be intact. The paint film will eventually burst, taking with it the fresh layer of paint. Blisters must be broken, scraped, dried out, primed, and repainted.

### Has the paint begun to peel?

Peeling represents the ultimate stage of paint failure. The paint has lost its grip on the wood, because of moisture in the wood, poor preparation, or improper application. At this stage, the wood is exposed to the elements, allowing for additional peeling and, more important, damage to the wood from water and sunlight.

Scraping off the peeling paint is only half the solution. Unless the cause of the problem is also corrected, the next layer of paint is apt to peel as well.

### Has the paint wrinkled in sections?

Like blisters, wrinkled paint is not a sign of old age, but of improper application. A fresh layer of paint will wrinkle if

- it was brushed on too heavy.
- it was applied before the previous coat was dry.
- it was applied on a bright, hot, sunny day.
- it was an oil-based paint applied over latex without a layer of primer between the two.

Since wrinkling is an indication that the paint has not adhered to the previous layer, the paint must be removed by scraping, sanding, or stripping before a new coat can be applied.

## How to Prepare Your Home for Painting

| *Steps* | *Tools and Materials* |
|---|---|
| 1. Repair any damaged boards, including the siding and trim, as well as leaking rain gutters and downspouts. | see #6 and #14 (pages 34 and 71) |
| 2. Caulk any separated joints, holes, splits, or any place where water could gain access to the wood. Make sure the caulking can be painted, and note how long it must cure prior to painting. | caulking gun exterior caulking see #15 (page 76) |

> TIP: Caulking at this stage prevents any water blown by a power washer from reaching the wood. It may be necessary to do minor touch-up caulking after priming.

| *Steps* | *Tools and Materials* |
|---|---|
| 3. Power wash your house to remove dirt and pollutants. | see #16 (page 81) |
| 4. Scrape, sand, or chemically remove any peeling, blistered, wrinkled, or alligatored paint. If you have reason to suspect that your house has lead-based paint on it, see #4. (page 20) | long-handled scraper wire brush |

> TIP: Buy a high-quality, long-handled wooden scraper. The extra weight will reduce the amount of pressure you have to apply. Look for the style with a replaceable double-edged blade. Remember that the blades soon become dull. Get into the habit of sharpening or replacing the blade once both edges lose their bite.

| | |
|---|---|
| 5. Feather the edges of any paint adjacent to bare wood. Fill low spots with an exterior surface compound. Sand when hard. | #80-grit sandpaper sanding block wide putty knife exterior surface compound |

> TIP: Apply a water repellent to bare wood that will be exposed to a great deal of moisture, such as boards around gutters and downspouts. Make sure the water repellent can be painted. Read the instructions carefully regarding drying time before painting.

| | |
|---|---|
| 6. Prime any bare wood. | alkyd primer wide brush |

TIP: Keep a caulking gun handy to fill any gaps that have opened during the scraping and sanding steps.

*Steps*                                          *Tools and Materials*

7. Paint.                                         paint
                                                  wide brush

## Tips for Painting

- When selecting a brand of paint, take your business to a store whose employees can do more than just read labels. Tap into their experience; ask them which brands have proven to be the most successful in your area. Your type of house, its exposure to the sun, your region's weather patterns, and its environmental pollutants will all affect your final choice. Talk to your neighbors, and get the advice of friendly professional painters in your area.
- Always stir the paint before using, even if the can was shaken at the store. Also, stir periodically during application to keep the pigments from settling to the bottom of the can and affecting the color.
- Pour the top third into another container to avoid spilling.
- Protect shrubs, decks, furniture, doors, and windows with drop cloths. If you plan for accidents, there may be no disasters.
- Keep a fresh rag handy at all times.
- Use a wide paintbrush, but be sure it feels comfortable to you. The size should be selected according to the width of the boards you are painting, the size of your hand, and your arm strength. A wide brush may carry more paint, but if your arm tires after 30 minutes of use, it's no more practical than a narrower, lighter brush.
- Brushes work the paint more deeply into the wood than do rollers.
- Don't try to carry too much paint on the brush.
- Work the paint into the wood, then remove any runs, drips, and brush marks by "tipping off." As your final stroke, hold the brush at a 45-degree angle and pull it toward you in the direction of the grain of the wood.
- To reduce evidence of overlapping, don't stop for lunch

with a board partially painted. Quit only when you reach a vertical projection, such as a window, door, or corner trim. Plan your work in horizontal rather than vertical sections. When you must pause in midboard to move your ladder, feather the edges of the paint to blend in the adjacent section.

• Check from the ground for bare spots—painters call them "holidays"—before moving your ladder and equipment.

---

### *Seven Days* Not *to Paint*
(or seven excuses for putting it off until tomorrow)

1. Early on a dewy morning when there is still a fine layer of moisture on your house.
2. The first day after several days of rain, fog, or high humidity. The old paint may feel dry, but the wood underneath is still damp. Trapping the moisture in the wood is sure to cause blistering.
3. The day after power washing your house, for the same reason as explained above.
4. On a hot, sunny day, when the sun dries the paint too quickly, trapping solvents next to the wood. This eventually causes the paint to blister.
5. On the same day you apply the first coat.
6. On the same day you seal the new wood with shellac or varnish to prevent knots from showing through the paint.
7. On a windy day, when there is dirt, dust, leaves, and pollen in the air.

---

### *Oil-based or Latex Paint?*

In the battle of the paints, latex has been declared the winner.

What began as an experiment to find an easy-to-use exterior paint for do-it-yourselfers has gradually won the approval of most professional painters. High-quality latex paints, with their acrylic resin binders (the "glue" that bonds all of the ingredients together in the can and on your house) and long-lasting pigments, have nearly shoved oil-based exterior paints off the shelf.

Dollar for dollar, stroke for stroke, exterior latex paints last longer, remain more flexible, allow the wood to breathe easier, resist the ultraviolet rays of the sun better, don't chalk as much, adhere to both oil-based and latex paints, are easier to clean up, and don't emit dangerous fumes.

But remember: Not all latex paints are high quality. Professional painters still argue over which brand is best, and you would be well advised to eavesdrop on their conversations. As a general rule, stick with nationally known brands with a proven track record.

High-quality paints are not cheap. But saving a few dollars may cut a few years off your paint job.

Kinda puts it in a different perspective, doesn't it?

# #18
# Tuck-point brick walls to keep them sound and attractive.

When my son Eric was four years old, his favorite bedtime story was "The Three Little Pigs." One night, at the conclusion of our reading, he turned to me and said drowsily, "Don't worry, Daddy. The bad wolf's not going to bother us."

"Why's that?" I asked.

" 'Cause we live in a brick house."

Naturally, Eric had no idea that the bad wolf could assume the identity a wide variety of "evil characters," including termites, dry rot, peeling paint, and adjustable-rate mortgages. But he was right to a certain extent. The bad wolf does have a harder time harassing people who live in brick houses; brick simply lasts longer and suffers fewer problems than wood.

Brick homes have been around for centuries, and will be for centuries to come. Judging from the number of historic brick structures, you might think that more 17th-, 18th-, and 19th-century homes were built of brick than of wood, but that's not the case. It's just that a higher percentage of brick houses have survived. Most pre-20th-century brick homes feature solid brick walls often three or four courses thick, so as to support the weight of the upper floors and roof. In contrast, brick homes built during the 20th century are more apt to feature a single layer of bricks attached to a wooden or concrete block wall that actually supports the roof. Brick veneer, as it is called, is the industry standard today. It is both faster and less expensive to build than solid brick homes.

Bricks, like lumber, are graded according to their quality, which is determined by the clay used and the length of time it is fired in the kiln. The three standard classifications are:

*SW*—capable of withstanding severe weathering

*MW*—capable of withstanding moderate weathering
*NW*—capable of withstanding only negligible weathering
(above-freezing temperatures year-round)

While water can eventually erode a brick-and-mortar wall, the greatest threat to a brick home is freezing water. A brick wall can absorb a good deal of moisture without suffering damage. But freezing water expands, and that sudden expansion can break off the face of a brick or loosen the mortar in a seam.

Bricks and mortar form an interesting relationship. As anyone familiar with brick buildings knows, mortar tends to crumble before brick does. But the mortar isn't flawed; it is purposely mixed to flex when the bricks don't. As substantial as it may appear, even a brick home moves: the foundation settles, the ground shifts, the bricks expand as the sun heats them and contract as the temperature drops. The mortar acts as a cushion to absorb any stress. If something has to give, the mortar breaks up first, not the brick.

But since it is relatively soft, mortar is also susceptible to excess moisture, wind, and pollution. Left unchecked, the mortar can actually erode to the point where the brick tumbles out. Damage, however, can occur long before bricks start to loosen. If eroded mortar is not repaired, water gains access to the interior of the wall, starting a cycle of weathering and decay. Freezing temperatures damage additional mortar and brick, enabling even more water to penetrate. Once it does, it is absorbed by the interior wooden framework and plaster, causing decay from the inside. By the time the damage is visible, the entire wall may be beyond repair and, in fact, may need to be replaced.

But before you become convinced that perhaps brick isn't such a great idea, realize that bricks and mortar require a minimum amount of maintenance in return for years of worry-free protection. Hairline cracks can be filled with an exterior caulking designed specifically for mortar joints. If you later discover that the crack has widened, look for a cause, such as the ground settling beneath the foundation or water entering the wall from another source.

Stable cracks wider than $\frac{1}{4}$ inch should be repointed with fresh mortar, a technique also referred to as tuck-pointing. Repointing is not beyond the capabilities of most homeowners, provided (1) you are patient and neat, (2) the extent of the damage is minimal, and (3) your home will never be a candidate for the National Register of Historic Places.

Owners of older brick homes face an additional challenge in repointing. They must match the color of the fresh mortar to that of the original. This is not a matter to be taken lightly, for a total disregard for the color of the new mortar can leave your home looking speckled. New, untinted mortars are often bright white in color, a far cry from the grayish hue of hundred-year-old mortar. You can adjust the color of mortar by mixing in powdered tints available from concrete supply firms. And this is where patience is a virtue. You must carefully mix, test (on an inconspicuous spot), and wait for the test spot to dry before repointing your house.

If your home is not just old, but truly historic, you should consult with a professional restoration expert on mortar colors, textures, and strengths before proceeding.

If you decide you do want to repoint your home yourself, take this final bit of advice: Don't experiment with mortar colors and your own skills on an obvious section of brick wall. Select a course of bricks hidden by shrubbery, or use an eroded section of brick wall in the basement as a classroom. And, as always, if the task becomes overwhelming, call in a professional.

## Mortar Warning Signs

- cracked or broken brick
- diagonal cracks running through mortar joints (generally a sign of a settling foundation, perhaps because of excess water around it)
- eroded mortar joints
- water and mud splashed up against the brick foundation after a rain
- moss growing on brick walls

## Mortar Do's and Don'ts

### Do

- make sure all gutters and downspouts are working properly and that the rainwater is diverted several feet away from the foundation.
- check horizontal brick surfaces, such as the tops of walls or bricks directly beneath a windowsill, for signs of deterioration.
- wear protective glasses while chipping out old mortar.

**Don't**

- apply a finish to bricks. The finish prevents brick from "breathing" and traps water.
- repoint your bricks until you have patched any leaking gutters or downspouts that contributed to the problem.
- risk damaging your bricks by using a power grinder to remove old mortar.
- sandblast brick; it destroys the hard protective facing.

## How to Tuck-point Mortar

| *Steps* | *Tools and Materials* |
|---|---|
| 1. Remove any loose or cracked mortar to a depth of 1 inch. | gloves |
| | protective glasses |
| | cold chisel |
| | heavy hammer |
| 2. Clean out the joint. | old paintbrush |
| | wire brush |
| | garden hose |
| 3. Mix a small batch of mortar, water, and if necessary, color tints. Use a measuring cup and record all ingredients for consistency. Mix to a stiff paste. | measuring cup |
| | mortar mix |
| | concrete color tints |
| | water |
| | plastic bucket |
| | trowel |
| 4. Mist the clean joint with water. | spray bottle or |
| |    wet paintbrush |
| 5. Place a small amount of mortar on the bottom of the trowel. | trowel |

*Steps*                                    *Tools and Materials*

6. Holding the trowel and mortar directly       repointing trowel
   beneath the clean joint, use a special
   repointing trowel to force the mortar
   into the joint. Deep recesses should be
   filled 1/2 inch at a time, allowing time for
   each layer to dry (approximately a half
   hour, or until mortar has begun to
   harden).

7. Use a damp rag to wipe mortar off            damp rag
   the face of the brick.

8. When the mortar is firm but not              pointing tool
   hardened, smooth the joint with a            paintbrush
   pointing tool that duplicates the
   profile of the existing joints. Use a
   damp paintbrush to feather the edges
   of the new mortar into those of the old.

9. Wipe or brush off any excess mortar.         dry rag
                                                soft bristle brush
10. If the new mortar is exposed to             misting bottle or
    sunlight, mist it occasionally for two        garden hose
    or three days to prevent it from
    drying too fast.

> TIP: Short patches of mortar are actually more unsightly
> than longer ones. When in doubt, chisel out additional
> old mortar, especially if it will lead to one longer section
> of new mortar rather than two or three unnatural-looking
> spots.

## *Recycled Brick: When Is a Bargain Not Such a Bargain?*

My parents still live in the 1911 foursquare where I grew up in New Windsor, Illinois. Like most rambling four-squares, the house is made of wood, but it does have a brick foundation and basement floor.

Once he was done paying for college tuitions, groceries, and dentists for four kids, Dad decided he was going to make his damp, dark basement more usable. In the process, he removed, one bucket at a time, hundreds of the original bricks from the basement floors and walls, and stacked them carefully in the backyard.

He and my mother decided that they would use the bricks to construct a sidewalk leading to their new garage. They marked the path, dug out the sod, tamped down a foundation of sand, and spent hours carefully setting the basement bricks in an attractive pattern.

It was about a year later, however, that they began to notice a problem. Several of the bricks had begun to disintegrate, leaving fair-sized chunks scattered about the sidewalk. They discovered the hard way that the original brick masons had delegated the softer bricks to the interior basement walls and ledges, saving the high-grade, tougher bricks for the exterior foundation. As long as they were in the basement, the softer bricks were fine, but once they were subjected to the harsh Illinois winters with frequent, sometimes daily, freeze-thaw cycles, they simply fell apart.

So what did my parents do?

Not much they could do, really, except to sweep a lot.

But knowing them as I do, someday my mother and father will be sitting out on their patio and Dad will say, "Let's tear out that brick sidewalk tomorrow."

And they will.

# #19
# Dig out decayed wood before the disease spreads.

Once wood becomes wet, it begins to rot. And once it begins to rot, it loses its strength. The adjacent boards or joints then have to assume the additional stress—if they can. Many times, this amounts to more than they were designed to withstand. If they can't handle the additional stress, they, too, will fail, which can lead to a minor disaster for homeowners.

If a board is protected with a coat of paint, clear finish, caulking, or glazing, water cannot penetrate into the pores of the wood. But once that outer layer of protection is broken, water can seep into the pores, where decay can begin and spread quickly without detection.

The first step in preventing expensive damage is in knowing where to look for water entry. Begin with those areas exposed to the greatest amount of water, such as the siding around downspouts, wood that is always shaded, posts that rest on concrete, and the bottoms of door casings and windows.

Windows are particularly vulnerable to small problems that can eventually lead to expensive repairs. Although they do not necessarily come in contact with more water than the siding that surrounds them, their protruding muntins, rails, and sill slow the descent of the water. Whether it is rain, melting snow, or condensation, the slow-moving moisture has more opportunity to test the effectiveness of the finish and find any gapped joints leading to exposed end grains. A typical double-hung window might have as many as 24 joints, each a potential entry point for water.

When magnified, the end grain of a board looks like hundreds of tightly bound soda straws. And like a soda straw, the ends are wide open and able to absorb far more liquid than the sides. Each joint in a window construction will conceal one or two sections of end grain. Unfortunately, they are not sealed when the window or casing is being assembled. Once the window is installed, a coat of paint or bead of caulking will cover the thin line marking the joint between two boards. But if that thin layer of protection is broken, water has easy access to the open end grain.

In addition to moisture and water damage, the joints in a window and its casing are also subjected to more stress than other external parts of your house. They must endure two types of movement: the opening and closing of the window and the wood's expansion and contraction. This is complicated by the fact that the temperature at each side of a window can differ by as much as 80 degrees. It's a good idea, then, to check the joints in a window regularly and make repairs immediately.

Despite good intentions, window joints often remain open for weeks, months, even years before they are repaired. When that happens, water seeps into the joint and is absorbed by the unprotected end grain, where it fosters decay-causing fungi. Just how long it takes for the wood to rot beyond repair is difficult to predict. The type of wood, the amount of water that flows into the gapped joint, how soon the fungi spores take root, and how much moisture is drawn out of the wood through evaporation all combine to determine how long the wood will last.

Regardless of the time factor, the best thing you can do is to check your windows, doors, and other exterior wood often for warning signs of deterioration. Once spotted, you can take one of the following courses of action:

- If the paint has begun to peel, but the wood is still firm, scraping, priming, and painting may be all that is necessary. (See #17 on page 85). Caulk any separated joints.
- If the wood has become spongy but is still intact, brush on one or more coats of wood hardener after scraping, but prior to priming and painting.
- If the wood has begun to decay, dig out the loose fibers and fungi with a knife, chisel, or screwdriver, apply wood hardener, and fill the gap with an exterior wood filler.

Although you might think it is time-consuming to regularly inspect all of your windows, doors, frames, and posts, there is one thing that takes much longer—having to replace them.

## Warning Signs of Deterioration

- peeling paint

- soft, spongy wood
- wood that breaks into soft chunks rather than long, springy splinters when pried with a knife
- a cupped windowsill
- deteriorated caulking or glazing
- gapped joints

## Do's and Don'ts to Preventing Wood Decay

### Do

- continue to caulk as needed.
- make sure storm windows and screens have weep holes at the bottom to drain off rainwater in the summer and moisture formed by condensation in the winter. Without these holes, the moisture remains trapped on the windowsill and can cause decay.
- take necessary safety precautions when working with consolidants and epoxies; some people are sensitive to the chemicals contained in them. Wear rubber gloves and eye protection when working with any liquid consolidant or soft filler, and use a particle mask when sanding the wood afterward.
- follow all labeled instructions carefully. Timing and techniques may vary from product to product. Dispose of all rags, brushes, and related materials in an outdoor trash can according to the labeled directions.

### Don't

- replace a wooden window on an older house with metal or vinyl. Compared to metal or vinyl, wood is relatively easy to repair.
- caulk over weep holes on aluminum track windows.
- expect the filler to be as strong as real wood. If a substantial portion of the board is missing, especially a portion that bears weight or stress, a new board may be required.
- convince yourself that a wood filler will accept a stain like real wood. It won't. Fillers are best disguised by paint.
- attempt to use consolidants or epoxies when the temperature is below 65 degrees. They cannot cure properly in cold weather.

## How to Make Repairs with Wood Hardeners and Fillers

| *Steps* | *Tools and Materials* |
|---|---|
| 1. Identify problem areas, probing with a knife or other tool to determine extent of decay. | awl, screwdriver, knife, or long nail |
| 2. Determine the source of moisture that has caused the damage. Make any necessary repairs to downspouts, storm windows, broken siding, and so on. | (See appropriate section for information on specific repairs.) |
| 3. Scrape away any loose paint. | paint scraper, chisel, or putty knife |
| 4. Drill a number of $^3/_{16}$-inch holes through the decayed area and into solid wood. Take care not to drill completely through the board. If you do, plug the exit hole with a sharpened dowel. | drill $^3/_{16}$-inch bit |
| 5. Clean out any loose wood. | dry paintbrush |
| 6. Allow the wood to dry. If necessary, cover it with plastic to protect it from rain or dew. | sunshine, hair dryer, or heat gun on low setting |
| 7. Inject the wood hardener (consolidant) into the holes, saturating the softened area. Repeat if necessary. | syringe or plastic squeeze bottle rubber gloves safety glasses |
| 8. Allow to dry according to manufacturer's directions. | |
| 9. If wood is missing, mix an appropriate amount of a two-part exterior filler. | exterior epoxy filler putty knife rubber gloves |
| 10. Pack the filler into the hole. | putty knife |
| 11. Shape the filler so that it rises just above the level of the surrounding wood. Scrape or wipe off any spills or excess filler before it dries. | putty knife |

| *Steps* | *Tools and Materials* |
| --- | --- |
| 12. After the filler dries, sand it smooth. | #120 sandpaper |
| 13. Prime and paint. | primer |
| | paintbrush |
| | paint |

TIP: Although some carpenters use automotive body putty for these types of repairs, it is too rigid to expand and contract with the wood. As a result, the patch is apt to break loose from the wood in about three years.

# #20
# Don't let little pests become big problems.

Every house is a potential home for more than just your family. Outside my office window, several bees constructed a honeycomb in the sill. Two boards separated just enough to give them access to the unpainted inner wood, and I suspect they found the soft, damp wood an ideal spot to spend the summer. Although I enjoyed watching them come and go for three or four days, I knew that if I allowed them to continue, their hive would have accelerated the decay the spring rains undoubtedly started.

Common household pests may seem harmless, but many can cause extensive damage if they are not discouraged from returning. I recall reading about a homeowner who had problems with paint peeling from a 16-inch-wide and 8-foot-long strip of clapboards. To his amazement, he discovered that over the course of several months, perhaps even years, honeybees entering through a hole in the top clapboard had constructed a gigantic honeycomb between two studs. The moisture from the honeycomb (and a rotted cornice) traveled through the sheathing and the clapboards, leading to the paint failure. It took two carpenters to rip off the siding and a professional beekeeper to remove the bees and their honeycomb. By the time the siding had been replaced and repainted, the bees had cost the homeowner several hundred dollars.

## Household Pests that Cause Damage

Here are several of the more common pests you should watch for and some suggested means of convincing them to move out.

### Carpenter Ants

The large carpenter ants commonly found around porches and in basements and crawl spaces do not eat wood, but they will bore into it to form their nests. In doing so, the reddish-brown or black ants provide channels for water and decay-causing fungi and should be considered a serious problem. They prefer wet, spongy wood, which is easier to bore through. Keeping the wood around your porch, foundation, and basement dry will go a long way toward preventing carpenter ants from riddling your columns, posts, and beams.

If you spot carpenter ants working around your house, don't kill them immediately. Instead, trace their route back to their current nest. Killing a few worker ants is not going to solve your problem. Only when the queen is eliminated, either by digging up the nest and/or saturating it with an insecticide, will the colony disperse.

### Carpenter Bees, Wasps, Hornets, and Other Bees

Carpenter bees look like miniature bumblebees, but they differ in that bumblebees generally build their hives in the ground or close to it, while carpenter bees will bore half-inch-diameter holes in unpainted wood. There they lay their eggs and raise their young. They prefer bare wood over painted wood and will opt for soft, partially decayed wood over hard, fresh wood. Their holes weaken the wood and provide a means for water and other insects to penetrate to the middle of a board.

When carpenter bees decided to bore holes in my boys' outdoor redwood play set, I had no choice but to use an insecticide to eliminate them. They posed both an immediate threat to my children and a long-term threat to their play set. But rather than paint the swing set, which I had finished with clear Watco Exterior Oil to highlight the color and grain of the redwood, I decided to watch closely for any signs of new tenants. I also now make it a point to mist the underside of the play set any time I have my hand-operated pump filled with a general household insecticide.

If carpenter bees, hornets, wasps, or honeybees insist on returning to a specific area, such as a cornice or railing, cover the area with ordinary screen wire and attach it with a staple gun or wire. An occasional misting of the problem area with a commercial insect or bee repellent (some aerosol cans will shoot a stream 20 feet or more) will also discourage the bugs from returning.

### Pigeons

See #11, "Don't let pigeons become windowsill pets," on page 56.

## Powder-Post Beetles

Several wood-boring insects, including *Lyctid* and *Anobiid* beetles, are commonly referred to as powder-post beetles. Although exterminators will distinguish between the many different species, most homeowners are understandably more concerned with their eradication than with their classification.

Powder-post beetles prefer moist wood and high humidity. When conditions are right, the beetles will live their entire lives, eating, sleeping, and laying their eggs, without ever leaving the beam, sill, or floor where they were hatched. The beetles rarely surface and often go undetected for years. Only if their exit hole and their trademark pile of fine sawdust, called frass, are spotted will you know if powder-post beetles are silently gnawing through your home.

If a colony of powder-post beetles has gone undetected for long in a section of floor or a supporting beam, the wood may have to be replaced. Killing the beetles is not an easy task; the unhatched larvae are often immune to insecticides. There are restrictions on the sale and use of strong insecticides by homeowners, so you must contact a professional exterminator if you find any sign of powder-post beetle activity.

## Rodents

Mice and rats can cause serious damage to your home by chewing wood, making nests in insulation, and gnawing on electrical wires. Traps have proven to be the most effective means of removing rodents, but if you are opposed to traps, contact an exterminator. You can discourage rats and mice by removing their sources of food, such as crumbs on the floor or counters, bags of garbage, and cardboard boxes of cereal. Rodents, however, are capable of finding food and water in places you might not even think about, such as in your pet's food dish or underneath your refrigerator.

Setting out poison is not recommended, especially in a house with pets or children. Keep in mind, too, that poison only kills rodents. It won't carry them out to the garbage can once they're dead. The lingering odor of a decaying carcass in your kitchen wall is one you won't soon forget.

## Squirrels

Squirrels are persistent little devils, and they can cause some serious problems if left to roam on their own through your cornice, walls, and attic. Like mice and rats, they gnaw on wood, insulation, even wires.

Squirrels don't necessarily enter a house in search of food. A warm, dry bed or a new adventure seems incentive enough for them. Obviously, if they can find food, they will return more frequently, and probably in greater numbers.

Your first step is to determine how the squirrels are getting into your house. Often, they begin by leaping from a nearby tree onto a gutter or the roof, although I have often watched squirrels scramble straight up the side of a house. Their first trip to your home may have been to forage for acorns or tree seeds. If you have squirrels in your attic, check around your gutters for a small hole in the fascia board or soffit. A chimney is also a common entry point, especially if it is no longer in use and if the mortar has been allowed to deteriorate. You may be able to find the opening by crawling around your darkened attic, looking for cracks of daylight in the eaves.

Before sealing up the entry, make sure that all the squirrels are out of your house. One way to rid a house of squirrels is to scatter mothballs in hard-to-reach recesses, or fill old socks with mothballs or flakes and hang them near suspected entrances and pathways. Another method is to soak rags with ammonia and place them in buckets or shallow pans next to entry holes or squirrel nests.

Once your feel confident that the squirrels have moved out, seal any hole with wood, wire, or metal. If the animals attempt to break in again, you might want to coat the patch with a commercial squirrel repellent until they get the message that they are not wanted.

Of course, you could always put a squirrel feeder in your yard and hope that they won't feel the need to dig through your attic in search of food.

### Termites
See #25 on page 131.

### Woodpeckers
While it doesn't happen often, woodpeckers have been known to target wood siding in search of a meal. These persistent wood borers can pepper a clapboard with holes in short order, giving both insects and moisture the opportunity to gain entry. Since woodpeckers don't normally attack wood simply for pleasure,

their consistent return should indicate that they are finding a ready meal in your wood siding. If you can eliminate the source of their food, you should also eliminate the woodpecker problem. Determine what insects have infested your siding, then spray it with the appropriate insecticide.

Other homeowners have reported that they have been able to discourage woodpeckers by covering the side of the house with plastic, which the woodpeckers have difficulty hanging on to. Rubber snakes, plastic owls, and rattling pie tins seem to be more effective on woodpeckers than on pigeons. But rather than treating the symptoms, attack the cause: eliminate the woodpeckers' free lunch and you should eliminate your problem.

> TIP: The common denominator in the majority of destructive household pests is moist wood. If you keep the wood dry by caulking, painting, and providing adequate ventilation, you reduce the odds that your home will ever be attacked.

# THE FOUNDATION

Ask any contractor, architect, or engineer what part of a house is the most important and chances are you'll hear one answer time after time: the foundation. These experts realize how important a firm foundation is to everything else in the house, from the wood floors and plaster walls to the rafters and roofing.

The majority of the most critical decisions regarding your home's foundation were made before the first shovel of dirt was turned. As a homeowner, there is little you can do now about the depth of the footings, the drainage at the base of the footings, the type of foundation material, or the way in which the foundation was constructed. In most situations, you can presume that the original architect and contractor designed and laid the proper foundation for your size of home and the ground on which it was built. Any mistakes that they may have made would have become painfully evident within the first year.

But like every part of your house, the foundation does require a certain amount of maintenance if you hope to avoid problems with sagging floors, cracked walls, or a wet basement.

There may be no other part of your home that costs so little to maintain, or so much to replace.

This chapter includes Home-Saving Guidelines 21 and 22.

*Page*

# #21
# Check the lay of your land
# to keep the basement dry.

The next time it rains, grab an umbrella and take a walk around your house. The neighbors may think you're crazy, but there's no better way to see just where the water goes once it lands on your roof or lawn. Besides making sure your gutters and downspouts are working properly, check the soil around the foundation. Whether it is covered with grass, decorative gravel, or bark, it should be landscaped to direct water *away* from the house. If you discover that water is running *toward* the foundation, rest assured, it won't simply disappear into the ground. It has to go somewhere, and water will always seek the path of least resistance. If it can't find one, it will try to make one, and oftentimes your foundation is easier to penetrate than several feet of compacted clay, rocks, and tree roots.

The foundation of a house can be compared to the hull of a ship; both are surrounded by moisture, seldom seen in their entirety, and horrible to repair. But unlike a ship, you can reduce the amount of water that your foundation has to resist simply by making sure that the grade of the surrounding land directs rainwater away from your house. If it doesn't, you're destined to be plagued by a wet basement and the distinct possibility that the foundation walls may eventually erode to the point where a costly rebuilding is mandated.

It is far easier and more cost effective to make sure that the rainwater is directed away from the foundation. Your options are rather limited, but simple: dig a drainage trench around your house or haul in several wheelbarrows of soil. If you ignore the problem, you are inviting a two-stage disaster: water in your basement and a deteriorating basement wall. Neither is easy to repair, but both are quite avoidable. So next time it rains, grab an umbrella and take a walk.

## Warning Signs of a Wet Foundation

- downspouts dumping water next to the foundation
- missing or leaking gutters
- puddles forming next to the foundation
- white stains on the *inside* of the foundation
- damp basement walls and floor
- bulging basement or foundation walls

## Do's and Don'ts to Keeping the Foundation Dry

### Do

- install splash blocks or additional downspouts to direct water away from the foundation.
- fill low spots with tamped topsoil.
- keep gutters clean and repaired.
- divert rainwater *before* it reaches your house, using terraces, raised planting areas, drainage ditches filled with decorative rock, and so on.

### Don't

- substitute landscape mulch for soil. Soil diverts rainwater; mulch lets it pass through.
- let plantings discourage you from making changes in the soil grade. Shrubs can be raised along with the grade. And remember, roots from mature shrubs can also tunnel through foundation walls.
- apply liberal amounts of fertilizer next to the foundation. It can be carried by the water into the foundation, where it can damage the bricks, mortar, or stones.

## How to Raise the Grade Around the Foundation

| *Steps* | *Tools and Materials* |
|---|---|
| 1. Identify areas where the grade slopes toward the foundation. Lay the two-by-four on edge, with one end touching the foundation and the | a two-by-four carpenter's level |

*Steps*                    *Tools and Materials*

other pointing away from the house.
Place the level on the board to
determine the slope of the ground.

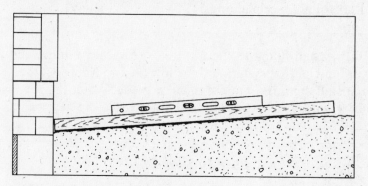

2.  Remove the grass or plantings in any          shovel
    low or improperly sloped areas.
3.  Option: In severe cases, consider             (recommend more
    installing a perforated drainage pipe            extensive
    in a bed of gravel at the bottom of              research before
    your foundation.                                 undertaking
                                                      this step)
4.  For buildups of 6 inches or less, use top-    topsoil or clay
    soil to restructure grade. To pitch the       shovel
    buildup away from the foundation,             wheelbarrow
    add soil in layers. Tamp down each            tamping device
    layer before adding another until the
    buildup is complete. For buildups
    greater than 6 inches, use clay for a

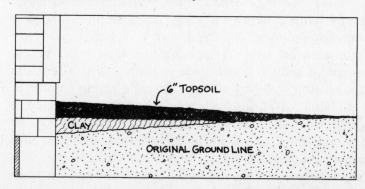

*Steps*                                    *Tools and Materials*

firmly tamped base, then cover with
6 inches of topsoil.
Again, firmly tamp down the topsoil.
5.   Replace grass or plantings.                    shovel

> TIP: When filling low grassy spots, carefully remove the
> turf and its root system, fill the low area with topsoil, then
> reinstall the turf on top of the new grade. Water the patch
> daily until the roots establish themselves in the new soil.

### Our Indoor Pool

Lydia and I once lived in a cute bungalow nestled into
the side of a gently sloping hill in Durham, North Carolina. The drop in elevation from the alley that ran across
the back of our property to the street out front was about
5 feet. We bought the house during a dry stretch of summer, when the one-room, partial basement looked as
normal as any.

We hadn't lived there long before one of those deep,
rumbling thunderstorms rolled across the Piedmont, dumping nearly 3 inches of rain on us in one torrid burst. A falling
tree limb had knocked out our electricity, so I grabbed a
flashlight and headed down the basement stairs looking for
the fuse box. When I hit bottom I knew I had a problem: I
found myself standing ankle-deep in water.

Next morning, I stood in line with a half dozen other
happy homeowners with soggy shoes waiting to rent a
sump pump. After pumping several hundred gallons of
water into the street, I took a closer look at my partial
basement and the crawl space surrounding it. The house
was basically a 30-by-50-foot rectangle sitting on a brick
foundation. A 12-square-foot area had been excavated to
a depth of 7 feet, then finished with a concrete floor to
create a small, one-room basement. In it stood an antiquated oil-burning furnace and a hot water heater. The
crawl space under the rest of the house reflected the original slope of the hillside. At the top end it narrowed to

about 18 inches, while at the downhill extreme I could almost stand up.

It was obvious from the silt spread across the bottom of the wet concrete floor that the water had run across the crawl space before cascading into the furnace room. I grabbed a flashlight and slithered into the dank, musty darkness, half expecting to bump into the skeletal remains of a previous homeowner. As I moved slowly toward the upper end of the house, the crawl space tightened until I knew that there was no way I could roll over or turn around should I come face-to-face with some hairy spider the size of my fist.

Keeping my mind on the task before me, I could see that the brick foundation was punctuated by dots of light coming through gaps in the mortar. Judging from the literal riverbed carved alongside the foundation, water had been running beneath our house for several years. The moment I could determine that the source of the water was not inside the house, I slithered back to the furnace room, content to turn the crawl space back over to its nocturnal inhabitants.

Once safely outside, the problem seemed obvious. The entire backyard served as a grass-lined funnel directing rainwater against the back of our house. To complicate matters, the roof had been stripped of its original gutter and downspout system years earlier. Hundreds of thousands of gallons of water had subsequently eroded the ground next to the foundation, leaving it nearly 6 inches lower than the rest of the yard. And just to complicate matters, a low deck built across the entire width of the rear of the house made it practically impossible for me to fill in one of the most vulnerable low areas next to the foundation.

Even though the task ahead of us seemed formidable, viewed as a series of logical steps, it wasn't terribly difficult. We began at the rear of the property, cleaning out the ditch that had filled with dirt and having a truckload of gravel dumped on the clay driveway. In one morning we effectively diverted any water running down the alley and onto our driveway safely into the ditch leading away from our property.

Our sparse backyard was in need of a sidewalk leading from the house to the garage, as well as some shrubs and planting beds. Having traced the path of the rainwater racing across the backyard toward our foundation, we knew precisely where to position our planting beds and how to angle our new sidewalk to serve as a diversion dam. Back at the house, new gutters and downspouts eliminated a second major source of water that had been entering our basement.

The ground around the foundation was so low, we decided to dig a trench around it and lay perforated drainage pipe. Once the plastic pipe was nestled in a bed of gravel, we proceeded to mound clay on the ground around the house until we were confident that any water would run away from rather than toward the foundation. A final layer of topsoil was provided for the grass and flowers.

Last, but not least, I tuck-pointed the bricks that had lost a portion of their mortar, reluctantly returning to the crawl space a few more times to make sure there were no more shafts of light peeking through.

The project consumed several weekends, and I did find myself back at the rental center several more times standing in line for a sump pump. But when we moved out, we left behind a dry basement.

# #22
# Patch any holes in your home's foundation.

Even if rainwater is diverted as it runs off your roof and the ground around your foundation is properly sloped, all of the water that is blown against the side of your house travels down and across the brick, concrete block, or stone foundation before it reaches the ground. Cracks and holes in the mortar between the bricks or stones can act as faucets, directing much of that water through the wall and into your basement or crawl space.

From a structural standpoint, minor cracks in the mortar are not a cause for alarm, but they must be caulked or repointed (or tuck-pointed) to prevent moisture from turning a minor problem into a major one. During the winter months, a warm afternoon sun can melt snow that has drifted against the foundation. If the water can work its way into cracks in the mortar, it will freeze and expand, causing even more damage to the mortar. In addition, acidic rainwater can penetrate a crack and saturate the interior mortar, where the acid attacks the mortar's lime, causing it to crumble. When it does, the weight of the bricks or blocks will cause them to come loose, which could affect the walls, doors, and windows above them.

The most severe cracks in the foundation will be obvious as you walk around your home. You can also check for cracks from within your basement. Block the light coming through the windows, then stand in the darkness and look for signs of light between the bricks, stones, or concrete blocks.

Exterior masonry caulking can be used to fill small cracks, but those larger than $1/4$ inch should be repointed with matching mortar. Foundation leaks are like roof leaks in that it is often difficult to determine precisely where the water is entering. As a precaution, repoint the problem area, not just one or two cracked joints. It is easier to do it now while all of your tools and materials are assembled, than to start again after the next rain.

## Warning Signs of Foundation Leaks

- soft, crumbling mortar
- loose bricks, stones or concrete blocks
- white stains on the inside of the foundation
- old nails or anchors in the mortar
- holes drilled in the brick or mortar
- gas and water pipes and vents passing through the foundation

## Do's and Don'ts to Patching Foundation Holes

### Do

- inspect the foundation each fall if you expect freezing temperatures during the winter.
- research means of tinting new mortar if you live in an older house whose original mortar is no longer white.
- pack the mortar in tightly, allow it to dry slightly, then strike a smooth, neat joint to repel water.

### Don't

- use power tools to remove old mortar. They can damage the bricks, stones, and adjacent mortar joints.
- use standard mortar mix to tuck-point 19th-century bricks. Modern mortar is too hard and actually causes the soft bricks to crumble during freeze-thaw cycles. Additional research is required before selecting the proper mortar for any historic house. For more information, consult back issues of *Old House Journal*.

## How to Patch Foundation Cracks and Holes

| *Steps* | *Tools and Materials* |
|---|---|
| 1. Inspect the foundation of your home, noting problem areas, cracks, holes, and entrances for water and gas pipes. Pay close attention to vine-covered sections, watching for any sign of damage to the mortar. If you detect any, it may be necessary to remove the vines to prevent additional damage. | notebook screwdriver pencil |

*Steps*                                     *Tools and Materials*

2. Use a caulking gun and an exterior masonry caulking that matches the color of the mortar to fill any cracks ¼ inch or smaller. Before caulking, clean out any dust with a dry paintbrush. Also caulk around any pipes or vents in the foundation.

caulking gun
masonry caulking
paintbrush

3. For cracks larger than ¼ inch, remove the crumbling mortar to a depth of 1 inch.

safety glasses
hammer
cold chisel

4. Clean out the recessed area.

wire brush or
    paintbrush
garden hose

5. Select the mortar appropriate for your home and region.

6. Prepare the mortar in small batches according to directions. Tint if necessary to match the existing mortar and test it in an inconspicuous spot.

plastic bucket
trowel
water

7. Dampen the joint with water.

spray bottle or
    wet paintbrush

8. Pack the mortar into the joint, but no more than ½ inch thick. When it begins to firm, but before it has completely hardened, apply another layer of mortar, if necessary.

narrow tuck-
    pointing trowel
flat trowel

9. Clean any excess mortar from the face of the bricks.

wire brush
damp rag

10. Smooth the mortar to match the adjacent joints.

trowel or striking
    tool

*Steps*　　　　　　　　　　　　　　*Tools and Materials*

11. Mist repaired sections for two or three days while the mortar cures.

12. (optional)
Carefully remove any mortar stains on the bricks using the solution given here. Rinse with water.

garden hose or
  misting bottle
Cleaning solution:
  1 part muriatic
    acid; take
    precautions
    listed on
    muriatic acid
    label.
  10 parts water
safety glasses
gloves
wire brush
rag
garden hose

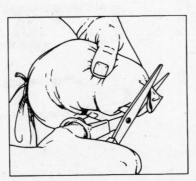 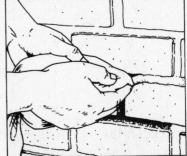

TIP: You can make your own version of a caulking gun for mortar by snipping off a small corner of a heavy-duty plastic bag. Add the prepared mortar to the bag, then twist the plastic until the mortar is forced through the hole. The size of the hole should be determined by the width of the space between the bricks, blocks, or stones. Finish by packing the mortar firmly in the seam with a narrow trowel.

# THE BASEMENT

Nearly all homeowners have looked longingly around their basements, wishing there were ways to make use of all that wasted space to alleviate some of the overcrowding upstairs. Who couldn't use an extra bedroom, an office, a second bath, or a spacious family room? Even the largest homes seem to have at least one shortcoming a dry, secure basement could rectify. The greatest problems in basements, however, seem to be inadequate headroom and water, either in the form of chronic dampness or occasional flooding.

Before a basement can be turned into usable living space—or even if it can't—every homeowner has to be on the alert for potential problems that could easily affect the remainder of the house. A damp basement floor or an open crawl space, for example, collects humidity that eventually works its way to the upper floors where it becomes trapped, leading to mold and mildew problems throughout the house. A beam riddled with insect tunnels causes floors to sag and doors to no longer open or close. And if not identified and properly protected, loose asbestos fibers could float on a stream of air up the basement stairway and into your first-floor rooms.

Unlike outdoor projects, basement repairs are perfect for rainy Saturdays at home.

This chapter includes Home-Saving Guidelines 23 through 27.

*Page*

# #23
# Identify the source of any unwanted water.

While a great deal of time has been invested in tracing the evolution of the American home, the lowly basement has received little more than passing notice. In the majority of middle-class houses, the basement evolved out of a crawl space when fireplaces were replaced by a central furnace. Although a fireplace was viewed as a decorative as well as a functional element, a massive, octopus-like, fire-belching, coal-eating, cast-iron furnace needed to be hidden from view. Since heat so conveniently rises, the most obvious location for the furnace was beneath the house, in that otherwise unused area inhabited by insects and stray cats.

Since basements were expensive to dig, the earliest versions were neither deeper nor larger than absolutely necessary. Heat vents snaked out across crawl spaces from the cavity dug near the center of the house. As people began to sense the potential of this area, basement excavations grew larger; floors and walls were finished with brick or concrete rather than packed dirt. But early furnaces were dirty contraptions, accompanied by a small mountain of oily coal a few feet away. As furnace designs grew smaller, neater, and more efficient, homeowners began moving other items into the basement: washing machines, an extra sink or toilet, water softeners, hot water heaters, and workshops.

The need for an extra bedroom, office, or family room has prompted many homeowners to take a close look at their basements. Unfortunately, many have discovered that their basements are frequently damp. A few, such as myself, have discovered that after a heavy rain their basements feature a miniature model of the Mississippi meandering across the floor on its way toward a pile of boxes in the corner. When you imagine what the ground surrounding your basement looks like after an afternoon thundershower—one authority compares it to a ship floating in a sea of mud—it should come as no surprise that many basements are wet a large part of the year.

A damp basement, however, can do more than just prevent you from laying down $20-per-square-yard carpeting on the floor. The moisture that permeates the air encourages the growth of mildew, wood-boring insects, and fungi. Ignoring the cause of the moisture-laden air can lead to some very serious problems, ranging from decayed beams in the basement to wet plaster in the rooms above it.

How does this happen? When water enters the basement (we'll talk about *where* in a moment), much of it is absorbed by the air. When the moisture-laden basement air comes in contact with a cool surface—such as an exterior wall, a beam, a cold water pipe, or a window—the moisture in the air condenses into droplets, which then attract insects and enable the spores of decay-causing fungi to take root, grow, and feed upon the wood cells.

Some homes only have a moisture problem in the summer, when warm, moist air enters the basement, cools, and forms moisture droplets. The solution may be as simple as installing a dehumidifier or providing additional air circulation to remove the moisture-laden air and to equalize the difference between the temperature of the basement and the incoming air.

The most obvious source of water is through the foundation. Even an intact foundation can serve as a source if the ground outside is saturated. To avoid what is called "rising damp," make sure rainwater is diverted away from your home's foundation by adjusting the pitch of the ground. (See #21 on page 109.) If you take measures to keep the ground on the exterior side of your basement wall dry, then you increase the likelihood that your basement will also be dry.

One of the most difficult things a homeowner can attempt to do is to stop incoming water once it has penetrated the foundation. Despite the multiple lessons to be learned from the story of the Dutch boy with his finger in the dike, many companies are prospering while homeowners are carrying out gallon after gallon of interior basement "waterproofing." Generally speaking, the only time these types of products work is when they really weren't necessary. Think about it for a moment: if hydrostatic pressure can force surface water through 4 feet of compact soil *and* 12 inches or more of brick, stone, concrete block, or mortar, how long can a brushed-on solution of varnish-thin waterproofing hold it back?

Before purchasing any basement waterproofing formula, take a few minutes to read the fine print on the back of the can. If you note the extent of the manufacturer's guarantee (if there is one), you may have second thoughts about the product. And remember, even if it were effective, you would have to treat every square inch of surface in your basement. The waterproofing does not eliminate the water outside the basement walls; it simply forces it to seek another access, such as an untreated spot.

So here's the bottom line: If the ground around your basement is saturated, it's just a matter of time before your basement will be, too. Don't treat the symptoms; cure the disease. The most successful cures to a wet basement are those applied to the exterior of the foundation, not the interior.

## Warning Signs of Water Infiltration

- items rusting in your basement
- dark stains on walls, floors, posts, or beams
- mold or mildew around windows or on beams
- condensation on basement windows
- swelled doors or windows
- peeling paint
- soft, spongy wood
- water marks located high on walls, posts, or furnace
- bowed walls
- crumbling bricks, plaster, or mortar
- crawling or flying insects
- musty odors
- powdery substance or incrustation on bricks

## Do's and Don'ts to Treating a Damp Basement

### Do

- consider using a dehumidifier along with other measures aimed at the source of the moisture.
- cover exposed pipes that "sweat" with special foam insulation designed specifically for pipes.
- insulate between exposed ceiling joists in the basement, but only after they have been cleaned of mold, mildew, fungi, and insects.
- circulate the air using fans.
- inspect all pipes for possible leaks that could be increasing the moisture in the air.
- make sure all basement drains are working properly.

- check the joint between the basement floor and the wall for possible seepage.
- cover any sections of bare ground with 4-mil plastic sheets.

### Don't

- use washing machines or dryers in the basement without good ventilation that routes the humidity to the outdoors.
- expect a dehumidifier alone to handle a serious moisture problem.
- cover a leaking wall with paneling or any other material before you are completely sure the infiltrating moisture has been stopped.
- apply fertilizer next to the foundation. Moisture can carry it into the bricks, where it can cause damage.

## Fifteen Ways to Cure a Wet Basement

Since no two homes are identical, selecting one cure for every wet basement is neither practical nor possible. Below are a number of different possible solutions for your particular situation, listed from the simplest to the more complex. Determining which ones will reduce or eliminate the moisture in the basement depends on your home, its foundation, and the soil surrounding it.

1. Make sure gutters and downspouts are clear and direct water away from the foundation. (See #6 on page 34.)
2. Install splash blocks beneath the downspouts.
3. Make sure the ground around your house slopes away from the foundation.(See #21 on page 109.)
4. Check basement window wells to make sure they aren't directing water into the basement.
5. Improve air circulation in the basement with screens and fans.
6. Insulate exposed pipes.
7. Inspect any water pipes for leaks.
8. Repoint any missing or cracked mortar in the foundation. (See #22 on page 115.)
9. Make sure all floor drains operate properly.
10. Install a dehumidifier.
11. Insulate between ceiling joists.

12. Replace any missing chimney caps to prevent rainwater from reaching the basement.
13. Cover any exposed ground or crawl space with plastic sheeting.
14. Install a drainage pipe along the exterior foundation.
15. Cover the exterior foundation wall (below grade) with tar, a membrane, or cement.

> TIP: Beware of fast-talking salespeople with one cure-all product for every wet basement. Wet basements are rarely the result of a single problem that can be solved with one simple (and expensive) solution.

# #24
# Use "sisters" to support weak or damaged beams or joists.

The wooden weight-bearing structure of our homes—the seldom-seen beams, joists, rafters, girders, and headers—are under constant threat of attack. Moisture, wood-boring insects, fungi, electricians, plumbers, and yes, even carpenters all have been guilty of undermining critical substructures. While fungi and insects see these beams as a source of food, workers often see them as obstacles to installing a new water pipe or electrical circuit. Rather than work their way around them, they take a more direct route, drilling, notching, or even removing them completely without considering the negative long-term effects.

Whatever the reason, the beams in your home's basement may weaken to the point where they no longer support sections of the floor above them. Eventually, the floors sag, doors won't operate properly, and plaster walls crack. There are many potential culprits. Critical beams and posts may have originally been laid atop foundation walls. There they eventually become wet, attract insects and fungi, and deteriorate. Posts may have been set directly on a brick, concrete, or dirt floor, through which the end grain will draw moisture and will begin to decay. Once the wood fibers deteriorate, the weight of the house will force them to compress, causing the floor to sag.

While a squeaky floor is not necessarily indicative of rotting joists, it can be a warning sign. If the problem is simply a slightly shrunken joist, a normal occurrence in older homes, you may be able to silence the squeaky floorboards by inserting a hardwood shim between the joist and the subfloor. Don't forget, however, to inspect the beams or posts supporting the joists to make sure the problem isn't occurring next to the basement floor or foundation.

If you discover that the joist or beam has been weakened either by insects, fungi, or workers, you have at least two options.

The more dramatic involves removing the weakened member and replacing it with a new board. In advanced stages of deterioration, this may be the only alternative; if that's the case, then you need the services of an engineer and possibly a contractor. But more often than not, you can strengthen a weak joist, beam, or post by "sistering" it.

A "sister" is a term for a new board attached to an existing beam, rafter, joist, or post. The sister provides additional strength without requiring that the original be removed. Obviously, if the joist or beam is so badly deteriorated it cannot provide support for the sister, then removal is in order. Sistering is most effective as a preventive measure, such as adding strength to a deck whose joists were spaced too far apart, or increasing the support capability of joists beneath a new fireplace, grand piano, or hot tub.

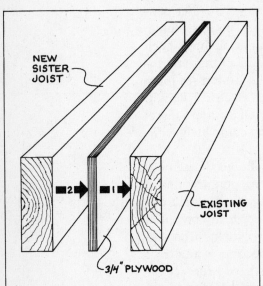

NEW SISTER JOIST

EXISTING JOIST

3/4" PLYWOOD

The thickness of the sister board is determined by how much additional strength is necessary. Many times a length of ³/₄-inch plywood is used as a sister to one or both sides of a joist (or, to be safe, a number of joists) to support construction of a new bathroom. Because of its inherent layering, plywood is stronger than the same thickness of hardwood or softwood.

If a joist or beam is badly weakened, or if it's going to carry a heavier load, then you may want to add a piece of new lumber of the same thickness. Another option is to apply a piece of a ³/₄-inch plywood before attaching the new lumber.

In extreme situations, a steel plate can even be added. For instance, when we enlarged our kitchen by partially removing a load-bearing wall, the architect determined that the wood beam would need to be sandwiched between two pieces of steel plate in order not to bend under the weight of the second-floor bathroom.

Knowing when to call in a professional, either an architect or an engineer, is critical; you certainly don't want to find that you underestimated the amount of weight the joists would have to bear when the bathtub is filled with water or when 20 people start dancing on your new deck. If it appears that (1) you are going to have to replace a beam or post, or that (2) you have widespread damage to a structural beam or post, or that (3) you will need to remove a load-bearing wall, beam, or post, then your first call should be to someone who knows how to calculate structural strength.

But if you simply need to reinforce an existing member, consider adding a sister to help support the weight.

### Warning Signs of Needed "Sisters"

- sagging or squeaky floor or steps
- enlarging cracks in a plaster wall
- doors that begin to drag on the floor
- windows that go out of alignment
- deteriorated joists, beams, or posts

### Do's and Don'ts to Keeping Beams and Joists Strong

#### Do

- inspect the foundation around any joists that rest on or in the foundation wall. A deteriorating foundation can cause the joists to slip below their intended level.
- check for gaps between the floor joists and the girder (the beam that supports the joists). Fill with hardwood shims.
- probe for softened wood fibers with a screwdriver or awl.

#### Don't

- assume that the original builder anticipated all present-day needs. Waterbeds, exercise equipment, a fireplace, or a new bathroom can put added stress on a series of joists or beams. If necessary, install a new metal jack post in the basement to provide additional support under critical areas. (See "The Adjustable Jack Post" on page 129.)
- install a supporting post on the first floor without installing an additional post directly beneath it in the basement to transfer the weight to the basement floor.
- remove any walls during a remodeling until it has been determined that they are not load-bearing.
- remove any beams or joists in your basement without first supporting the weight of the upper floor with two jack posts and a crossgirder spanning the affected area.

## How to Install a "Sister"

| *Steps* | *Tools and Materials* |
|---|---|
| 1. Determine the cause of the deterioration of the beam, such as moisture, insects, fungi, or termites, and correct the source of the problem. | flashlight (see appropriate sections in this book) |
| 2. With chisel and hammer, remove any portion of wood infected with fungi. | wood chisel hammer safety glasses |
| 3. Treat the original beam with a wood preservative. | wood preservative brush |
| 4. Cut the sister to the desired size. | saw |
| 5. Apply construction adhesive to the sister. | caulking gun tube of adhesive |
| 6. Nail the new board in place. | hammer 8d or 10d common nails |
| 7. Drill a series of staggered $3/8$-inch holes 9 inches apart through both boards. Do not drill a hole closer than 2 inches to the edge of the boards. | drill $3/8$-inch bit |

EXISTING JOIST

3/4" PLYWOOD

SISTER JOIST

STAGGER HOLES

3/8" DRILL BIT

BOLT ASSEMBLY

| *Steps* | *Tools and Materials* |
|---|---|
| 8. Treat the sister with a coat of wood preservative. Squirt preservative into the bolt holes. | wood preservative<br>brush<br>plastic squeeze bottle |
| 9. Bolt the two boards together. | $3/8$-inch galvanized bolts, washers, and nuts<br>wrench |

---

TIP: If you have to drill a hole through an existing joist or beam for an electrical line or water pipe, select the spot carefully. Select a bit no larger than absolutely necessary to let wires and pipes thread through easily, and drill as close as possible to the supporting post. Avoid placing holes or notches near the edge of a board, or where the board has little support.

---

## The Adjustable Jack Post

Many homeowners discover that a load-bearing wall needs additional support under a deck or in a basement to compensate for the added weight of a hot tub, piano, exercise equipment, cast-iron stove, or even second bathroom. While you could accomplish the task using a wooden beam and shims, most contractors agree that the fastest, easiest, and safest solution is a metal jack post.

A jack post should be used to provide additional support rather than to raise a sagging floor. It is best utilized as a preventive measure; attempting to reverse a severe sag in a floor using a floor jack can crack plaster, buckle floorboards, or even break water lines.

The steel jack post consists of three primary parts. The bulk of the post is made up of two heavy, telescoping tubes. The inner tube has a series of holes through which a bolt is passed to lock the two tubes at the appropriate height. On top of the inner tube is a screw jack with a rod that enables you to raise the height of the top plate until it

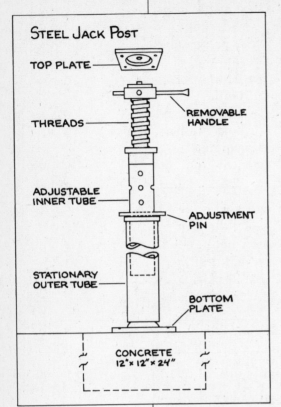

STEEL JACK POST

TOP PLATE

THREADS

REMOVABLE HANDLE

ADJUSTABLE INNER TUBE

ADJUSTMENT PIN

STATIONARY OUTER TUBE

BOTTOM PLATE

CONCRETE
12"× 12"× 24"

presses against the beam or joist. The top plate should have holes for attaching it with nails, screws, or bolts to the joist or beam. This is an important safety feature that prevents the heavy jack from tipping.

The base of the jack can be attached to the concrete floor using lead expansion anchors. Keep in mind that any weight you place on the jack is going to be transferred directly to the floor beneath. If the stress is significant, it will quickly damage a wood floor, crumble a thin layer of concrete, or crush bricks.

If the bottom of the jack post is not firmly resting on at least 5 inches of concrete, you must break through the existing concrete, dig a hole approximately 12 inches wide by 12 inches long by 24 inches deep, and pour a new footing. It won't be fun breaking a hole in the concrete, but if you don't, the jack post probably will in time—and the result can be disastrous.

The building codes in your area may dictate whether or not you can use a jack post as a permanent support post without building a box around it or modifying it to prevent someone from unscrewing it. If you intend to use the jack post to raise a joist while you install a wood post, be sure to position the jack slightly off center so the permanent beam will be in the correct spot. Do not set a wooden post directly on the concrete, as it will absorb moisture and eventually decay. Instead, set it on a specifically designed metal plate available at building centers.

# #25
# Don't be eaten
# out of house and home
# by wood-boring insects.

Wood-boring insects are the silent killers of basement beams, sills, and joists. Termites, the most feared member of a rather large family of such insects, can jeopardize the support structure of your home without even disturbing you and your family. Other insects, such as powder-post beetles and carpenter ants, can also turn your home's beams and joists into little more than hollow shells incapable of supporting the weight of the floor above them.

Once you understand the habits and needs of termites and other wood-boring insects, controlling them is simply a matter of prevention and inspection. All wood-destroying insects require moisture, either in the wood itself or, as in the case of subterranean termites, from the nearby ground. With the exception of the drywood termite found in southern Florida and in the Southwest, termites, powder-post beetles, and carpenter ants either prefer moist wood or require moisture for their continued existence. Insects are so drawn by moisture, in fact, that experience has proven that a wet basement either is currently hosting a family of wood-boring insects or is going to be in the very near future. One of the first and most important steps in eliminating the threat of wood-boring insects is to eliminate the source of moisture in your home's basement.

Subterranean termites, the most damaging of their group, are found throughout most of the United States. Only the coldest, northernmost areas escape their threat. Subterranean termites normally build nests approximately 4 to 7 feet below ground, safely below the frost line, in moisture-rich soil. While you may never see any of them, a mature colony can number more than 50,000. In addition to moisture, the termites are drawn to wood lying on the surface or buried in the ground, which supplies them with nutrients. Moist, soft, partially decayed timbers, the kind you might find under a porch, forgotten beneath a thick, spreading evergreen, or buried around the foundation of your house, can provide termites with both food and moisture. Once the wood has been consumed, the termites seek the nearest fresh source, which just might be your home.

If part of your house, such as a bottom clapboard or a support post under the porch, is in direct contact with the ground, the termites will be able to burrow from their nest to the wood (and beyond) without being seen. When they do encounter a nonedible barrier, such as a brick or stone foundation, they build mud tunnels to protect themselves as they travel back and forth from the nest to the beams resting on the foundation. Subterranean termites can also enter your home through cracks in the foundation. They weave their way through the bricks, stone, or concrete blocks until they come in contact with the sill plates or beams. Termites typically retreat to the ground for life-sustaining moisture every day or so, but if they can find sufficient moisture in the beams, joists, sills, and lumber in the basement, they don't have to make the trip back to their underground nest.

Unlike termites, carpenter ants don't consume wood, but they will carve nesting areas in soft, rotted boards. These large ants, both winged and unwinged, are not as destructive as termites, but they can still cause problems. Porch pillars and supports seem especially susceptible to carpenter ants, which do not require mud tunnels to protect themselves from the dry air. Carpenter ants are also drawn to soft, rotted wood beneath leaking gutters and around soffits and eaves. If you find a steady stream of carpenter ants working feverishly on your home, follow them back to their queen and the colony, which you can destroy using readily available chemicals. Be sure to read and follow the directions carefully. Even though the chemicals may be purchased and applied by homeowners, the ingredients are often toxic to humans, especially children.

Powder-post beetles, a category that commonly includes wood-boring beetles of both the *Lyctid* and the *Anobiid* families, can live their entire lives eating their way through a beam or rafter. These beetles prefer to lay their eggs in damp, moist wood, ensuring that the infestation continues beyond their life cycle. Round or oblong exit holes, approximately $1/16$ inch in diameter, are a sign of their presence. Active infestation is generally indicated by fine, fresh sawdust, called frass, in and around the holes.

Since the majority of chemicals, such as chlordane, used to

effectively destroy colonies of subterranean termites and powder-post beetles are highly toxic and are restricted in their sale and application, you should leave the treatment to professionals. However, you should take it upon yourself to watch for the early warning signs of termite or other insect infestation. If you don't, a professional exterminator can eliminate the insects, but it will take a small army of workers to replace rotted beams, joists, or supporting sills.

## Warning Signs of Infestation

- swarms of termites in the spring or early summer
- large numbers of termite wings discarded during the swarming process
- mud tubes attached to your foundation
- hollow-sounding beams
- termite fecal material either inside the wood or on the floor beneath it
- round or oblong holes ($1/16$ to $1/8$ inch) in beams and joists
- fine powdered wood around cracks or exit holes

## Do's and Don'ts to Preventing Infestation

### Do

- pick up wood lying on the ground, especially in crawl spaces and basement recesses and under your porch.
- use pressure-treated lumber for construction less than 12 inches from the ground.
- use a screwdriver or awl to probe for internal damage in beams or joists.
- eliminate any source of moisture in your basement and under the eaves.
- keep the attic and crawl spaces well ventilated.
- watch for warning signs any time you are working in your basement, around the foundation, or in a crawl space.
- have your home professionally treated at the first sign of infestation.

### Don't

- store firewood near or against the foundation or a wall of your house or garage.

- bury wood construction scraps when backfilling the foundation.
- allow latticework under your porch to rest on the ground or to become even partially covered with leaves, dirt, and debris.
- assume that termites can't hurt you. If you plan to eventually sell your house, know that most home buyers and lending institutions today require a termite inspection—and complete repair and eradication—before they will close a sale.
- attempt to treat your house yourself. The only chemicals proven effective on termites and powder-post beetles are highly toxic and should be handled only by competent professionals.
- rely solely on chemicals. Also check your foundation regularly for signs of insect infestation.

## How to Prevent Infestation

| *Steps* | *Tools and Materials* |
|---|---|
| 1. Scour the inside of the basement, including any crawl space and under the porches, removing scraps of wood. | flashlight garden rake trash can |
| 2. Pick up any scraps of wood around the outside of your house. Stack firewood away from foundation and exterior walls. | trash can or    garbage bag |
| 3. Inspect both sides of every square foot of the foundation, looking for mud tunnels, actual insects, cracks in the foundation, and other telltale signs of infestation. | flashlight |
| 4. Inspect water and natural gas pipes leading into your home for termite tunnels. | flashlight |
| 5. Probe support sills on the foundation and adjacent joists for soft, rotted areas. | screwdriver or awl |
| 6. Inspect sills, joists, and supporting members for powder-post beetle holes, telltale sawdust, and pellets of termite feces. | flashlight |

*Steps*                                 *Tools and Materials*

7.  Pay careful attention to joists and sills      flashlight
    near water pipes and under bathrooms.
    Look for signs of chronic dampness from
    slow leaks or condensation. Wet wood
    attracts decay-causing insects.

> TIP: Landscape timbers and old railway ties can attract
> and foster thousands of termites. If your locale is subject
> to termites, consider using brick or stone in your land-
> scaping plans.

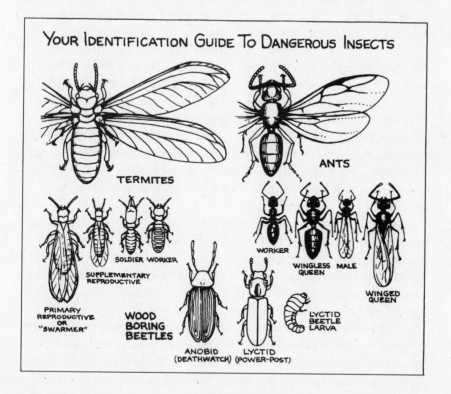

YOUR IDENTIFICATION GUIDE TO DANGEROUS INSECTS

TERMITES

ANTS

SOLDIER  WORKER

SUPPLEMENTARY
REPRODUCTIVE

WORKER

WINGLESS  MALE
QUEEN

PRIMARY
REPRODUCTIVE
OR
"SWARMER"

WOOD
BORING
BEETLES

WINGED
QUEEN

ANOBID      LYCTID
(DEATHWATCH) (POWER-POST)

LYCTID
BEETLE
LARVA

# #26
# Learn how to handle asbestos.

If your home was built before 1980, chances are it contains asbestos somewhere: in the shingles, in the attic insulation, in the heating ducts, beneath the floor tiles, or behind the fireplace or wood-burning stove. But the most obvious—and the most dangerous—evidence of asbestos generally is found in the basements of older homes, where it may be wrapped around hot water or steam pipes leading from the furnace to the radiators.

The fibers of asbestos, a natural mineral, are fire-resistant, durable, flexible, and versatile. For years, it was believed that asbestos was the long-awaited "miracle cure" to home-building problems where both insulation and fire resistance were required. During much of the 20th century, asbestos has been shredded into insulation to be blown into attics and walls, molded into shingles for both roofs and siding, pressed into sheets of brittle wallboard, even woven into theater curtains. Until the 1970s asbestos was still being sprayed as a textured insulation in homes, schools, and public buildings.

As incidents of lung cancer and similar diseases began appearing among workers who were in daily contact with asbestos, medical researchers began taking a closer look at the popular material. What they discovered proved startling. When released into the air, the microscopic fibers are nearly invisible and can float long distances on currents winding their way through a building. The tiny asbestos fibers are easily inhaled and settle in the lower portion of the lungs. Unlike many foreign substances, the asbestos fibers cannot be broken down and flushed out of the body. They remain lodged in the lungs, where they can cause cancer.

The threat from asbestos, however, occurs only when the fibers are released into the air. Asbestos that is securely sealed, intact, and stable does not pose a threat to your family. But once the asbestos fibers are released from deterioration or improper removal, they can threaten the life of everyone.

Asbestos that is "friable," a term used to describe material that crumbles when you touch it, needs to be properly removed, since it can easily send dangerous, invisible fibers floating throughout your home. Asbestos fibers can also be carried from distant points in the basement to other rooms on your shoes, your clothes, even your hands and hair.

Nonfriable asbestos, such as unbroken insulation on heating pipes, is generally considered safe, as long as it remains intact. Once it is cut, ripped, or broken, it can instantly become friable and dangerous. Those of us living in homes with asbestos insulation, wallboard, floor tiles, or shingles aren't risking our lives, *unless* we manage to turn nonfriable asbestos into friable asbestos, releasing hundreds of thousands of invisible fibers into the air in our homes.

Asbestos removal should be handled only by trained, licensed professionals armed with the proper equipment. Your state or local health department maintains a list of certified asbestos abatement firms and can provide additional information regarding removal and disposal of asbestos. While homeowners are not prohibited by law from attempting their own asbestos removal, no one should take asbestos lightly. One mistake can contaminate your entire home with invisible, dangerous fibers, risking your life and your children's.

Asbestos maintenance, however, is the responsibility of every homeowner and is clearly within most homeowners' abilities. The first step is a thorough inspection to identify potential sources of asbestos fibers and analyze their current condition. If what you find gives you cause for concern, call your local health department immediately to learn how you can go about getting your home's asbestos evaluated by a licensed professional.

## Warning Signs of Asbestos

- thick, grayish coating applied to the outside of an older furnace
- cloth-wrapped whitish insulation on older heating pipes
- broken, exposed insulation on furnaces or pipes
- discarded asbestos-wrapped pipes in crawl spaces and basements

## Do's and Don'ts to Maintaining Asbestos

### Do

- call your public health department for the name of the local agency or department who can help you analyze your asbestos risk factor and develop a plan for asbestos removal or containment.
- work carefully around asbestos-insulated pipes in your basement.
- supervise plumbers or other tradespeople working around asbestos in your home. (See "Harley, the Plumber" on page 140.)
- mist any pieces of asbestos that have been discarded in your basement with water before picking them up. Always bring a garbage bag to the asbestos; never attempt to carry the asbestos to your garbage bag, as you risk breaking it into smaller pieces.

### Don't

- *ever* use a vacuum to clean up crumbling asbestos. The filters in household and shop vacuums are too coarse to catch the microscopic fibers. The vacuum actually blasts the fibers across the room, increasing your odds of inhaling them.
- attempt to remove any asbestos yourself from pipes. Asbestos removal is a job for trained professionals.
- assume that a conventional particle mask will catch asbestos fibers; it won't.
- store wood or other items on top of asbestos-wrapped pipes. You could easily rip the asbestos, releasing fibers into the air.

## How to Seal a Rip in Asbestos—Temporarily

The following steps are to be used only in the event you, a worker, or someone in your family accidentally punctures or rips the asbestos insulation around one of the heating pipes in your home's basement. This is intended as a temporary repair, not a permanent solution. If a large amount of asbestos has been released into the air, do not attempt to repair the rip yourself. Seal off the area from the remainder of your house and call a professional asbestos abatement firm. As mentioned earlier, asbestos removal should be undertaken only by a trained, qualified professional.

| *Steps* | *Tools and Materials* |
|---|---|
| 1. If you think asbestos or fibers may have been released into the air, immediately leave the room. Do not reenter without a respirator. | respirator |
| 2. Seal off any doorways, windows, vents, registers, or openings to other rooms. | plastic drop cloths<br>duct tape |
| 3. Set up a vaporizer in the room. The mist will saturate any fibers in the air, causing them to fall to the floor. Run the vaporizer for 24 hours. | vaporizer |
| 4. Wearing a respirator, use a damp mop or wet rags to wipe up the floor and the asbestos fibers. Pick up any pieces of asbestos that have fallen on the floor. Carefully place them in a plastic garbage bag to avoid creating any dust. If the pieces crumble, immediately mist with water. Spray water into the bag to prevent any asbestos fibers from escaping. | water<br>mop<br>rags<br>disposable gloves<br>plastic garbage bag<br>misting bottle |
| 5. Mist any friable asbestos in the punctured, ripped, or broken area to prevent the fibers from becoming airborne. | misting bottle<br>water |
| 6. In preparation for patching the tear, wipe the moisture and dirt off the insulation around the damaged area. Take care not to disturb any exposed asbestos in the tear. | dry rag |
| 7. Beginning several inches away from the tear, begin wrapping the insulated pipe with duct tape, making sure to overlap each previous wrap for a tight bond. Continue wrapping until you have gone several inches beyond the damaged area. | duct tape |

| *Steps* | *Tools and Materials* |
|---|---|
| 8. Wipe down the floor and any affected area one more time with a damp cloth. Deposit the dust, the rag or sponge, and your gloves in the garbage bag. Label and seal the bag tightly. Contact your local health or sanitation department for proper disposal. | damp cloth or sponge<br>disposable gloves<br>garbage bag<br>label<br>duct tape |
| 9. Paint the tape and, as a precaution, the adjacent insulation with a latex paint. | latex paint<br>paintbrush |
| 10. To prevent the asbestos from flaking, periodically repaint the insulated pipes. | latex paint<br>paintbrush |

TIP: If you suspect you have inhaled asbestos fibers, immediately drink several glasses of water. The water will carry any fibers in your mouth and throat past your windpipe and into your digestive system, where they will not cause any harm. Contact your physician for further advice.

### Harley, the Plumber

Our house has asbestos.

Fortunately, it seems to be confined to the basement, where we have several hundred feet of asbestos-wrapped heating pipes crisscrossing the ceiling. Someone, either a previous owner or the original contractor, took the time to coat the pipes with a paint or whitewash, which hardened and prevented the asbestos from contaminating the basement.

Since we purchased our home several months before we were able to move in, we had rented it out to some young men from California. That winter they thought that they were doing us a favor by turning both the heat and the water off before they flew back to Los Angeles. One week later, on Christmas Day, the thermometer never rose above 20 degrees. The freezing water burst six cast-iron radiators and as many steel and copper pipes. Vowing never to play landlord again, we hired a plumber over the telephone to make the necessary repairs to get heat back into the house.

Several months later, after we had begun to settle into our new house, something unusual amid the maze of pipes and wires suspended from the basement joists caught my eye. One old pipe had been cut off and capped by Harley, our plumber. Apparently, it was either non-functional or no longer needed. What alarmed me, however, was the shredded, crumbling mass of exposed asbestos dangling around the capped metal pipe. It reminded me of one of those grisly Mathew Brady photographs taken of a crude amputation in a Civil War field surgery.

My reaction was about the same had I discovered a hornets' nest between the joists. I instinctively stepped back to a safe vantage point and surveyed the situation. It had been more than six months since the plumber had left, and there was no sign of any asbestos on the floor beneath the exposed pipe. I needed to do two things: stabilize the crumbling asbestos and contain it. Since I knew that touching it with a brush would immediately knock loose the dry, crumbling asbestos, I dug around in my moving boxes until I found an aerosol can of shellac. From a range of about 18 inches I carefully misted the asbestos without disturbing it. The fast-drying shellac latched onto the dry asbestos and acted like a surface glue. Once the first layer had dried, I applied another, repeating the process until I had created a hard, thin shell of shellac over the asbestos. Any fiber that might have broken loose would have dropped harmlessly to the floor encased in shellac.

While the final coat was drying, I went to the kitchen and returned with two heavy-duty food storage bags. I opened the first and carefully placed it over the end of the asbestos-wrapped pipe, taking care not to bump or touch the exposed (but now sealed in shellac) asbestos. The bag easily extended several inches past the danger area. Holding it tightly against the "good" asbestos, I carefully secured it with several feet of duct tape. Just to be safe, I then pulled the second bag over the first and taped it a few inches farther down the pipe. By the time I finished wrapping it with duct tape, I knew that no asbestos fibers were going to be able to escape.

Looking back, I now realize that while the shellac did create a thin shell over the exposed fibers, it would not have penetrated as far into the asbestos as water. I have since found a few punctures in our asbestos pipe wrapping and am preparing to patch and paint them, as well as the stump left by my plumber. As for Harley, I caught sight of him on another job not long afterward and asked him if he wasn't worried about the dangers of asbestos. Harley laughed, then reached into his pocket for a fresh pack of Camels.

# #27
# Cover your crawl space to prevent moisture damage.

Ask anyone who has been in one and he will tell you that a crawl space is an appropriate name for that low, dark, dirty piece of real estate lurking beneath many homes. While owners of new houses may never have experienced the sensation of lying on their backs in a puddle of mud in a cramped, black, spider-infested tunnel while trying to install the water supply line for a new refrigerator, believe me, it is an experience no one should have to struggle through more than once in his lifetime.

I lived in a new house for several years and didn't miss wondering if anyone had ever died in its crawl space. We later lived in a 1927 bungalow that had only a token basement and a large, uninhabitable crawl space that I practically lived in during our kitchen and bathroom remodelings. I grew so tired of filling my clothes with dirt, ripping my elbows on old construction debris, and worrying about rats crawling up my pants that I began wearing a long-sleeved, one-piece snowsuit I could zip up to my Adam's apple and wrap tape around my ankles and wrists. With my high-top work boots, leather gloves, and stocking hat pulled down over my ears, I looked more equipped to scale Mount Everest than slither on my belly across 20 yards of no-man's-land. Actually, it wouldn't have been so bad if I hadn't watched that snake disappear into the crawl space our first week in the house.

Our present house has a full basement, but it still has a large crawl space reaching out into a far corner I have no desire to explore. Unfortunately, like most crawl spaces, it has a dirt floor that is littered with discarded lumber, old pipes, broken glass, shrapnel-like pieces of bricks and mortar, and several small, suspicious-looking holes. It is a stark reminder that despite all our pretensions and attempts at civilization, a few feet below us Nature is ready to take back that which we naively think we own.

Until that day comes, however, you must make sure that your home's crawl space is not acting as an open door for moisture, insects, foul air, fungi, cold air, and termites. Since it is rarely practical to pour a concrete floor in a crawl space, the next best thing is a plastic vapor barrier that will prevent moisture from rising out and filling your home.

Before you can begin to take control of the crawl space, you must first clean it out. The crawl space under our bungalow was so infested with spiders and crickets, not to mention at least one snake, that I began by buying a half dozen aerosol "bug bombs" at the grocery store. I then slithered as far back into the crawl space as I felt comfortable, popped the top of each of the canisters, and lobbed them like hand grenades into the various dark recesses.

The following day I unsealed the basement door and prepared to clean out the crawl space at least mildly confident that anything left alive after my lethal gas attack would be very sick or very mad.

## Warning Signs of Crawl Space Problems

- a damp basement
- large number of insects in basement or throughout home
- persistent musty odor
- mold, mildew, or fungi growing on floor joists

## Do's and Don'ts to Maintaining a Crawl Space

### Do

- clean out the crawl space.
- open the crawl space vents in the summer, then close them in the winter to conserve energy.
- make sure the crawl space has adequate ventilation. A full-size crawl space should have one vent on each side of the house for maximum ventilation. Smaller crawl spaces can get by with no fewer than two.
- keep the plastic vapor barrier in good condition for it to remain effective.

### Don't

- block vents in the foundation with plastic sheets or insulation.
- use the crawl space as a place to store junk.
- expect a plastic vapor barrier to solve a serious groundwater moisture problem.

## Steps to Keeping a Crawl Space Clean and Dry

| *Steps* | *Tools and Materials* |
|---|---|
| 1. Remove all trash, construction debris, and wood from the crawl space. | leather gloves<br>old work clothes<br>garden rake<br>trash bags or cans |
| 2. Make sure the foundation vents are clear. Make any necessary repairs, and insert new screens if necessary to keep out snakes and small animals. | heavy galvanized<br>  screen<br>tin snips<br>wire<br>pliers<br>flashlight |
| 3. Inspect for insect infestation, fungi, or termites. (See #25, "Don't be eaten out of house and home by wood-boring insects," on page 131.) | |
| 4. Check the floor joists, beams, and sills for damage, mold, or mildew. (See #13, "Trim bushes and limbs away from your house," on page 66, and #24, "Use 'sisters' to support weak or damaged beams or joists," on page 125.) | flashlight<br>screwdriver |
| 5. Inspect water pipes, drains, and electrical wires. Make any necessary repairs. | flashlight |
| 6. Patch any holes or cracks in the foundation. (See #22, "Patch any holes in your home's foundation," on page 115.) | caulking or mortar |
| 7. Beginning at the far end, spread sheets of 4 or 6 mil plastic over the dirt floor. Use bricks as weights while you arrange the plastic and cut it to size if necessary. | plastic sheets<br>bricks<br>utility knife |
| 8. Try to attach the plastic sheets to the foundation to form a tight barrier. If the duct tape refuses to adhere to the foundation, use additional bricks to hold the plastic as tightly as possible against the foundation. | duct tape<br>bricks |

*Steps*                           *Tools and Materials*

9. Overlap each sheet by 6 inches and      duct tape
   tape the joint securely to form a vapor
   barrier. Tape any holes in the plastic.

TIP: To remove smaller debris from a crawl space, use a shallow wooden or plastic box with a length of rope attached to either side. One person assigned to clean out the crawl space pulls the empty box in and fills it; another person at the entry to the crawl space then pulls the box back and empties the contents into a trash can. This two-person operation saves a great deal of time and energy, making the job less tedious.

## To Insulate or Not to Insulate?

Deciding whether or not to insulate your home's crawl space deserves special consideration. Naturally, if the crawl space is unheated and is an annoying and expensive source of cold air, then you would want to consider installing insulation between the floor joists. One problem, however, is that insulation becomes nearly useless when it's wet. In fact, insulation can trap moisture between the floor joists, where it can eventually rot the joists and the subflooring. If the crawl space has an unsolved moisture problem, you have to take care of that before you start installing insulation.

A heated crawl space does not need a layer of insulation between it and the first floor. If it remains dry year-round, you can attach insulation at the top of the foundation and unroll it down the wall and across the vapor barrier. In effect, you would be insulating the walls and the floor of the crawl space, but would leave the joists above it unfilled. This procedure is not recommended in the northern states, where severe cold could damage the foundation in this situation. Obviously, if the crawl space is subject to moisture problems in the summer, then insulation is again out of the question.

An obvious problem with insulation on the floor of the crawl space (always installed on top of a plastic vapor barrier) would come when you have to gain access to telephone lines, water pipes, or heat ducts at the far end. Working your way on your elbows and knees across this narrow space is difficult under ideal situations (which rarely occur), but it is nearly impossible to crawl across a layer of insulation without damaging it and rendering it ineffective.

In short, it is possible to insulate a crawl space, but only if every other problem, especially the presence of moisture, has been proven to be under control.

# WOODEN PORCHES AND DECKS

Porches and decks often play contradictory roles: They provide many of the conveniences of an interior room, yet they must withstand the daily abuses of the sun, rain, snow, fog, and wildly fluctuating temperatures.

Wooden porches have been around longer than decks and enjoy the added advantage of being painted rather than left exposed or finished with only a thin, watery sealer. On the other hand, decks rarely have moisture-related problems rising from the ground beneath them, whereas low porches have been known to rot from the bottom up.

Either way, wooden porches and decks do need extra attention. Unlike your home's roof, exterior walls, or foundation, your porch or deck consists of hundreds of short boards, plus twice that number of exposed end grains. And it's at the end grain where a board is most vulnerable, since that's where the wood most easily absorbs water.

As is true for other parts of your home, water is the number one enemy of a wooden porch or deck. Water encourages decay-causing fungi, rot, and wood-boring insects, and it can peel paint off a board in less than a week.

So rather than take a break on your deck or porch this afternoon, do yourself a favor: Take one under it.

This chapter includes Home-Saving Guidelines 28 through 32.

*Page*

# #28
# Protect your home's deck against rot and decay.

Porches once dominated the entrance to nearly every home, spreading across the front from corner to corner or even wrapping around one or two sides. As people began spending more time in their backyards, the need arose for a similar structure on the rear of the house. Until the latter half of this century, back porches had been little more than stoops, steps, or perhaps an enclosed utility room. The need for an all-weather, open platform set above the ground and suitable for relaxing, entertaining, and just being outdoors prompted the evolution of the deck, which now generally dwarfs any remnant of the former front porch.

While porch boards were always painted, decking boards are often left natural. Natural wood decks can be attributed to the present popularity of interior hardwood floors. But the desire to enjoy the grain of wood *outdoors*—something a 19th-century carpenter would have scoffed at—brings with it a set of problems no one has yet solved to everyone's satisfaction.

At the root of the problem is the simple fact that wood pores absorb moisture. And moisture, as we know by now, encourages the growth of wood-destroying fungi and insects. Some woods, most notably cedar and redwood, are more resistant to moisture and insects than others. Even so, if you hope to derive several years of satisfaction from your deck, you have to help the wood resist its natural inclination to absorb water.

At the same time, the ultraviolet rays of the sun take their toll. Left unprotected, the wood cells first sacrifice their natural color to the rays of the sun, gradually turning gray. The heat also robs the cells of their natural oils, causing them to dry out, crack, and split. This leaves an opportunity for moisture to enter. The detrimental effect is compounded in areas where the temperature drops below freezing. When it does, water inside the wood freezes and expands, further damaging the wood.

The most effective barrier against moisture, fungi, insects, and the sun is paint, but few people want a painted deck. For those of us who enjoy the beauty of wood grain, paint is a last resort.

So the question arises: What finish will protect your deck without obscuring the grain of the wood?

Most deck finishes, other than paint, fall into one of four categories:

- water repellents
- water-repellent preservatives
- semitransparent deck stains
- clear finishes

**Water repellents** are thin-bodied liquids that penetrate into the pores of the wood and increase a board's resistance to water. (See #5 on page 28, for a do-it-yourself recipe.) They do not make wood waterproof. They generally are less toxic than **water-repellent preservatives**, which contain dangerous chemicals, such as chromated copper arsenate or pentachlorophenol, intended to kill and prevent the spread of harmful fungi.

The toxic ingredients in water-repellent preservatives cause many people to avoid them. Theoretically, if a water repellent is used properly, the moisture that the fungi depend on will not be present in the wood; hence a water-repellent preservative would not be necessary. In some areas, however, where recurring fungi or harmful insects are a serious problem, this theory may not apply. In such cases, a water-repellent preservative may be needed. If so, be sure to read and follow the manufacturer's instructions carefully; the ingredients can be harmful to humans, pets, and plants.

**Semitransparent deck stains** add color to wood. Always make sure the stain is specially designed for decks—stains meant for siding simply cannot withstand foot traffic. Some brands also include special pigments that protect the wood from the sun's ultraviolet rays. Since a semitransparent stain seals the pores of the wood, it acts as a water repellent. A stain also offers a partial solution to two deck problems. First, if a deck is badly weathered or discolored, a semitransparent stain can partially disguise the signs of age. Second, it can help blend new deck boards with the originals. Even so, experts recommend you give any new deck boards several weeks to begin to age before applying a stain to the entire deck.

For additional protection, you can use both a water repellent and a deck stain, provided, of course, the labels clearly indicate that the two may be combined. When applying two different products, it's safest to use two that are produced by the same manufacturer and are thus more likely to be compatible.

**Clear finishes** have two categories of their own: penetrating oil finishes and surface finishes, such as spar varnish. Experts rarely recommend spar varnishs for a deck because it is simply too difficult to remove when it begins to wear out. A penetrating oil finish, on the other hand, doesn't have to be removed before additional coats can be applied. Penetrating oil finishes, however, are expensive and for that reason have not been as popular as water repellents.

The strengths and weaknesses of the four categories could be debated endlessly. What is more important than which finish you select is that you (1) apply a finish, (2) stay with the same finish, and (3) apply it as often as necessary to maintain a barrier between the wood and the water.

Before applying any finish, however, it is advisable to power wash your deck, especially if it has been ignored for years, to blast off any loose finish, stubborn dirt, mold, and mildew. By exposing the fibers of the wood, power washing increases the effectiveness of the finish you apply. The only drawback, besides the minor expense of renting a power washer (your garden hose just is not powerful enough), is that the washing causes loose nails to pop above the surface of the wood. But a half hour with a hammer and nail punch solves that problem. (For more on power washers, see page 81.)

## Warning Signs of Possible Water Damage

- nails popping out of deck boards
- cracks developing in the boards
- warping
- dark stains
- gaps in railing joints
- unprotected end grain
- support posts with softened fibers
- fungi growing on joints
- warped or cracked steps
- accumulation of leaves, twigs, and pine needles between deck boards

## Do's and Don'ts to Maintaining a Deck

*Do*

- protect plantings and shrubs around your deck when power washing or applying any bleaches, stains, or finishes. If the label indicates that the product is toxic to plants, you may need to catch the excess liquid in plastic sheets. Simply covering the leaves won't prevent the roots from absorbing the chemicals that soak into the ground.
- use galvanized nails and zinc-coated bolts, washers, and nuts for repairs to prevent rusting. Rust stains are among the most difficult to remove from wood.
- use disposable foam brushes to apply repellents, preservatives, or finishes between deck boards.

*Don't*

- allow debris to accumulate between deck boards, where it can hold moisture and foster decay.
- assume that pressure-treated lumber is invulnerable to decay. It has a higher resistance to moisture, but it, too, rots when exposed to water over a period of time.
- permit mildew to grow on your deck. It makes the boards slippery and dangerous for your guests and family.

## How to Maintain a Deck

| *Steps* | *Tools and Materials* |
|---|---|
| 1. Do a deck inspection, listing all the deck problems you find. | notebook and pen |
| 2. Check for rotted posts and joists. | awl, screwdriver, or pocketknife |
| 3. "Sister" new boards alongside any cracked or weakened joints or posts. (See #24, "Use 'sisters' to support weak or damaged beams or joists," on page 125.) Remove and treat any sign of fungi before attaching the new wood. (See #5, "Fight fungi with simple, proven methods," on page 28.) | pressure-treated wood galvanized nails ½-inch carriage bolts, washers and nuts (zinc-plated) drill and bit wrench |

*Steps*                                      *Tools and Materials*

hammer
water-repellent
   preservative
brush
tape measure

4.  Remove and replace any badly    pry bar
    cracked, rotted, or unsafe boards.  hammer
saw
galvanized nails
nail punch
tape measure

5.  Power wash your deck (See #16,  rented power
    page 81).      washer

6.  Countersink any nails that have  hammer
    popped up.    nail punch

7.  (optional) Apply a deck brightener/  commercial
    reviver/cleaner according to    product
    directions. Be sure to follow all safety  cool, cloudy day
    precautions and instructions.  paint roller
bristle brush or
   broom
plastic sheets
garden hose and
   water
safety glasses
gloves
old shoes and
   clothes

8.  (optional) Apply a stain designed  paint roller or
    specifically for decks. Be sure to    brush
    follow all safety precautions and  rags
    instructions.    bristle brush or
   broom
plastic sheets
safety glasses
gloves
old shoes and
   clothes

9.  Apply a finish designed for decks.

TIP: Once a nail pops out of the wood, it's likely to do so again despite your repair efforts. To keep the nail head below the surface, install a galvanized deck screw adjacent to the nail. Position the screw so that the head of the screw overlaps the head of the nail, locking it in place.

## *Cedar, Redwood, or Pressure-Treated Wood?*

Time has proven that certain types of wood last longer than others when used outdoors. Two of the most common are redwood and cedar. Each has naturally occurring chemicals that resist water and insects better than oak, pine, maple, or other familiar woods. Teak also falls into the same category as redwood and cedar, but it is too expensive for most homeowners to use for new decks.

Many people incorrectly assume that redwood and cedar do not need a water repellent, but that simply is not the case. Even though these two woods have a higher resistance to water and decay, they are not impervious forever. The sun and water can eventually weaken the chemicals that resist water. If you have a cedar or redwood deck, begin a regular program of treating it with a water repellent to increase its life expectancy.

Theoretically, any wood can be pressure-treated, but since pine is readily available, inexpensive, and receptive to chemicals, it is the most common. Generally, the pine is treated with chromated copper arsenate, which turns ordinary wood into lumber that is both decay and water resistant. Depending on the process, the lumber may or may not have water-resistant properties. To be safe, treat a pressure-treated deck with a water repellent.

When making repairs to your deck, select the same type of wood as was used originally. If you will be working with pressure-treated lumber, realize that the toxic chemicals contained in the wood can pose a threat to you and your family if the following precautions are not taken:

• Avoid buying or handling any lumber with excess chemicals visible on the surface.
• Wear a mask when cutting, sanding, or creating wood dust. This prevents you from inhaling toxic chemicals.

- Always cut pressure-treated lumber in a well-ventilated area, preferably outdoors.
- Clean up all dust and scraps at the end of each day.
- Do not use pressure-treated lumber for countertops or cutting boards, or anyplace it will come in contact with food or drinking water.
- Do not burn pressure-treated wood. Heating or burning such wood in a fireplace or wood burner releases toxic chemicals and can create a dangerous situation. Scraps should be disposed of in a landfill.
- Wash thoroughly after working with pressure-treated lumber; the chemicals can be absorbed through your skin.

Finally, how do you know when it is time to treat your deck with a fresh application of water repellent? The same way you know when your car needs a fresh coat of wax: when rainwater no longer beads on the surface.

# #29
# Cover all exposed end grain on your home's porch.

Wood porches come with their own set of problems. Consider for a moment the number of individual pieces of wood used to construct a typical porch. The structure could easily require 300 floorboards, 50 or more balusters, a half dozen top and bottom rails, 4 columns, several brackets or corbels, two dozen joists, and numerous other miscellaneous pieces. Once you estimate the number of boards used to construct a porch, which might be as high as 400, multiply that by 2 and you have the number of places where water penetration can cause serious problems.

To understand why exposed end grains are so vulnerable to decay, compare a board to a bundle of soda straws glued together. Water has trouble penetrating the sides of the straws, but once it reaches the open ends, it meets no resistance. If water penetrates the end grain of a board, it can travel several inches through the interior pores, eventually causing the wood to swell, break the bond with the paint, and decay.

Most carpenters rely on a tight joint and a coat of paint to prevent water from reaching the end grain, but as the wood continues to dry, especially over the course of a hot summer, it shrinks. Joints separate, paint cracks, and water—rain, ice, mist, or melting snow—seeps in. And that's when trouble begins. The paint around the end grain soon begins to peel, allowing more water to penetrate. As more water penetrates, more paint peels off the wood. The combination of moisture, wood, and air provides an ideal environment for fungi that can quickly turn a perfectly sound board into a soft, crumbling mess.

One place where this happens on a regular basis is along the end grain of the porch boards. Most porches are designed to pitch away from the side of the house. Thus, when a hard, blowing storm drives gallons of water onto the porch, the water drains away from the main structure of the house. The floorboards are laid perpendicular to the side of the house, so water is channeled along the joints toward the ends of the boards.

At the end of each board, the water cascades over the exposed end grain. Unless an extra coat of paint is applied to the end grain, chances are that some of the water will be absorbed by the board. As the board swells, its bond with the paint is tested. A fresh coat of paint might flex under the stress, but older paint will crack. When the next rain comes, more water is absorbed and more paint breaks loose, and before long the ends of the boards are saturated with moisture. Decay-causing fungi will find an ideal home here, and soon the boards will begin to deteriorate.

At that point, your only solution is a major, and expensive, rebuilding project. But all that's required might be nothing more than a few tubes of high-quality exterior caulking, some protective half-round trim, and a couple hours of your time.

## Warning Signs of Water Penetration

- separated joints
- paint blisters around the ends of boards
- exposed end grain on floorboards
- water dripping from the underside of a joint
- sagging handrail
- loose balusters (spindles)
- soft, crumbling wood

## Do's and Don'ts to Preventing Water Damage

### Do

- make sure the floorboards are sloped away from your house.
- repair any leaking gutters to reduce the amount of water on your porch.
- allow joints to dry before caulking.
- sweep off standing water and snow after each storm.
- use pressure-treated lumber to replace badly damaged wood.

### Don't

- buy cheap caulking material. It breaks down too easily and, therefore, doesn't save you money.
- store a partially used tube of caulking. Instead, find a spot that needs repair, and use up the remaining caulking—partial tubes invariably harden.

- ignore fungi or insect damage. Caulking won't cure dry rot.
- use a shovel to clean snow off your porch—unless, of course, you want to repaint the porch in the spring.
- forget the porch roof. Make sure it isn't directing moisture to your porch.

## How to Cover and Caulk Exposed End Grain

| *Steps* | *Tools and Materials* |
|---|---|
| 1. Clean out any separated joints with an old paintbrush. Allow damp wood to dry in the sun, or use a heat gun or hair dryer if necessary. | old paintbrush<br>heat gun, hair dryer, or sunshine |
| 2. Scrape blistered paint off the wood around the joints. | paint scraper |
| 3. Renail any loose joints. Use galvanized nails to prevent rust spots. | hammer<br>galvanized finish nails<br>nail punch |
| 4. Glue and nail half-round trim onto exposed end grain of floorboards. | half-round trim<br>exterior adhesive<br>hammer<br>galvanized finish nails<br>nail punch<br>fine-tooth saw<br>tape measure |

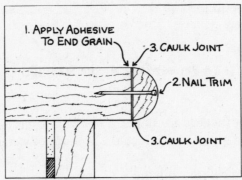

1. APPLY ADHESIVE TO END GRAIN
3. CAULK JOINT
2. NAIL TRIM
3. CAULK JOINT

| | |
|---|---|
| 5. Caulk all joints and seams where water could enter. | exterior caulking<br>caulking gun<br>rag |
| 6. Prime and paint. | paintbrush<br>primer<br>paint |

TIP: Cut the tip of the caulking tube at a 45-degree angle for a neater, more effective bead.

# #30
# Take a closer look
# at your steps.

If you take a close look around your neighborhood, you will probably notice preformed concrete steps where there once were
wooden sets of stairs. Wooden steps suffer many of the same
problems as porches because they have lots of exposed and very
vulnerable end grain, yet they seldom have a protective roof to divert rainwater and melting snow. When you also consider that
many carpenters, former and still swinging, don't fully understand how quickly exposed end grain can deteriorate and what
extra precautions have to be taken to protect the open pores of
each board, it's a wonder any wooden stairs are left at all.

But if your house or deck has a set of wooden stairs, you can
restore them rather than replace them with concrete, and you
certainly can extend their life expectancy. Most of these tips are
intended for exterior stairs, but if you have a set of wooden
steps in the basement, you would be well advised to apply many
of the same principles to them as well. Water is water, and
whether it's indoors or out, it can cause serious and expensive
problems. Basement stairs often suffer from problems associated with high humidity and dampness: mold, mildew, fungi,
and wood-boring insects. Increased air circulation and lots of
water repellent (or a water repellent containing a fungicide)
may be necessary to prevent further damage.

Stairs leading to decks generally don't suffer problems associated with lack of air circulation and constant dampness, but enclosed porches on older homes often do. Many homeowners tend
to neglect the undersides of wooden steps simply because they
seem so inaccessible. Since the steps are well attached to the
framework of the porch, you may have to remove some of the latticework around your porch to gain access to them. Your other
option may involve inching across the crawl space. As unpleasant
as the task may be, it's important to inspect and treat the underside of your steps if you hope to save them. Chances are, the

stringers and support posts were never treated with a water repellent or preservative. They may also be in direct contact with the ground or may have become infested with termites.

All of which are very good reasons for taking a few minutes to take a closer look at your steps.

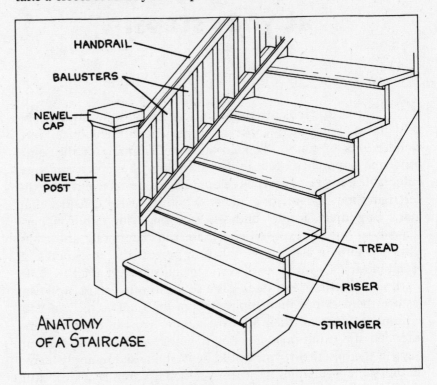

HANDRAIL

BALUSTERS

NEWEL CAP

NEWEL POST

TREAD

RISER

STRINGER

ANATOMY OF A STAIRCASE

## Warning Signs of Worn Stairs

- stair treads that are cupped and hold water
- stair risers that have pulled away from the notched stringer
- cracked boards
- soft or crumbling wood
- peeling paint
- separated joints
- ineffective or missing caulking material
- stringers pulled away from the house or deck

### Do's and Don'ts to Maintaining Stairs

**Do**

- watch for boards that hold water rather than shed it.
- use pressure-treated lumber for repairs.
- apply extra finish, paint, or water repellent to any exposed end grain.
- make sure there is adequate air circulation under wooden steps.
- caulk, caulk, caulk.

**Don't**

- sacrifice ventilation for beauty. You can have both.
- let wood rest directly on concrete; it can absorb moisture and quickly rot.
- forget to look under and behind your stairs, especially if they are enclosed over open, moist ground.

### How to Save Wooden Stairs

| *Steps* | *Tools and Materials* |
|---|---|
| 1. Closely inspect your stairs for places where water can enter a board or a joint between two boards. | |
| 2. Replace any badly decayed wood with pressure-treated lumber. | saw<br>hammer<br>galvanized nails<br>tape measure |
| 3. Apply a water repellent to all new and exposed wood. | brush<br>water repellent |
| 4. Drill ½-inch drainage holes, 9 inches apart, in cupped stair treads. Apply water repellent. If the steps are painted, paint the interior of each hole. | drill<br>½-inch bit<br>water repellent<br>primer and paint<br>paintbrushes |
| 5. Provide ventilation for any enclosed stairs with holes or decorative shapes, such as stars or circles, in the risers | drill<br>bit<br>saber saw |

*Steps*                                          *Tools and Materials*

or stringers. Use a drill bit to make a
starter hole for the saw blade. Apply a
water repellent to any newly exposed
wood in each cutout. After it dries,
paint to match the surrounding wood.

water repellent
paint brush
primer and paint

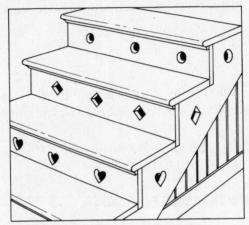

6. Nail sloping trim on horizontal
   boards and in right-angle corners
   that hold water.

saw
trim
hammer
galvanized nails
tape measure

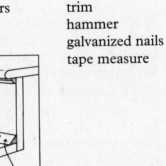

7. Tighten any loose or separated joints.

hammer
nail punch
galvanized nails

8. Caulk any nails or screws set below
   the surface of the wood to prevent
   them from holding water.

caulking gun
exterior caulking

*Steps*                                             *Tools and Materials*

9. Nail nosing trim over exposed end
   grain on each tread.

half-round trim
tape measure
saw
hammer
galvanized nails
exterior adhesive

10. Caulk, caulk, caulk. (See #15, on
    page 76, for details on the right way to
    caulk.)

caulking gun
caulking tubes

---

TIP: To test the endurance of your stairs during a rainstorm, use a garden hose to simulate a downpour, and
watch where the water goes.

# #31
# Guard against decay in your porch columns.

Wooden columns are prone to deterioration for several reasons. First, the end grain of the boards that form a column is vulnerable to moisture. Rainwater can seep into the boards at the top or, more often, be absorbed by the end grain at the bottom. Second, the hollow core of the column can trap condensation, causing the wood to rot from the inside.

The danger of a rotting column is obvious. Most columns are intended not merely as purely decorative features, but as supporting members of a porch roof. If a column is permitted to rot, the weight pressing down on the wood crushes the softened pores, and the roof above sags. As a result, the boards resting on the column may crack, split, or develop a permanent bow. Removing a badly damaged column may require the services of an engineer and a construction crew, so preventive maintenance is always a good idea.

Some of the moisture that accumulates inside the hollow core of a column can escape as vapors, passing harmlessly through the wood and the paint. Ironically, too much paint on a column can cause moisture damage just as readily as too little. If several thick layers of paint prevent moisture vapors from escaping, water is trapped in the wood and eventually causes the paint to peel and the wood to deteriorate. To guard against this, moisture vapors can be vented through ½-inch holes drilled strategically near the top and bottom of each column. Holes should be positioned where they cannot provide an inlet for rainwater. If that is unavoidable, install special vent caps in the holes. And if insects or bees find the vent holes inviting, you can block their entrance with ordinary screen wire tucked neatly inside.

Holes also need to be drilled at the bottom of the plinth (the square base) or beneath the column to allow complete drainage of any moisture that does accumulate in the hollow core. Check the plinth as well to make sure standing water does not accumulate after a downpour. Given time, a puddle of water around the plinth can make its way into the end grain of both the plinth boards and those of the column. If a new column is being installed or if an older one has been removed for repairs, it should be positioned on a manufactured metal base specially designed to provide ventilation for the hollow core and to prevent standing water.

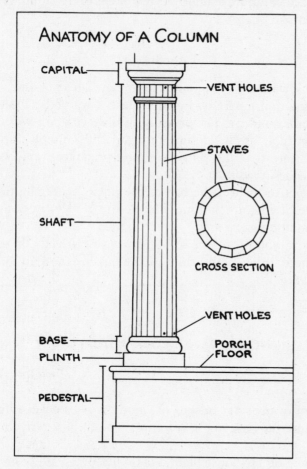

### Warning Signs of Decaying Columns

- peeling paint, especially around the base
- large seam separations between the staves
- staves that have come loose
- soft or rotted wood
- woodpeckers, which eat insects found in wet wood

## Do's and Don'ts to Preventing Decay

### Do

- keep a protective layer of paint on each column.
- caulk all joints, cracks, and seams on or around each column.
- coat the inside of any drilled holes with a water repellent.
- check columns regularly. Movement of the house can cause joints to open.

### Don't

- let several layers of paint accumulate on a column.
- think that a wire wrapped around a warped stave will correct a problem. The protruding stave can be a warning sign that moisture is building up inside the column. It may also indicate that the pillar is supporting more weight than it was designed to hold.
- forget to inspect the top of the pillar, especially the gutter over it and any flashing intended to prevent rainwater from penetrating the top.
- allow wood columns or plinths to rest directly on masonry, where they can absorb moisture passing through the porous material.

## How to Save a Column from Decay

| *Steps* | *Tools and Materials* |
|---|---|
| 1. Identify any soft portions of wood around the base of the column. | pocketknife, screwdriver, or ice pick |
| 2. Scrape off any loose paint. Allow the wood to dry before treating it with a water repellent. | scraper or steel wool water repellent paintbrush |
| 3. Drill a ¼-inch test hole through the pillar wall to determine the thickness of the staves. | electric drill ¼-inch bit |
| 4. Wrap a piece of tape around the bit to keep it from completely penetrating the staves. | masking tape |

*Steps*

*Tools and Materials*

5.  Drill a number of holes into the soft wood ¼-inch apart, making sure the bit does not pass through the back of the board. Drill the holes at an angle so they cannot hold liquid.

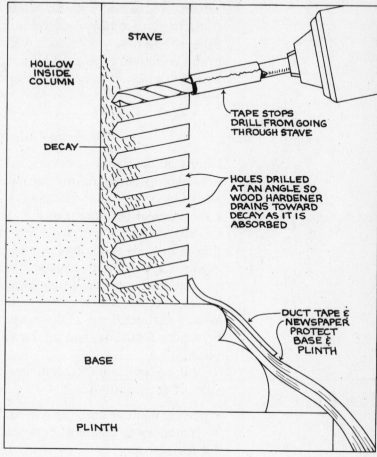

STAVE

HOLLOW
INSIDE
COLUMN

DECAY

TAPE STOPS
DRILL FROM GOING
THROUGH STAVE

HOLES DRILLED
AT AN ANGLE SO
WOOD HARDENER
DRAINS TOWARD
DECAY AS IT IS
ABSORBED

DUCT TAPE &
NEWSPAPER
PROTECT
BASE &
PLINTH

BASE

PLINTH

6.  Using a syringe or plastic squeeze bottle, fill each hole with a liquid wood hardener (also called a wood consolidant).

wood hardener
syringe or squeeze
 bottle

7.  Refill the holes as the wood absorbs the hardener.

8.  Allow the hardener to cure, then fill the holes with an exterior wood filler, following manufacturer's instructions. Let dry, then sand it smooth.

wood filler
sandpaper

9.  Before painting the column, make sure vent holes and drainage holes have been drilled and the exposed wood is coated with a water repellent.

electric drill
½-inch bit
water repellent
paintbrush or
 squeeze bottle

TIP: To saturate a slightly separated joint with water repellent, wedge one end of a short cotton string into the seam, then place the other end in a container of water repellent. The rope works like a wick, transferring repellent from the container to the end grain. Allow three or four days for the wood to become saturated.

### My Two Columns

I must admit that I've never paid close attention to the two columns marking the formal front entrance of our 1914 Georgian-Tudor brick home. The columns support a semicircular pediment, so they serve more of a decorative than practical purpose. Nevertheless, they're wood, they're original to the house, and, as it turns out, they're at a critical point in their preservation.

One morning I took time away from my research and writing to conduct an impromptu inspection of the columns. What I discovered was so distracting I was tempted to forgo my writing for the day and get started on a Save the Columns project.

My columns, in fact, exhibited several classic warning signs of deterioration:

- peeling paint around the base and the plinth
- separations in the joints between the staves
- a few soft spots
- several open joints
- a poorly designed flat spot at the top of each column that could hold rain and snow, and, most alarming,
- no sign of any drainage or ventilation holes

My plan of attack was to scrape off loose paint and treat any exposed wood with a mixture of my homemade water repellent: 1 quart of boiled linseed oil to 1 quart of turpentine. I then drilled ventilation holes in the top and combination drainage-ventilation holes in the bottom.

I also considered printing up some Save the Columns T-shirts and organizing a Column Watch program with my neighbors, but I reluctantly admitted that was just a way to avoid going back to work at my desk.

# #32
# Provide ventilation under your porch or deck.

The cool, shaded ground under your home's porch or deck is a constant source of moisture and can cause chronic problems for the joists and flooring above. The problem is especially prevalent in older homes, where untreated pine boards were painted only on the visible side. The undersides of the boards were left unsealed, ready to absorb the moisture that inevitably leads to rot and decay.

Competent carpenters and architects, however, realized that without adequate ventilation, the moisture escaping from the ground beneath the porch would be absorbed by the posts, joists, and flooring. To compensate, they installed latticework or, on low porches, left open space between the ground and the outside joist. This allowed for the adequate ventilation that was critical to preventing moisture from being trapped in the enclosed area.

Leaking gutters and overgrown plantings, however, can punish the fragile latticework around many porches. Rather than repairing, repainting, or replacing the lattice, many homeowners have enclosed their porch or deck foundations with solid materials, such as plywood, siding, bricks, metal, or concrete blocks. In other instances, mounds of dirt, landscaping mulch, and lush groundcover have prevented air from circulating under low porches. Without the necessary air circulation, the moisture from the ground accumulates beneath the porch, is absorbed by the unprotected boards, and causes invisible decay.

If the lattice is missing from around your home's porch, you can purchase lattice panels at a lumberyard or, even better, make them yourself. The lattice sold by many lumberyards is neither sturdy enough nor appropriate for many homes. If you cannot find high-quality lattice, take a look at the November 1983 issue of *Old House Journal*. There you'll find easy-to-follow instructions for designing and building lattice panels. If you own a historic home, you need to do some research first to make sure the lattice you install is appropriate for the age and style of your home.

Remember: If you seal off your home's porch or deck foundation, you'll also seal the fate of the joists and flooring to a lifetime of decay.

## Warning Signs of Poor Ventilation Under the Deck and Porch

- solid, nonvented foundation skirting
- mold and mildew underneath the porch or deck
- peeling paint on porch flooring
- warped flooring
- soft spots in the floor

## Do's and Don'ts to Improve Air Circulation

### Do

- level any mounds of dirt, gravel, or decorative bark that are hindering air movement beneath a low deck or porch.
- trim back any vegetation that blocks air circulation.
- replace any nonoriginal solid skirting with lattice.
- install vents in original solid foundation material.
- cover the ground beneath the porch or deck with a plastic moisture barrier.

### Don't

- forget to inspect the lattice regularly for damage.
- expect thin, inexpensive, lumberyard lattice panels that are constructed with staples to last more than two or three years.

## How to Provide Ventilation Under the Deck or Porch

*Steps*                                      *Tools and Materials*

1. Study homes of similar age and style to determine which lattice pattern is appropriate for your home. You may want to refer to an article in the November 1983 issue of *Old House Journal*.

| *Steps* | *Tools and Materials* |
|---|---|
| 2. Adjust the grade of the soil around the foundation to divert rainwater away from your porch or deck. (See #21, "Check the lay of your land to keep the basement dry," on page 109.) | shovel |
| 3. Make or purchase the appropriate lattice. Prime and paint. | primer<br>paint<br>paintbrushes |
| 4. Cover the ground under the deck or porch with plastic. Weigh it down to hold it in place. | plastic<br>rocks or bricks |
| 5. Attach the lattice, hinging one panel for easy access to the underside of your porch. | screws<br>hinges<br>screwdriver<br>drill |
| 6. Prevent vegetation and dirt from coming in contact with the lattice. | shovel<br>pruning shears |

TIP: Screw, rather than nail, lattice in place so it can be easily removed for repairs and repainting.

## 1959

My parents' sturdy white foursquare has a wide, sprawling porch that dominates the front of the house. When I was growing up, it was a wonderful place that adapted to our changing needs. On rainy days, it was where my brother and I played blind man's bluff or Monopoly with our friends. On hot summer nights, it was where we slept on old canvas army cots and listened to the murmur of neighbors across the street, dogs down the block, or crickets camped under our dusty tennis shoes. Each Sunday morning without fail our cousins, aunts, and uncles would meet on our porch to form a processional for the one-block trek to the First Presbyterian Church, where we proudly filled the entire back row. Afterward, the men would gather around the porch swing, loosen their ties, and discuss the crops, the weather, new tires for a tractor, and plans for the next week.

I remember, too, the summer when my best friend and I discovered that one section of the sturdy lattice under the porch was hinged, not nailed, along its top. We would crawl behind the boxwoods, lift up the lattice, and slip unseen into the dry, dimly lit crawl space. We laughed quietly while my unwanted younger brother and his friends raced around the yard looking for us, unaware that we were watching them from behind the lattice under the porch.

The ground was mounded in the center, where workers 50 years earlier had tossed shovelfuls of dirt as they dug the footings for the five brick pilings that supported the weight of the porch. The earth was dry and would crumble under our weight as we slithered from one end of the crawl space to the other, exploring every corner in hopes of finding a lost treasure, an Indian arrowhead, or a German Luger brought home, we reasoned, by one of the town's many war veterans. All we ever found was a 1907 Indian head penny.

The joists on which we bumped our heads countless times that summer were amazingly sound. We encountered few insects, no snakes (though we lived in fear of coming face-to-face with one), and no rotting boards. With a breeze gently blowing through the lattice panels, our secret hideout offered an escape from the hot August sun, as well as pesky brothers. What I did not realize, and had no concern with as a nine-year-old, was that the lattice around our porch did more than just provide us with a hiding place. It enabled the wind to erase any sign of moisture escaping from the ground and, like myself, looking for a place to hide.

The porch on my parents' house is now more than 80 years old, but it looks today just as it did in 1959. The yellow pine joists are still straight, the flooring firm, and the ground beneath it just as dry as I recall.

Good design lasts almost as long as good memories.

# THE ATTIC

Long before homeowners started worrying about energy conservation, heat loss, R-values, and utility bills, attics were simply storage rooms, filled with everything from scrapbooks and old dishes to wedding dresses and broken chairs. No one thought too much about them, except on a rainy Sunday afternoon or when it was time to drag the suitcases down for a summer trip.

The oil embargoes of the 1970s suddenly changed all of that. People stayed home and weatherproofed their doors and windows. Upstairs, boxes of old clothes, books, and magazines were thrown out. Drafty attics were sealed and saturated with insulation. And in the process some new problems were created—and a few old ones were overlooked.

Today, many homeowners avoid venturing into their attics. Now transformed into sterile, dusty caverns, attics have been stripped of their charm and nostalgia. Nevertheless, they cannot be ignored, since they can be the target of moisture problems ranging from ice dams on the roof to condensation on the rafters.

So, whether you grab a flashlight and a dust mask or simply open the door and switch on the light, inspect your attic every fall and spring. It could be trying to tell you something.

This chapter includes Home-Saving Guidelines 33 and 34.

*Page*

# #33
# Prevent ice dams and
# rotting rafters.

For years, homeowners paid little attention to their attics. The extra space served as a convenient storage room for old trunks, winter clothes, broken lamps, and back issues of *National Geographic.* Larger attics often had an open stairway and a pine floor, making it possible to store furniture that might otherwise have been hauled to the dump. Some were even pressed into service as makeshift bedrooms for cousins, grandchildren, and rebellious teenagers.

The energy crisis of the 1970s signaled the end of sentimental, yet inefficient, attics. When the price of heating oil skyrocketed, homeowners began looking for ways to conserve energy, and attics were an obvious target. Far easier to access than walls, attics could be cleaned out, insulated, and sealed off from the rest of the house. While generations of children might be denied a rainy Saturday exploring the contents of dusty boxes and faded photo albums, home heating bills were reduced as energy conservation measures took effect.

Even though your home's attic might now be blanketed in insulation or accessible only through a small hatch in the ceiling, you need to inspect it twice a year. While your heating bills may have dropped, the rafters in your attic may be soaking up moisture trapped by the extra insulation.

So why go to the trouble of insulating your attic now that the price of fuel has stabilized? For two good reasons. First, you have no guarantee that the supply or price of fossil fuels is going to remain constant. Conservation, not complacency, is the best way to reduce energy consumption.

Second, a poorly insulated attic can weaken more than just your household checking account. If you live in the snowbelt, heat lost through your home's roof could cause harmful ice dams.

In an underinsulated home, the attic is warmed by air escaping from the rooms on the lower floor. This heat is transferred to the roof, where it melts any accumulated snow. As the snow turns to water, it trickles down the roof, until it reaches the unheated overhang and gutters. There it freezes, forming a ridge made of ice. The weight of the ice can bend or even snap metal or vinyl gutters. Just as dangerous, the ice dam blocks the descent of additional water from the heated portion of the roof. At the critical point where the warm water encounters the ice dam, the water accumulates, backing up beneath the shingles. If the water finds a loose nail or rises above the top of a row of shingles, it is going to drain into your home.

The wood sheathing beneath the shingles is going to absorb much of this water, which eventually causes it to rot. In addition, water is going to penetrate the rafters in the dark, seldom-seen recesses of your attic. The pool of water caused by ice dams accumulates only a few inches above interior walls. Given enough snow on the roof and warm air in the attic, water will soon be dripping from your ceiling and running down your plaster walls. And once it starts, there is little you can do to stop the flow of water that ruins plaster, wallpaper, and paint.

The solution to ice dams is very simple: Insulate your attic before, not after, it begins to snow. If you can create a heat shield between your plaster ceiling and the air in your attic, you can keep your roof from becoming a virtual hot plate. Most experts recommend the equivalent of 10 to 20 inches of loose-fill fiberglass or cellulose insulation above the ceiling to prevent heat loss into the attic. Any less and you increase the risk of water damage to your home's sheathing, rafters, walls, and ceilings.

Insulation also creates a special problem that must be dealt with if you hope to avoid damage to your attic rafters from condensation. Attic floors are often punctured by a variety of necessary structural elements, such as chimneys, vent pipes, doors, plumbing, and electrical lines. Each hole provides a means by which warm, humid air can rise into the attic. In an uninsulated attic, this moist air passes harmlessly outdoors through cracks in the siding, the roof, or the soffit, or through loose windows. Once an attic is tightened and insulated, however, moist air can become trapped. When the captive warm air comes in contact with the cold rafters, the moisture in the air condenses on the wood, where it will crystallize or form water droplets, depending on the air temperature. Regardless, the rafters soon absorb the water and eventually weaken.

Once again, the solution is neither as difficult nor as expensive as repairing the damage water and decay-causing fungi can cause. First, eliminate, as much as possible, the sources of warm, moist air. Caulk around pipes, holes drilled for electrical lines, and gaps around chimneys. Second, provide ventilation ports so moisture can pass harmlessly out of your attic. Since building codes vary, consult a local contractor to determine how many vents your attic may need. Vents can be located in the soffits or on the roof itself. Since installing vents may involve cutting holes in the roof or soffits—both potentially dangerous situations—you should consider this a project for a professional.

There's nothing nostalgic about an attic filled with loose insulation, but perhaps the next generation can find other means of staying in touch with their heritage.

## Warning Signs of Ice Dams

- icicles hanging from the gutters
- heavy accumulations of snow and ice in the gutters and along the edge of the roof
- large bare spots on a snow-covered roof that correspond with the boundaries of the attic
- water stains on the sheathing and rafters
- water stains at the point where the ceiling meets the wall
- frost crystals on rafters
- dust accumulated on floor insulation around pipes, indicative of air rising through the insulation

## Do's and Don'ts to Working in the Attic

### Do

- inspect your attic every winter, preferably after an accumulation of snow, for warning signs of ice dams.
- check for leaks during a summer shower.
- pick a cool day to work in your attic.
- for an unfinished attic, cut pieces of ¾-inch plywood to span the joists so you can stand or sit safely while you work.
- wear a particle mask when working around insulation.
- make sure all electrical boxes in your attic are properly sealed.

**Don't**

- wait until winter to insulate your attic.
- take chances hopping from joist to joist. One misstep can send your foot crashing through the ceiling of the room below.
- pile insulation on top of recessed lights that require ventilation of the heat produced by the bulb.
- work in what you believe may be old asbestos insulation without first having it checked. Call your local health department for information on testing services.

## How to Prevent Heat Loss Through the Attic

| *Steps* | *Tools and Materials* |
|---|---|
| 1. Inspect each rafter in the attic, looking for signs of moisture, decay, or insect damage. | flashlight |
| 2. Clean out any accumulation of boxes, papers, old clothes, and potential fire hazards. | trash bags |
| 3. Wearing gloves and a particle mask, pull the insulation back from pipes and other protrusions rising into the attic. Check for evidence of air leaks and feel for drafts. Leave the lights on in the room below the attic while you conduct your inspection. Any sign of light is a sign of an air leak. | gloves<br>particle mask<br>flashlight |
| 4. Caulk or plug any air leaks. (See #15, "Buy a gun—a caulking gun—and use it," on page 76.) | caulking gun<br>caulking material |
| 5. Caulk and/or insulate around the chimney passing through the attic. Check for missing or deteriorating mortar. Repair as needed. (See #18, "Tuck-point brick walls to keep them sound and attractive," on page 92.) | |
| 6. Insulate and weather-strip where needed, including around the hatch or door leading to the attic. | insulation<br>weather stripping |
| 7. Make sure soffit vents remain open. | flashlight |

*Steps*                                    *Tools and Materials*

8.   Check with a contractor to determine
     your home's ventilation needs.

TIP: One way to create a tight-fitting seal around pipes rising through your attic floor is to drill a hole the same diameter as the pipe in a piece of pine 2 inches by 4 or 6 inches. Cut the hole and the board in half, then position each half around the pipe. Rather than nailing the boards and risk damaging the plaster or splitting the block, glue each half in place around the pipe. To complete the seal, caulk between the wood and the pipe.

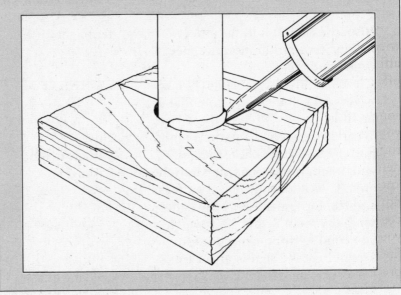

# #34
# Get more out of your home's attic space.

When handed a lemon, make lemonade.

That simple slogan has helped me muddle through more than a few disappointing discoveries, and it may help you solve two chronic problems with one solution. Attics can be lemons, with problems ranging from excessive heat loss and no insulation to exposed electrical lines and excessive condensation. When combined with an acute shortage of living space in your home, an unfinished attic might seem like just another problem, but this problem may offer a solution that can also increase the value of your home.

If your attic is an accessible haven of wasted space lined with some serious problems threatening the future of your home, then you should consider turning that wasted space into a finished room. In doing so you also solve the problems of heat loss, condensation, and exposed electrical lines. And as building experts know, it is far less expensive to improve existing space in your home than it is to build a new addition. When compared to the cost and inconvenience of buying a new home, moving, changing your work schedules, and uprooting the kids from their schools, finding a few hundred more square feet of living space in your present home will feel like a gift.

Many 20th-century homes, such as bungalows and towering foursquares, were designed with large, unfinished attics, perhaps to compensate for the tiny closets the architects so begrudgingly handed out. For three generations, most of these attics remained virtually sealed, dusty tombs opened only by curious children on rainy Saturdays and parents in search of a box of Christmas decorations or an old photograph. It was not until the energy crisis of the 1970s that homeowners began scrutinizing their attics, not as a source of additional space, but as a means of reducing energy consumption. I returned home from college one year to find my father methodically prying up the wide pine floorboards in our third-floor attic. He filled the long empty chambers between the floor joists with insulation, then carefully renailed each board in place. With his children about to leave the nest, he didn't need an extra bedroom, but he had learned that each cold Midwestern winter was pulling valuable heat out through his attic. His solution prevented warm air in the bedrooms from ever reaching the attic.

Depending on its size, attic space can be converted into a children's playroom or bedroom, an office, a family room, a master bedroom and bath, or quarters for live-in help. But before you rush off to the lumberyard for a load of lumber and plasterboard, take the time to accurately assess your attic's true potential and to compare it with the basic requirements for an attic conversion.

### Basic Requirements

- an existing or potential stairway
- a finished ceiling height of at least 7.5 feet over most of the area
- sufficient finished square footage to justify the investment
- floor joists capable of handling the additional weight
- access to heating, electrical, and plumbing systems

### Checklist for an Attic Conversion

__ 1. Access

*Is there an existing staircase to your attic?*

This is one of the most crucial questions, since it is far easier to deal with even a small, narrow, unfinished staircase than no staircase at all. A ceiling hatch or pull-down folding staircase is no substitute for an actual staircase. These substitutes are often the cause of accidents and could trap children in the attic in the event of a fire. If a staircase is the only major obstacle in the path of your attic conversion, try to find a convenient place in your home where a staircase could be installed. You may be able to annex space at the end of a bedroom, alter basement stairs, or sacrifice an existing closet. Call in an architect for a fresh approach and technical expertise.

__ 2. Usable space

*Is there a sufficient amount of usable vertical space to make the conversion worthwhile?*

Don't be fooled by what may appear to be an abundance

of unused floor space in your existing attic. Where to put your head is more important than where to put your feet. Attic space quickly falls into three categories: storage, seating, and standing. To determine just how much of each the attic has, make a topographical map. With a tape measure, pencil, and paper, sketch an outline of your attic. Now, using a 4-foot piece of trim as a measuring rod, determine where the ceiling and the floor are 48 inches apart. By connecting those points with a series of lines on your drawing, you can approximate the location of the new walls and create a room within the attic. The area less than 48 inches in height is good only for storage. That above 48 inches can be considered usable living space, although 90 inches is required for standing space.

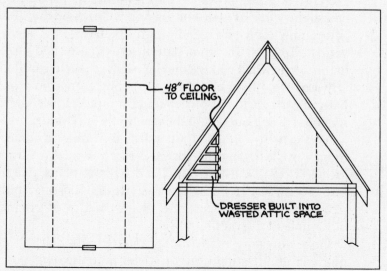

Using the tape measure or another length of trim, determine where the ceiling and floor are a minimum of 90 inches apart. This is a somewhat arbitrary height based on practical experience. You should call your local building inspections department to determine what the governing code mandates and use that measurement as your guide. By connecting the dots on your drawing, you can see exactly how much standing space your attic has to offer.

If you are encouraged by what you see, transfer your measurements to graph paper. Draw a preliminary floor plan showing the approximate location and size of each piece of furniture you envision in this room. Placing chairs, desks, and beds near the walls will reserve most of the vertical space for walking and standing. Your drawing will give you an accurate idea of how much floor space will remain once the furniture is in place. Remember: The sloping ceiling will affect the location of a tall chest of drawers, a bookcase, or a bed with a headboard.

___ 3. Utilities

*Will you be able to extend existing utility lines into your attic?*

Bringing water, heat, and electricity into an attic generally isn't a major obstacle, especially if your plans don't call for an additional bathroom. But if there is only one bathroom, bear in mind that the value of your home will increase to reflect the cost of a second one. Even a partial bathroom will increase the value of your home—and will reduce the stress on your family on Monday mornings. If you have the space and your budget can accommodate it, the time to add a second bathroom is while you are making an attic conversion, not afterward. If nothing else, have a plumber rough in a second bath so you or a future owner could complete it at a later date without tearing out any of the new walls or flooring.

You can save yourself a good deal of time, trouble, and money by designing the space so that the new bathroom is located over an existing one. In addition to being able to tap into nearby water lines, you can use the existing soil vent pipe, saving you the cost and inconvenience of cutting another hole in the roof.

Once you have made a preliminary plan, call a licensed plumber and heating expert to determine the demands your new room will make upon the existing systems. Then decide what work you can do yourself and what must be done by an expert.

___ 4. Lighting

*Can your new room be lit without disturbing the exterior structure of your home?*

The original plans for your home probably did not call for many windows or lights in the attic. A typical attic might have a window in a dormer or gable and a bare bulb hanging from a rafter, but that's about it. If you're fortunate, your home's attic has an acceptable number of existing windows that you can supplement with interior lighting. Your next least expensive option would involve cutting a hole in the roof for a skylight. If you need both additional floor space and more lighting, a dormer would be another option, although a far more expensive one. Besides the cost, consider the impact a new dormer would have on your home's appearance. You won't have to drive far to find examples of inappropriate dormers that have ruined the lines of a home. Skylights and dormers have to be carefully considered in light of a home's historical value as well. Many home buyers will walk away from an older house whose character has been compromised by a hastily conceived alteration or addition.

As an alternative to a skylight, some owners install fluorescent light panels between the ceiling rafters. When framed and covered with a textured Plexiglas panel, they nearly duplicate the appearance of a skylight for a fraction of the cost.

## __ 5. Ventilation

*Can you provide proper ventilation to reduce the amount of heat accumulating in and around your attic conversion, as well as eliminating any condensation problems in the winter?*

On a clear, sunny day in July an attic can become a hothouse. Warm air that rises from lower floors can collect in an unvented attic, where the stale air is heated even higher by the rays of the sun beating down on the roof. An attic conversion does not eliminate this problem because it is simply a process of building a room within a room that has its own conditions. So even though your attic—that is, the storage space—is reduced to triangular-shaped areas tucked down near the eaves, you still could create a condensation problem if you don't provide proper ventilation and insulation.

Exhaust fans, vents, and insulation are far easier to install before you frame out the new walls than after. The insulation and ventilation requirements are determined by your home, the design of the new room, and your local building codes. The best person to determine those requirements is someone who has experience with attic conversions, such as an architect, contractor, energy consultant, or heating technician. Your best course of action is to anticipate any problems and their solutions before you begin hammering even the first nail.

## Do's and Don'ts to Attic Conversions

### Do

- have an architect or engineer inspect your home's existing attic to determine if the structural components are adequate for your planned conversion.
- become familiar with local building codes to determine the feasibility of finishing your attic. The most important questions you will want answered are (1) What legal requirements must be satisfied by an attic conversion? (2) What steps are necessary for any permits and inspections? and (3) How much of the work can I do myself?
- try to locate a new attic bathroom above an existing bathroom to reduce plumbing expenses.

### Don't

- seal off the triangular space between the eaves and the new walls, since this can still be used for storage. Insulate, line the area with plywood, and provide an access door at one end. This would also be the ideal time to install lighting for this area.
- simply extend the present heating system without having a qualified technician determine if the existing blower or pump can handle the extra load. The same advice applies to the electrical and plumbing systems.
- forget about the excess heat that accumulates in an attic in the summer and condensation that often forms in the winter. Plan accordingly.
- ruin the exterior appearance of your home with inappropriate dormers or skylights. Instead, consult an architect experienced in attic conversions before installing these features.

> TIP: Since space will always be in demand in an attic room, design dressers, bookshelves, desks, and closets as built-ins tucked behind the new walls. (See illustration on page 181.)

# THE PLUMBING

Hot and cold running water is a convenience we all take for granted—provided, that is, the only place we see it is between a faucet and the nearest drain. The remainder of the time we quite naturally want water to remain hidden from view in either a copper supply line or a plastic drain pipe.

But water never seems quite satisfied with our plans. Given the slightest opportunity, it comes running over the side of the sink, tub, or toilet, sprays across the basement, or drips, drips, drips all night.

The best way to avoid a plumbing emergency is to plan for one. Begin by identifying and clearly marking the location of the main water shut-off valve. Each of the faucets and major appliances should have one as well, but if you know where the main shut-off valve is, you can go to it first in an emergency and look for the others after the water has stopped spraying.

Before that happens, take a few minutes to see what else you can do to avoid an emergency that could leave you and your home dripping wet.

This chapter covers Home-Saving Guidelines 35 through 40.

*Page*

# #35
# Learn how to open
# a clogged drain.

While getting water into your home is seldom a problem, getting it out often is. Waste water systems can suffer from a host of problems, any one of which can cause a minor—or major—disaster.

The most difficult problem to overcome is improper installation. Older homes seem to suffer more than newer ones from this malady; in many instances, pipes, drains, and vents have been installed after the house was built. Chronic slow-draining tubs and sinks may be the result of improper venting or inadequate sloping of the waste piping. In either case, the services of a professional plumber may be required to identify the problem and solve it.

Other plumbing problems can be avoided simply by watching for critical warning signs. A common problem is a slow-running drain, usually the result of some blockage. It is much easier to dislodge a partial blockage using a plunger (also called a plumber's helper) than it is to remove a complete blockage with a hand auger (commonly referred to as a snake). Electrical or even hand-cranked augers can damage or puncture old pipes, so avoid using them if you can. A buildup of hair or grease may be responsible for a slow-acting drain and can be dissolved with a commercial drain opener. Be sure to read the label on any product and follow directions carefully. I never use a commercial drain opener once the blockage is complete. At that point, the toxic chemicals in the liquid or crystals will only collect in the trap, where they can harm you or your plumber if you then switch to a plunger or snake, or if you end up removing the trap.

A trap is the bent pipe directly beneath a sink or tub that is used to collect water, effectively preventing the passage of toxic sewer gases. You can remove a clogged trap using a pair of large pliers with jaws that can reach around the nut at either end of the trap.

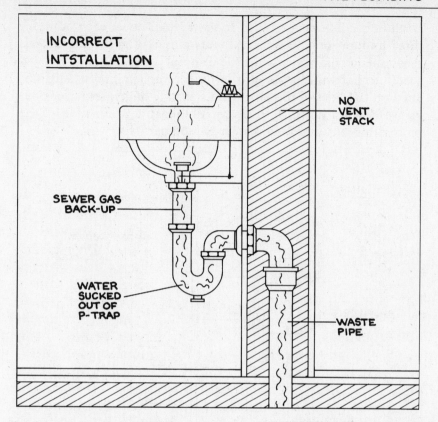

It's always a good idea to run water at least once a week in every sink, tub, shower, or floor drain to ensure a sufficient amount of water in the traps. If the water evaporates or drains out through a leak in a trap, dangerous sewer gases can build up. If you smell sewer gas, the drain may not have been vented when it was installed. Without proper venting, a rush of water coming from another sink on the same drainage line can literally suck the water out of the trap and into the sewer system. You won't know it has happened until you step into the room and smell sewer gases escaping from the drain. Since vent systems are often difficult to understand and impossible to see, you should seek the advice of a plumber if you suspect that a drain has been improperly vented.

There are several ways you can avoid ever having to wrestle with a clogged drain. One is to make sure that all sinks have strainers in place to catch hair, food particles, bottle caps, and other small items. The second is to run hot water down each drain for three minutes once a week. Manufacturers of garbage disposals recommend cold water while the disposal is running, but you can switch to hot water afterward to flush away any grease accumulated on the sides of the pipe. And speaking of grease, never pour grease down a drain. It cools rapidly, coating the inside of the pipe with a sticky residue that traps food particles.

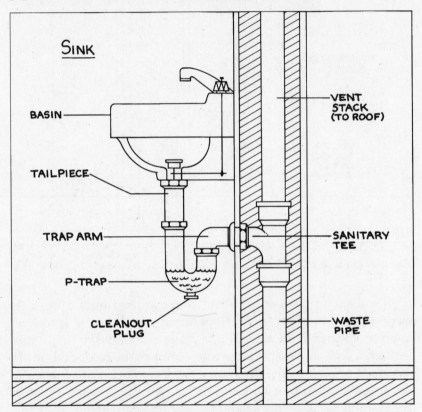

## Warning Signs of a Clogged Drain

- slow-draining sink or tub
- sewer gas odor
- sinks without strainers

## Do's and Don'ts to Keeping Drains Clear

### *Do*

- keep the strainer basket in the kitchen drain, not under the sink or on the counter.

- run cold water when operating a garbage disposal to wash food particles out of the trap. Follow with hot water to dissolve grease inside the drain.
- occasionally run water down a seldom-used basement drain to be sure that all of the water in the trap has not evaporated.
- keep a pair of extra trap gaskets taped to the inside of each sink in your house, in case an old gasket breaks when you remove the trap to clean it or to remove something that's lodged in the pipe.
- buy extra traps the next time you're in the hardware store. They're inexpensive, take up little space, and will make you look like a hero to your family the next Sunday morning an old trap springs a leak.

### Don't

- dispose of paint thinner, latex or oil-based paint, or paint and varnish remover down a drain. They cause clogs.
- pour a caustic drain opener into a drain that is completely clogged. Chances are, it won't work and it can harm you or your plumber when you have to resort to more effective measures, such as a snake or plumber's helper.

## How to Clear a Clogged Drain

| *Steps* | *Tools and Materials* |
| --- | --- |
| 1. Identify a slow-acting drain. | |
| 2. Run water in other drains to determine if the blockage is in the main waste water pipe leading from your house to the street. If the other sinks also back up, call a professional plumber. | |
| 3. Position a plunger over the drain, making sure it fits snugly. On sinks and tubs with an overflow hole, plug the hole tightly with a damp rag, piece of plastic, or tape. | plunger<br>cloth, plastic bag,<br>  or duct tape |
| 4. Push down slowly on the handle of the plunger, expelling the air under the | |

*Steps*                                                      *Tools and Materials*

rubber dome and creating a vacuum.
If no vacuum is created, the plunger
cannot be effective. Check to make sure
the seal around the plunger is airtight.

> TIP: Coat the lip of the plunger with petroleum jelly to
> help create an airtight seal.

5. Pull up on the handle. The force of
   the vacuum should reverse the
   blockage.
6. Repeat steps 4 and 5 about 10 to
   15 times in steady succession.
7. Remove the plunger to see if the
   water begins to drain.
8. If not, repeat the procedure several
   times, making sure that the plunger
   is creating a vacuum over the drain
   opening.
9. If the blockage persists, the next step      pliers
   is to remove the trap.                       small bucket or
   Position a bucket or dishpan under              dishpan
   the trap. While holding on to the trap,
   loosen two large nuts with pliers.
10. Unscrew the nuts by hand. Carefully
    pour the water out of the trap into
    the bucket. Be careful not to lose
    sight of the rubber gaskets on the
    trap or adjacent pipes.
11. Clean out the trap. If it is apparent
    that the blockage was not in the trap,
    the next step is to insert a flexible
    snake into the drain pipe. Depending
    on your skill level and available tools,
    this may be the point at which you
    will want to call a plumber.

## How to Use a Snake

*Steps*                                          *Tools and Materials*

1.  Push the spiral end of the snake into        snake
    the pipe until it reaches the clog.
    Lock the snake in the handle.

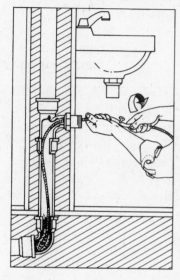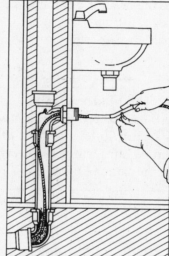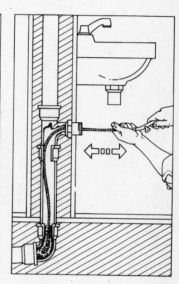

2.  Grasp the handle and begin turning it in
    a clockwise direction to rotate the
    snake. Loosen the set screw to feed
    more of the snake into the pipe. Work
    the snake back and forth until you feel
    no resistance.

3.  Pull the snake out of the drain, wiping      rags
    it off as it emerges.

4.  Push a garden hose into the drain and        garden hose
    slowly turn it on. Keep the pressure low
    until you determine whether or not the
    clog has been dislodged. *Option:* If a
    garden hose is not available or is
    impractical, proceed to steps 6 and 7,
    then test the drain with tap water.

5.  If the water flows unimpeded, the
    clog is gone. If it backs up, repeat the
    process or call a plumber.

| *Steps* | *Tools and Materials* |
|---|---|
| 6. Reassemble the trap. Inspect the trap and the gaskets closely; this may be the best time to replace these items if they are worn out. | trap<br>gaskets |
| 7. Tighten snugly. Run the water to make sure the drain is clear and there are no leaks. | pliers |
| 8. Clean up. | rags<br>hand cleaners |

TIP: The best time to buy a plunger is before you need one. Rest assured you won't wear it out. Invest a few dollars in two different styles of plungers (bell-shaped and standard cup), since not every sink design will accommodate the same plunger.

# #36
# Thwart those nasty overflows.

While a plugged toilet may not seem as threatening to your home as a colony of termites in the basement, chronic toilet problems can lead to more serious difficulties than just a few hours of inconvenience. A leaky toilet tank or a regular overflow of a toilet bowl can eventually cause the flooring and joists supporting the bathroom to deteriorate. Repairing or replacing them would cost hundreds if not thousands of dollars, which could have been saved had a few simple steps been taken.

Small, steady leaks can go undetected for months, especially if your bathroom is carpeted, by which time serious damage may have occurred. There are three important connections in a toilet you need to check regularly, since water from any of these joints could quickly disappear into the flooring without your noticing. The first is between the vertical drain pipe and the base of the toilet. This joint is sealed with a special wax ring that normally lasts for years. Nevertheless, check around the base regularly for leaks, especially just after a toilet has been installed.

The second important joint is between the toilet tank and the bowl. The rubber seal between these two porcelain parts is secured by three bolts. Check to make sure the nuts beneath the tank are tight and that no water is seeping out. The third possible escape is on the bottom of the tank where the cold water supply enters. This hole is sealed with a rubber gasket between the internal toilet mechanism and the threaded pipe. Make sure that the gasket is not leaking either from age, improper installation, or a loose nut.

The more obvious problem associated with toilets is caused by obstructions in the toilet bowl. Households with young children are more prone to such problems than others. Disposable and cloth diapers, as well as toys, can clog a toilet—as my two boys have demonstrated more than once. Most obstructions can be prevented. We continued to have problems with one toilet in our home until I discovered that my recently toilet-trained son was using several yards of toilet paper each time he went to the bathroom.

Since a parent's advice often goes unheeded, it's a good idea to have a snug-fitting plunger on hand, not buried somewhere in the basement, and a special toilet auger. Often called a closet auger (a term derived from water closet, an old name for a toilet), it is designed to direct the flexible metal line around the unique bends in the toilet drain. It is possible to use a standard drain auger to unplug a stopped toilet, although you would need to place your hands in the water to direct the hook around the first bend.

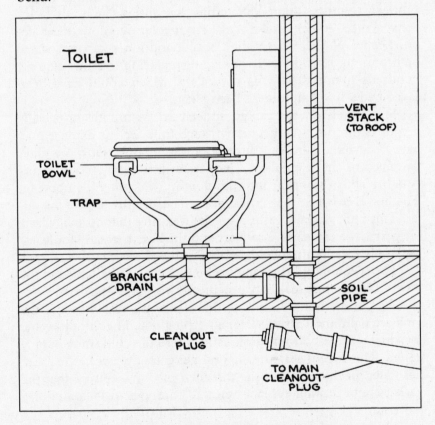

## Warning Signs of Toilet Troubles

- regular obstructions in your toilet
- a slow-draining toilet
- damp flooring around your toilet
- water dripping from the toilet tank

## Do's and Don'ts to Preventing Toilet Troubles

### *Do*

- keep the lid closed on the toilet to prevent items from accidentally being dropped into the bowl.
- make sure that the style of plunger you have on hand will fit snugly inside each of the toilets in your home.
- have a plunger for each toilet.
- invest in a special toilet auger, especially if you have young children in your home. It will cost about the same as 30 minutes of your plumber's time.
- get the advice of a plumber if a toilet becomes plugged on a regular basis. You may have an ineffective toilet design or a problem with tree roots penetrating the sewer line.
- inspect the floor around the base of the toilet to make sure that the wax seal between the toilet and the drain pipe is not leaking.
- make sure that water is not leaking from the toilet tank. A slow but steady drip may not be noticeable, especially if the floor has been carpeted, but the water will weaken the surrounding flooring and joists.
- tighten the nuts attaching the toilet to the drain pipe in the floor. If they become loose, the toilet may rock, breaking the seal with the wax ring and allowing water and sewer gases to seep into the room.

### *Don't*

- use the bathroom as your infant's playroom.
- allow soaking diapers to accumulate in the toilet bowl, especially if you have another child who has just been toilet trained.
- attempt to use a commercial drain opener to unplug a stopped toilet. The design of the drain and toilet prevents the toxic chemicals from ever reaching the obstruction. Instead, the chemicals will remain trapped in the bowl, where they can harm you or your plumber.
- use your toilet as a wastebasket. Keep paper towels, sanitary napkins, hair, and other nonflushables out of the toilet.

## How to Clear a Plugged Toilet

| *Steps* | *Tools and Materials* |
|---|---|
| 1. If necessary, bail out enough water from the toilet bowl to prevent it from spilling over as you work on removing the obstruction. | bucket<br>plastic cup or glass<br>rubber gloves |
| 2. Insert a plunger into the toilet bowl, making sure that you have a complete seal between the lip of the plunger and the bowl. | plunger<br>rubber gloves |
| 3. Push down slowly on the handle of the plunger, expelling the air under the rubber dome and creating a vacuum. If no vacuum is created, the plunger cannot be effective. Check to make sure the seal around the plunger is airtight. | |
| 4. Pull up on the handle. The force of the vacuum should reverse the blockage. | |
| 5. Repeat steps 3 and 4 approximately 10 to 15 times in steady succession. | |
| 6. Remove the plunger to see if the water begins to drain out of the toilet. | |
| 7. If not, repeat the procedure several times, making sure that the plunger is creating a vacuum over the opening. | |
| 8. If the obstruction persists, insert a toilet auger into the bowl and slowly begin turning the handle. Try to snag the obstruction and pull it backward rather than attempt to push it forward (which may make it more difficult to remove). | toilet auger<br>rubber gloves |
| 9. Gently pull on the auger to see if its end has engaged the obstruction. | |

*Steps*

*Tools and Materials*

10. If you feel that the obstruction has been broken up or removed, carefully pour water from a bucket into the toilet bowl to see if the passage is open.

bucket
water

11. If the toilet fails to drain, the obstruction may be in the main pipe (called a soil pipe). At this point, you may wish to call a plumber. If not, you can locate the cleanout plug (generally in the basement), remove it, and attempt to break up the obstruction. Use an auger, a long metal rod, or a garden hose and low water pressure. Afterwards, replace the cleanout plug and repeat step 10. If this fails to work, call a plumber.

large wrench
auger, metal rod,
    or garden hose

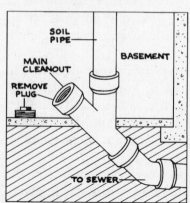 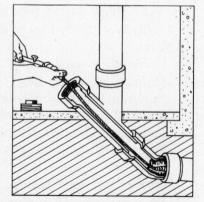

TIP: If you have an emergency but no auger, you can fashion a crude substitute from a coat hanger. Cut the coat hanger beneath the hook, then straighten the wire, forming a 3-foot-long probe with a hook on one end. Wrap 6 inches of the opposite end with duct tape or electrical tape for a firm grip.

### *The Case of the Perspiring Toilet Tank*

One nagging problem that homeowners often discover in their bathrooms is condensation forming on the outside of the porcelain toilet tank. When warm, humid air comes in contact with the cooler porcelain tank it condenses and forms water droplets. If the bathroom is well ventilated or does not contain a shower or bathtub, the droplets may evaporate before they can accumulate. But if the room is often filled with steam that is not pulled out of the room either through a window or an exhaust fan, condensation droplets on the toilet may form. As a result, carpeting beneath the tank may begin to mildew and the wood flooring may actually begin to deteriorate.

The quick fix to a minor condensation problem is a terry cloth tank cover. The inexpensive cover prevents much of the humid air from reaching the tank and absorbs the few droplets that do form. Once the shower or bath is finished, the bathroom door opened, and dry air begins to circulate, the water evaporates from the cloth fibers.

More serious condensation problems can be solved in a number of ways. The first is to limit and control the amount of warm, humid air in the bathroom. If you keep windows and doors open and the exhaust fan running when bathing or showering, the amount of moisture in the air is reduced significantly.

The problem can also be solved or reduced at the other end. If you can raise the temperature of the porcelain tank, the moisture in the air will not be as likely to condense on the outside of the tank. You can achieve this in one of two ways. The first is to raise the temperature of the water by mixing a small amount of warm water with the cold water that enters the tank each time the toilet is flushed. A special valve, called a tempering valve, is inserted into the cold water supply line. An additional line is run from the nearest warm water pipe (generally under the sink or at the end of the tub) to the tempering valve. The tepid water warms rather than cools the toilet tank and the bowl, effectively eliminating the condensation problem.

The second option calls for a layer of foam insulation on the inside of the tank. Easier and less expensive to install than a special valve and hot water line, the foam sheets are sold in a kit available through plumbing supply firms. Installation involves shutting off the water supply valve, flushing the toilet to remove most of the water, then drying out the inside of the tank with rags. The interior of the tank is then lined with the insulation, which prevents the cool water from lowering the temperature of the outside of the porcelain tank. As long as the tank remains at nearly the same temperature as the surrounding air, condensation is not a problem.

# #37
# Caulk around your shower and tub.

As has been emphasized throughout this book, moisture is a major threat to our homes. More often than not, however, homeowners concentrate on moisture in the form of rain, snow, leaky pipes, dripping faucets, overflowing toilets, and high humidity. But there is one other source of moisture you might never suspect until it is too late. The bathtub or shower is probably used on the average of twice each day. Add a few children and the number can quickly double. While we would like to hope—and expect—that all the water that flows into the tub or shower exits through the drain, this is not always the case. If the thin bead of caulking that spans each of the joints between the tub or shower and the wall beside it happens to wear out, break, or be punctured, water can literally pour out of sight and into the wall or floor adjacent to it.

What makes these joints particularly troublesome is that they span two dissimilar materials: They must bond a stationary wall or floor with a tub or shower that expands and contracts, even flexes, as it is filled with water. Add to that the natural deterioration that is associated with water and it's a wonder that caulking manages to last more than a few weeks.

The good news, however, is that you have plenty of opportunity to inspect the seal around your tub or shower, including the most important one—the joint around the drain. Remembering to come back later that day and make the repair is generally the toughest part of this job. If you simply remind yourself that the water being absorbed by the surrounding drywall, studs, flooring, and joists may soon ruin the plaster ceiling downstairs, you probably won't have any trouble remembering to pick up a couple tubes of tub and tile sealer on your way home from work.

## Warning Signs of Deteriorated Caulking

• peeling or discolored caulking

- caulking that has shrunk or pulled back from the tub, surrounding drywall, floor, or drain
- gaps in the caulking
- low spots along the joint that hold water after a bath or shower
- loosened tiles
- water stains on the ceiling below the shower or tub

### Do's and Don'ts to Caulking the Shower or Tub

**Do**

- inspect the caulking each time you bathe or shower.
- store a tube of tub and tile caulking in a safe place in your bathroom.
- alert your family when you are about to recaulk the joints; the caulking requires 36 hours to completely cure.
- check for a tinted caulking that matches the grout.
- remove the worn caulking before applying a fresh bead.

**Don't**

- use ordinary caulking around bathtubs and showers. Select a brand designed specifically for this application.
- caulk over old caulking.
- wear shoes in your tub or shower unless you have first put down a towel to protect the fiberglass or porcelain surface.
- attempt to apply the caulking until the surface is completely dry.

### How to Recaulk Tub or Shower Joints

| *Steps* | *Tools and Materials* |
|---|---|
| 1. Lay an old towel in the bottom of the tub or shower. | towel |
| 2. Carefully pry out any pieces of loose caulking or grout with a screwdriver or dental pick. | narrow screwdriver or dental pick |
| 3. Scrape the surface of any intact grout for better adhesion to the new caulking. | pocketknife or narrow screwdriver |
| 4. Vacuum or rinse off all dust and | vacuum with |

*Steps*                                    *Tools and Materials*

pieces of grout and caulking.                bristle brush
                                             attachment or
                                             dry paintbrush
                                           wet rag or sponge
5. Thoroughly wash any soap residue        rags
   from the joint.                         rubbing alcohol
6. Let the area dry completely.            fan
                                           hair dryer
7. Trim the tip of the tube of special     tub and tile
   tub and tile caulking to the desired       caulking
   bead size.                              utility knife

8. Beginning at one end of the joint,      caulking
   apply a bead of caulking in one
   continuous application, making sure
   to overfill the joint slightly.

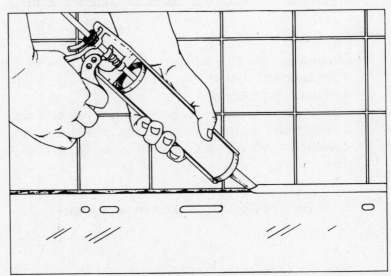

9. If you have to stop in the middle of a
   run, overlap slightly when you begin
   applying more caulking.
10. For a smooth, blemish-free joint, wet
    your index finger and slowly run it the

*Steps*                                    *Tools and Materials*

    length of the fresh bead of caulking.
    Keep your finger wet to avoid pulling
    the caulking out of the joint.

11. Wipe up any spills before the                 wet rag
    caulking begins to dry.

12. Allow 36 hours for the caulking to
    cure before it comes in contact with
    water.

TIP: Use a hair dryer to speed the evaporation of moisture in the joint you are about to caulk, but don't use it in an attempt to speed the curing of the freshly caulked joint. Proper curing takes time, not heat.

# #38
# Don't let a dripping faucet drive up your water bill.

Rest assured, a leaky faucet is not going to bring your house crashing down around you. But it can drive you and your spouse crazy at night, raise your water bill each month, and if there is a high mineral content in the water, leave unsightly, permanent stains in the sink basin.

Is this the most important of all the 50 checkpoints covered in this book? Absolutely not, but that doesn't mean you should ignore a dripping faucet. Besides wasting money, a leak wastes a valuable resource. The faucet in my basement workshop has been leaking steadily for some time now, but it wasn't until this morning that I calculated exactly how much water I've wasted. At an average of one drop of water every two seconds, I collected 1 cup in one hour. Sixteen hours later, the amount had risen to 1 gallon. That averages 1.5 gallons of water a day, 10.5 gallons in a week. It doesn't take a master's degree to figure out that that comes to 546 gallons of water wasted in a year. If you have additional faucets that leak, the figure just keeps multiplying.

What generally keeps homeowners from immediately attacking a dripping faucet is the deep-seated fear of suddenly becoming part of an old "I Love Lucy" gag. What someone conveniently forgot to tell Lucy was that you're supposed to turn off the water before disassembling the faucet, not after. (Of course, repairing a leaky faucet the correct way wouldn't make for very good comedy.) Today's homeowners are also faced with another obstacle, since the days of the ordinary washer-type faucets have almost vanished. Modern faucets have cartridges, rather than simple washers. Fortunately, manufacturers have stepped in to produce replacement kits that contain new cartridges and detailed instructions for disassembling every major brand of faucet.

The first step, then, in repairing a modern leaky faucet is purchasing the correct kit from a plumbers' supply firm. Find the brand name on the faucet, then use your phone, not your car.

Rather than spend half a day driving from store to store only to discover you also need a particular style number, use the telephone to find the right parts. If you're still in doubt and have a Polaroid camera in the house, take a snapshot of the faucet with you to the store, or better yet, take along the installation instructions that originally came with the faucet.

The older washer-type faucet actually requires you to partially disassemble it in order to take the old washer with you to the plumbers' supply store. Naturally, this mandates that you start this project in the morning on a day when the stores are open. And watch out—many supply firms close at noon on Saturday, 10 minutes before you discover that you bought the wrong washer. Only by taking the old washer with you, or by buying extras while you are there, can you be sure you can reassemble the faucet successfully and correctly.

## Warning Signs of a Leaky Faucet

- steady leak from the faucet
- water around the base of the faucet
- water seeping from beneath the cap or spout
- mineral stains in the sink
- improper mixing of hot and cold water

## Do's and Don'ts to Repairing a Faucet

### Do

- find out everything you can about the brand and style of your faucet before you leave the house.
- buy extra kits and washers.
- ask if any special tools are required for installation.
- make sure you turn off the water before you disassemble the faucet.
- protect the external faucet parts from the pliers by padding with a dishcloth or rag.

### Don't

- start this project late in the day or right before you want to use the sink.
- ignore the installation instructions that come with the faucet repair kit.

## Steps to Repairing a Leaky Faucet

| *Steps* | *Tools and Materials* |
|---|---|
| 1. Write down the brand name and any model numbers associated with your faucet. Check under the sink for information. If the faucet is a washer style, follow steps 2 through 7. If it is a cartridge style, follow steps 8 through 12. | paper<br>pencil<br>flashlight |
| 2. Washer style: Shut off the nearest water supply valve. | |
| 3. Remove the retaining screw or nut in in the handle. | screwdriver<br>adjustable wrench |

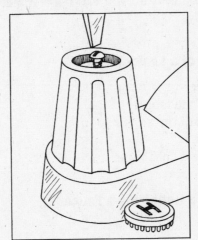 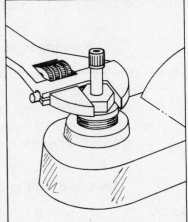

| | |
|---|---|
| 4. Remove the handle and the valve stem beneath it. | pliers |
| 5. Carefully place the valve stem and any replaceable washers in a food storage bag. | food storage bag |
| 6. Take the information and/or the parts with you to the plumbers' supply store. Buy extra parts. | |
| 7. Remove the old washers and replace with new ones. Carefully scrape any grit off the valve seat inside the faucet. Reassemble carefully. Turn on the water supply valve and check for leaks. | screwdriver<br>pliers |

*Steps*                                    *Tools and Materials*

8. Cartridge style: Shut off the hot and cold water supply valves under the sink.

9. Follow the instructions in the kit for disassembling your particular style of faucet.

kit instructions
screwdriver
pliers

10. Lay the parts out carefully in the order in which you removed them.

11. Install the new cartridge and any new O-rings or other parts included in the kit.

12. Reassemble carefully, taking care to line up any notches in the cartridge, stem, or other parts. Turn on the water supply valves and check for leaks.

TIP: A sink acts as a large funnel for small screws, as well as for water. When working on or around a sink or tub, be sure to stuff a rag into the open drain so small parts can't fall into it.

# #39
# Drain your hot water heater twice a year.

Hot water heaters generally do not make any demands on us; if installed properly, they will operate quite efficiently for several years with only minimal maintenance. Most homeowners, however, don't even provide minimum maintenance for their hot water heaters, preferring instead to simply replace them when they finally wear out.

You can extend the life of the hot water heater and reduce the cost of operating it simply by giving it a few minutes of your time twice a year. Particles of lime, iron, and calcium traveling through the cold water line enter the hot water heater daily, where they settle to the bottom. As the sediment accumulates, the burner must run longer so the heat can pass through the layer of sediment between it and the water. In extreme cases where the water is loaded with particles and the sediment is never drained, the water capacity of the heater can be dramatically reduced.

Removing the sediment from the bottom of your hot water heater is facilitated by an external drainage valve located at the bottom of each model. Eliminating the sediment is not quite as simple as just turning a valve; you have to make sure that (1) you provide a place for the water to go and (2) you don't burn yourself in the process. If there's a drain in your basement or if you can divert the water outdoors, a garden hose can be attached to the threaded valve. If that is not a practical alternative for you, the water and sediment can be captured in a small bucket or shallow pan.

The temperature and pressure relief valve located near the top of the water heater should not be confused with the external drain at the bottom. The pressure valve should be opened only briefly once a year to make sure it's operating correctly. Do not attempt to use it to drain sediment from the tank, as this will not work and could result in a serious injury from the blast of hot water.

In areas where lime and iron are present in the water supply, it's not unusual for deposits to form on the interior sides of the hot water heater. Periodic draining does not remove these scale deposits. If the deposits begin to affect the operation of the hot water heater, contact a manufacturer's representative to inquire about a chemical cleansing.

Owners of gas hot water heaters need to remember that vapors from open containers of paint and varnish remover, gasoline, and other flammable liquids are often heavier than air. The fumes from an open can settle to the basement floor and can be drawn toward and into the gas burner unit. The flames will immediately ignite the fumes traveling back to the container, causing an explosion and fire. To avoid a major catastrophe, make it a rule never to store or use any flammable materials, including refinishing supplies, in the same room as the gas hot water heater.

## Warning Signs of When a Hot Water Heater Needs Draining

- a pounding or rumbling sound from the heater indicating the accumulation of sediment at the bottom of the tank
- a sizzling sound caused by moisture condensation above the burner
- unpleasant odors in the water
- periodic discharges from the temperature and pressure relief valve
- uneven flame (gas burners only)
- smell of natural or liquid propane gas (gas burners only)
- water leaks around any of the pipe fittings and valves
- flammable liquids used or stored in the same room as the gas hot water heater (gas burners only)
- unusually high hot water pressure when a faucet is first turned on (gas burners only)

### Hot Water Heater Do's and Don'ts

*Do*

- check the dial to determine the temperature of the water. Water heated above 125 degrees can scald. Set the dial to the lowest temperature that meets your family's needs without posing a danger to anyone.
- check the temperature and pressure relief valve once a year. Caution: This will release hot water. Stand behind the valve and take the necessary safety precautions outlined in the owner's manual for the heater. When in doubt, have the

valve checked by a plumber.
- make sure that the vent pipe and the fresh air intake are unobstructed.

### Don't

- ever plug the temperature and pressure relief valve or any pipe or hose attached to it.
- shut off a hot water heater during cold weather without also draining the tank. The water in the tank could freeze, expand, and burst the heater or pipes. When completely draining a hot water heater, be sure to first shut off the cold water inlet valve.
- attempt any cleaning or repair of the burner without first turning off the gas valve.
- store or use aerosol paint cans, gasoline, paint and varnish remover, swimming pool chemicals, waxes, or other flammable liquids near a gas hot water heater. Fumes from these products can be drawn into the gas burner, where they can ignite and corrode the flue, leading to possible asphyxiation of anyone in your home.
- use a gas hot water heater if any part of the burner mechanism has been submerged during a heavy rain, flood, or break in the water line. Have the unit inspected by a qualified technician before relighting.
- install carpeting under your hot water heater; it represents a fire hazard.

## How to Drain a Hot Water Heater to Remove Sediment

| *Steps* | *Tools and Materials* |
|---|---|
| 1. Do NOT shut off the cold water inlet valve during a partial draining to eliminate sediment. Additional water is necessary to replace that which is removed with the sediment. | |
| 2. If possible, attach a hose to the external drain valve at the bottom of the hot water heater. Insert the opposite end of the hose into a sink or floor drain to avoid contact with the hot water. | garden hose |

| *Steps* | *Tools and Materials* |
|---|---|

3.  Otherwise, place a small bucket     small bucket or pan
    or shallow pan beneath the external
    drain valve.

4.  Slowly open the valve completely,
    taking care not to come in contact
    with the hot water.

5.  Allow the water to run for three to
    five minutes. It may be necessary to
    drain off more sediment-loaded water
    if the hot water heater has not been
    partially drained for more than a year.

6.  Close the external drain valve.

7.  Carefully empty the bucket or pan.
    Remember that the water will be
    very hot.

8.  Repeat this process every six months
    or more often if the water carries an
    unusual amount of sediment.

---

TIP: If you suspect a gas leak in a pipe fitting or valve, brush on a solution of soapy water. If gas is escaping, tiny bubbles will form over the site of the leak. If this happens, do not turn on a light or appliance, since any spark that's generated could cause a gas explosion. Go immediately to a neighbor's house and call the gas company.

# #40
# Insulate your pipes to prevent freezing.

If you're in the mood for an easy, rainy-day project that gives you instant gratification and a quick return on your money, keep reading.

The ceiling in your basement is probably overflowing with yard upon yard of pipe: copper pipe, steel pipe, plastic pipe, cast-iron pipe, but hopefully no lead pipe. Some of these are drain pipes, which we have no interest in at the moment. The vast majority are hot and cold water supply lines, although you may well have a maze of supply and return pipes if you also have a radiator heating system. Older heating pipes are often wrapped in asbestos and, generally speaking, should be left that way. As long as the asbestos is intact, you're safe. Disturbing it, as explained in detail in #26, on page 136, causes far greater problems for you and your family. Besides, thick asbestos wrap, as dangerous as it might be when disturbed, is probably a better insulator than what you can now buy.

Insulating water supply lines is worth the small investment it requires in time and money because it saves energy, which translates into dollars. Here's why:

When hot water leaves the hot water heater or the furnace, it immediately transfers a portion of its heat to the cooler pipe surrounding it. If the pipe is uninsulated, it transfers that heat to the cooler air around it, which is constantly changing. As a result, heat begins and continues to escape from the hot water the moment it enters the pipe system. In the hot water heating system, this means that the water that reaches a radiator is several degrees cooler than when it left the boiler. Hence, the furnace must run longer and hotter to supply the radiators with adequate heat.

Nearly the same thing happens in the hot water supply line. Since every foot of uninsulated pipe robs the water of some of its heat, the water arrives at a faucet several degrees cooler than when it left the hot water heater. To obtain water at the temperature you want, the hot water heater actually has to heat it to a higher temperature before it can leave.

The cold water supply lines are not without their problems. When warm, humid air comes in contact with a cold water line, either a supply line or a return pipe from the radiators (which remain cool during the summer months when they're not in operation), the resulting condensation causes water droplets to form on the outside of the pipe. The droplets don't remain on the slippery surface, but instead fall to the floor below. In some cases, they may fall harmlessly, but they may also land on furniture, carpeting, storage boxes, or your tools. Regardless, they contribute to the moisture in the basement and your home and encourage the growth of mold, mildew, and decay-causing fungi.

Besides energy loss and condensation, water pipes are involved in yet a third dilemma. If a pipe travels through an unheated portion of the basement or crawl space, or through an exterior wall that was not properly insulated, then the water inside it may well freeze in the winter. And when water freezes, it expands with a tremendous force. It required four workers to carry one of our cast-iron radiators out of our house, but only a little water and subfreezing temperatures to blow out a chunk of the heavy metal.

The solution to all three problems comes in the form of lightweight foam tubes. At first glance, the foam tubes look like black pipes, but they're split the entire length to slip easily over a bare pipe. The snug-fitting tubes are available in two or three different diameters to fit standard supply pipes. Drain pipes do not require insulation. Since they're empty the majority of the time, they don't burst even when the temperatures drop below freezing (unless, of course, the pipe is plugged). And without cool water to lower the temperature of the pipe, the drain pipes don't prompt humid air to leave condensation droplets on them.

So, how do you distinguish one pipe from another? Since both drain pipes and supply pipes can be made of copper, plastic, steel, or iron, we have to find a useful means of identification. Generally, drain pipes are at least 1¼ inches in diameter. In the basement, they may be six inches or larger. Most water supply lines however, are much smaller. It's unusual to find a water pipe larger than 1¼ inches in diameter. In addition, if you follow a water supply line, it leads you to a hot water heater, main water line, sink, shower, toilet, or appliance. And, unlike drain lines, most hot and cold water lines run parallel to one another. Finally, plumbers avoid installing drain lines that travel horizontally. When they must, the pipes are angled to encourage the water to flow toward the main soil stack.

It's not always necessary to insulate every foot of water line. You can select which pipes you want to insulate, depending on which of the following problems you anticipate in your home:

**Heat loss**
- hot water pipes branching out from the hot water heater
- hot water pipes leading from the furnace to the radiators
- return pipes leading from the radiators to the furnace (reduces the amount of energy required to reheat the water)

**Condensation**
- cold water supply lines
- any pipe with moisture droplets forming on it, not to be confused with drips from a leak

**Freezing**
- hot and cold water lines passing through an unheated area

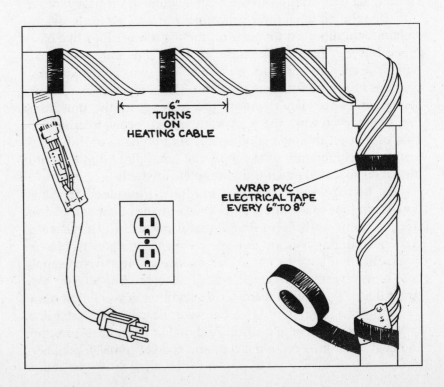

TIP: Foam pipe insulation may not prevent pipes from freezing in unheated areas when the temperature stays well below freezing for an extended period of time. Problem pipes should first be wrapped with electric heat tape according to the manufacturer's instructions, then, unless prohibited on the tape package, covered with foam pipe insulation. Leave the plug in plain sight so it can be plugged in only when needed in the winter.

## Warning Signs of Needed Pipe Insulation

- uninsulated supply pipes that are warm to the touch (indicative of heat loss)
- any pipes that "sweat"
- supply pipes passing through an unheated crawl space in regions where freezing temperatures can occur

## Do's and Don'ts to Insulating Pipes

### Do

- insulate pipe connections also.
- wrap joints between sections of foam insulation with duct tape.
- check for leaks in pipe connections as you install the foam insulation.

### Don't

- remove any ground wires attached to the water pipes. These serve as protective devices against electrical shocks that could occur in the telephone or household wiring.
- disturb asbestos insulation on your pipes. (See #26 on page 136.)

## How to Insulate Pipes

| *Steps* | *Tools and Materials* |
|---|---|
| 1. Note the diameters of the different pipes and measure how many feet of insulation you need for each. | tape measure notebook pencil |
| 2. Purchase the foam pipe insulation. If more than one brand is available, | notebook |

*Steps*                                    *Tools and Materials*

compare prices and R-values. The
higher the R-value, the better the
insulation.

3.  Take out the first tube and locate          your finger, a
    the partially scored slit. Open the            knife, or a
    slit by running your finger, a knife,          screwdriver
    or a screwdriver the length of the tube.

4.  Slip the tube over a section of pipe.

5.  Measure and cut any short pieces of          tape measure
    tubing. Cut 45-degree joints for             utility knife
    90-degree turns in the pipe.

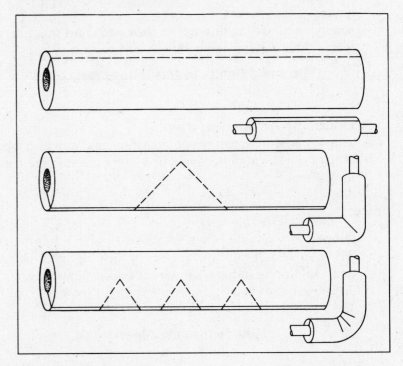

6.  For curved ends in the pipe, cut           knife or scissors
    wedge-shaped pieces out of the foam
    sleeve.

7.  Make all joints as tight-fitting as
    possible. Don't attempt to stretch the
    insulation.

TIP: For additional protection, wrap each foam joint with duct tape. Also seal the slits with duct tape or an adhesive recommended by the manufacturer.

## Quick Tips for Thawing Frozen Pipes

If you discover that water has frozen inside one of the pipes, take immediate action; you may be able to prevent the ice from bursting the pipe. Begin by opening the faucet nearest the frozen section. This will provide an escape route for any steam or water created during the thaw. Starting at the faucet, apply heat to the pipe with whatever means you have: a heat gun, hair dryer, clothes iron, heat tape, heat lamp, or propane torch.

A propane torch must be handled with care to prevent the ice from turning into steam. If the steam becomes trapped between two blocked sections, it can burst the pipe just as easily as the ice. That's why you should always start the thawing process next to an open faucet. Regardless of your means of melting the ice, if the pipe becomes too hot for you to grasp with a bare hand, you have applied too much heat too quickly. Excessive heat may damage the pipe or soldered joints and can create powerful and dangerous pressurized pockets of steam.

Once the ice has melted, inspect the pipe for any signs of leaks. Close the faucet to produce pressure in the pipe, then check along the entire length. The leak could be slow, so wipe the pipe dry, then watch and feel for any drips. If you detect a bulge in the pipe, it most likely was caused by the ice. If it isn't leaking, you don't have to replace that section of pipe immediately, but you should as soon as possible if you wish to avoid an untimely eruption.

# ELECTRICAL AND HEATING SYSTEMS

Most homeowners don't know the difference between a watt, a volt, and an amp, but wait. Before you think about skipping this section, read one more sentence.

You don't *have* to know the difference to save your house.

Electricity can be complicated, so don't feel guilty for not understanding exactly what goes on behind the panel box or why your two-way switch turns on the hallway light only if the other switch is in the "on" position.

You don't need to be a licensed technician to own a home, but you need to be able to recognize the warning signs that indicate that there's a problem with the electrical or heating systems. These two systems are the lifeblood of your home, and ignoring the warning signs places you, your home, and your family in danger from fire.

This chapter shows you how to pinpoint problems before they become too big. Once you've discovered a problem, contact a licensed electrician or heating specialist to make the repairs. If you're not experienced in electrical or heating systems, do not attempt to make the repairs yourself. The homeowners who get themselves into trouble are those who think they know more than they really do.

So read this section carefully and treat your home's electrical and heating systems with care and respect.

This chapter includes Home-Saving Guidelines 41 and 42.

*Page*

# #41
# Map out your electrical system.

If you have ever had the opportunity to walk through a new home while it is under construction, especially just after the electricians have finished but before the carpenters have sealed up the walls, you know what a maze of wires is required to meet all of our electrical needs. What begins as a thick sheath of wires entering through an exterior wall quickly divides, subdivides, and subdivides again, not unlike our body's system of the aorta, arteries, veins, and capillaries.

And like our body's arterial system, our home's electrical system generally does not require special daily maintenance. We get up each morning, flick a switch, and the light comes on. Fill the coffee maker, push a button, and the water begins to heat. Open the refrigerator and cool air pours out. But just as we have each learned our body's basic functions, how to get the most from it, how to make it last longer, and how not to overload its capacity, we also need to understand the basic pattern and functions of our home's electrical system. Doing so enables it to run safely and efficiently for years to come.

It is not necessary to become an electrician to understand how your home's electrical system works—and why it sometimes doesn't. Recognizing its basic elements and knowing their functions and limitations enables you to spot a potential problem before it could cause a disastrous fire. Electricity is dangerous, but one thing even more dangerous is ignorance. As one of my favorite bumper stickers reads, "If you think education is expensive, try ignorance."

You need to begin right where the electrical service begins—where it enters your property. The thick sheath of cable-clad wires that directs a continuous, powerful surge of electricity from the street to your house may travel either above or below ground. Regardless, you need to know its precise route; if you were to scrape the wires with an aluminum extension ladder while trimming trees or painting your house or to cut through them with a spade while preparing a new rose bed, your death would be instantaneous.

Above-ground cables are easy to identify, as they are much heavier than either telephone or television wires. A buried cable, however, is difficult to trace without a metal detector. If you call your local power company, a representative will come to your home and mark, using a brightly colored aerosol paint, the route across your yard. The paint remains visible for a few weeks, but then gradually disappears. Before it does, draw a map of your property and indicate on it the path the electrical service takes. Your representative can also give you an idea of how deeply it's buried, but don't rely on that data completely. Rocks, pipes, and other underground obstructions may have prevented the installers from burying the line as deeply as they prefer. To be completely safe, avoid doing any digging around a buried cable.

The main electrical lines enter your home either above or below the familiar glass-encased meter that records how much electricity your family uses. At this point, the cable is encased in a metal or plastic pipe for your protection. Nevertheless, take care in working around the service entrance, especially if you're planting shrubs or flowers next to the foundation. You don't want to risk slicing into the cable with a shovel or trowel. Inside your home, generally close to the service entrance, is a service panel, a gray metal box mounted on the wall. The main power lines enter the service panel and immediately pass through the master switch. It is imperative that you find and clearly mark the master switch. In the event of an emergency, this switch cuts off all power to every part of your house.

From the master switch, the electricity is routed to a number of circuits, each marked by either a fuse or circuit breaker. The actual wires are located behind a metal shield, which should be removed only by a certified electrician. The shield, which is attached to a service panel box with four screws, is not to be confused with the hinged door. The door keeps dirt and water out of the service panel box and protects the fuses and circuit breakers mounted in the metal shield. Homeowners have no business removing the protective shield. Doing so only increases the odds that your name will be added to the list of people who die each year in home-related accidents.

The fuses and circuit breakers behind the service panel door are safety devices that prevent the wires that wind through your home from carrying more power than they're capable of handling. Were it not for fuses and circuit breakers, a wire behind a wall might overheat, melt the insulation covering it, and ignite the adjacent dry dust and wood. Fuses and circuit breakers are rated by amperes (amps), which are matched to the size of the wires in each circuit. People who bypass this protective device by placing a copper penny behind a fuse or by installing a larger capacity circuit breaker in the panel only increase the odds that an unseen wire overheats and starts a fire.

If you have a circuit breaker that often "breaks" (the internal switch opens and shuts off electricity to that particular circuit) or fuses that frequently blow, consider it a warning. In lay terms, when this occurs, a wire is carrying more electricity than it is equipped to handle. If plugging in an appliance, vacuum sweeper, or lamp into a different outlet does not solve the problem, have the service box analyzed by a certified electrician. He or she may be able to redistribute the power demands by rearranging some of the wires behind the protective shield. *Do not attempt to do this yourself.*

What you can and should do, however, is to make a map of the different circuits in your home, identifying each of the outlets, appliances, lights, and other devices drawing their power from each circuit. With this information in your household notebook and written on the inside of the panel box, you can (1) identify potential problem circuits, (2) protect yourself from a dangerous or deadly shock, and (3) prevent a fire from destroying your home.

Determining if a circuit is overloaded is often difficult and mathematically complex. Simply counting the number of outlets can be misleading, as an empty outlet makes no demand. If, in setting up an office in an extra bedroom, you plug in a computer, printer, fax, answering machine, photocopier, three lamps, a stereo, and a television set all into the same circuit guarded by a 15-amp breaker—and use several of these simultaneously—you may be making regular trips to the basement. Ideally, the circuit breaker or fuse announces if you have attempted to overload the circuit, but the danger is that a previous owner may have switched to a larger circuit breaker or fuse (anything greater than 20 amps) than was intended for the wires. In that case, you could be overloading the circuit without throwing the circuit breaker or blowing the fuse. As long as you were using only one machine at a time in your new office, you might not be in danger, but if several were to be used at once, you could set off an electrical fire in the wall.

If you sense that you're overloading a circuit or that someone might have tampered with the service panel, don't take a chance. Call in a licensed electrician to analyze the service panel, the circuits, and your electrical needs.

### Warning Signs of a Neglected Electrical System

- fuses or circuit breakers that often shut down the power to a particular circuit
- a service panel box with unmarked circuits
- a missing door on a service panel box
- large-capacity (greater than 20 amps) circuit breakers on general circuits (meant for outlets and lights, but not large appliances)
- a light or a television that flickers or dims when another appliance is turned on
- appliances that are not able to operate at full power
- numerous extension cords in full-time use

### Do's and Don'ts to Maintaining the Electrical System

*Do*

- call in a certified electrician if you suspect any problem within the system.
- keep a flashlight on top of or next to the circuit box.
- buy extra fuses of the same type and size as those in the circuit box.
- place a rubber mat (such as an old car floor mat) or wooden pallet beneath the panel box if the floor there is ever damp.
- disconnect the main power switch before replacing a blown fuse.
- buy two or three inexpensive voltage testers so you always have one nearby to make sure the power is off when you work on a problem outlet or set of wires.
- keep one hand firmly jammed in your pocket while replacing a fuse or working on an outlet or socket. Touching a metal pipe or the side of the panel box creates a ground, which enables electricity to pass through your body. And it takes very little electricity to stop your heart.

**Don't**

- stick a screwdriver into any part of a circuit box.
- stand on a wet basement floor while doing any electrical work, including replacing a fuse in the service panel box.
- use a metal stepladder or metal extension ladder for electrical work. A wooden ladder is less apt to provide a deadly ground for you and a live wire.
- replace a fuse or reset a circuit breaker until you have determined the cause of the overload.

## How to Map Out the Electrical System

| *Steps* | *Tools and Materials* |
|---|---|
| 1. Draw a diagram of each room in your house, allotting one room per sheet of paper. Do not include furniture. | household notebook or clipboard and paper<br>pencil<br>ruler |
| 2. Mark the location of each outlet, switch, ceiling light, or semipermanent large appliance (washer, dryer, dishwasher, stove, television, computer, and so on). | diagram<br>pencil |
| 3. Make sure the floor beneath the service panel is dry. To be safe, wear rubber-soled shoes and stand on a board or rubber mat. | tennis shoes<br>board or rubber mat |
| 4. Turn off the first circuit breaker. | |
| 5. Test switches and outlets throughout the house. | table lamp, radio, or small appliance |
| 6. Whenever you find a switch, outlet, light, or appliance that does not come on, mark it on the diagram as "circuit #1." | diagram |
| 7. Return to the service panel, turn breaker #1 back on, and turn #2 off. | |

*Steps*                                              *Tools and Materials*

8. Repeat steps 5 and 6 to identify the next round of nonfunctioning outlets and appliances as "circuit #2."

9. Repeat steps 4 through 8 until you have tested all the circuits and have labeled each outlet, light fixture, and appliance with a circuit number on the diagram.

10. Label all of the circuit breakers in the service box with the circuit's general location (master bedroom, guest bath, and so on).

adhesive labels
pencil

11. On a single sheet of paper, list each outlet, fixture, and appliance under the respective circuit number. Attach this sheet to the inside of the service panel door.

paper
typewriter or
     computer

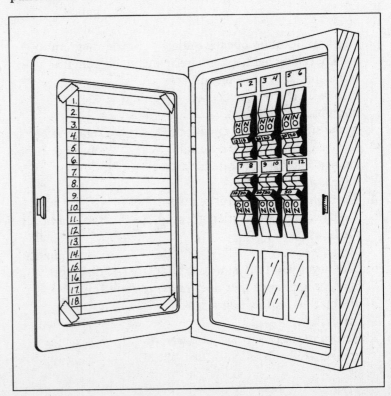

*Steps*                                    *Tools and Materials*

12. Study the diagram and list to determine if any of the general circuits appear to be overloaded. General circuits are those that serve primarily outlets and ceiling lights. Dedicated circuits are meant to serve only one major appliance, such as a furnace or electric stove.

13. If it appears that a general circuit is nearly overloaded, hire a licensed electrician to transfer some of the demand to another circuit.

---

TIP: When working alone in a large house, an easy way to know if you have turned off the proper circuit breaker is to plug a radio into an outlet that is on the circuit you want to turn off. Return to the basement and, one at a time, begin flipping breaker switches. When the radio goes off, you have found the right circuit breaker. Confirm your decision with a circuit tester.

# #42
# Don't let a faulty furnace become a silent killer.

Each year, hundreds of people die from carbon monoxide poisoning caused by faulty or inadequately vented furnaces. Ironically, incidents of carbon monoxide poisoning have risen as a result of our efforts to make our homes more energy efficient. Old drafty houses had no problem supplying a furnace, fireplace, or wood-burning stove with adequate oxygen for efficient combustion and with fresh air to whisk away any trace of dangerous carbon monoxide. But as we have filled our walls and attics with insulation, installed storm windows and weather stripping, even sealed the wall openings behind outlets and light switches, our homes have become nearly airtight. As a result, our heating bills have decreased, but the threat posed by a faulty furnace has actually increased.

We most often think of carbon monoxide as the by-product of incomplete combustion. Automobile exhaust, cigarette smoke, barbecue grills, kerosene heaters, wood-burning stoves, fireplaces, and gas furnaces are some of the most common sources of carbon monoxide. Normally, carbon monoxide dissipates in the air, but when it accumulates in concentrated levels, it poses a danger. When you inhale carbon monoxide, the invisible gas enters your lungs, where it virtually wraps itself around red blood cells, which carry oxygen to vital organs. The carbon monoxide effectively prevents red blood cells from absorbing life-sustaining oxygen. When high levels of carbon monoxide are inhaled for several minutes, the victim loses consciousness, then dies.

It is impossible for you to avoid inhaling some carbon monoxide, but as long as it remains below a 2 percent level in your bloodstream, you won't suffer any detrimental effects. What helps to keep it at a safe level is the fact that the carbon monoxide does not accumulate in your body. Fresh air and outdoor exercise, both of which pump additional oxygen into the bloodstream, will dilute any small amounts of carbon monoxide that you've inhaled. Nevertheless, you must eliminate or substantially reduce the amount of carbon monoxide that your body absorbs each day in order not to damage your central nervous system.

The symptoms of carbon monoxide poisoning are similar to those associated with the flu, but one of the critical tests is whether or not the symptoms persist once the affected individual leaves the house. If the nausea, dizziness, and headaches begin to diminish when you are outdoors or at work, then rather than suffering from the flu, you—and your family—may be suffering from carbon monoxide poisoning. Children, elderly people, and expectant women seem particularly susceptible to carbon monoxide poisoning. Since carbon monoxide in the bloodstream can be detected only through a specific blood test, speak to your doctor about the possibility, especially if any of the warning signs listed on page 228 are evident.

In our homes, the major sources of carbon monoxide are heat producers: oil-, gas-, or wood-fueled furnaces; stoves; hot water heaters; gas dryers; and fireplaces. Homeowners with attached garages also need to realize that warming up a car in the morning with the garage door closed can fill the garage and the house with deadly fumes. During the winter months, furnaces produce the most carbon monoxide in our homes. When the heating system is operating properly, the level of carbon monoxide is decreased and that which is produced is directed out of our homes through chimneys.

Several things, however, can happen to disrupt the normal operation of a furnace. First, the chimney can become plugged, forcing deadly fumes back into your home. Second, the furnace burners can also become plugged or misaligned, increasing the amount of carbon monoxide inside the furnace. Third, critical elements of the furnace can crack or fail, allowing dangerous gases to escape. Fourth, the necessary stream of fresh air required by the burners for efficient operation can be reduced or cut off by overinsulating the furnace room or the entire house, causing what is referred to as "backdrafting."

Backdrafting occurs when the flame in a gas furnace or hot water heater actually pulls fresh air down a chimney simply because all the windows, doors, and vents have been sealed shut and the chimney becomes its only source of fresh air. When that happens, the downdraft of air in the chimney reverses the flow of toxic carbon monoxide. Rather than escaping out the chimney, the carbon monoxide remains in the house, where it can quickly accumulate to deadly levels. Backdrafting can happen without warning and can easily go unnoticed. If you suspect that your home is extremely airtight and that you might have a problem supplying enough fresh air to your furnace, conduct a backdraft test, as detailed on page 230.

Avoiding carbon monoxide poisoning is relatively simple and worth the effort, especially when you consider that ignoring the warning signs could turn your home into a gas chamber.

## Carbon Monoxide Warning Signs

- persistent odor of exhaust fumes
- unexplained stale air
- soot on the floor or wall around a chimney clean-out door
- soot around the furnace or fireplace
- weak draft up the chimney
- occasional downdraft from the chimney into your home
- excessive moisture condensation on the windows, indicative of unseasonably high humidity in the air
- a wood-burning heater with loose-fitting doors and joints
- orange-colored flame, rather than blue, on the burner in the furnace or hot water heater

## Symptoms of Carbon Monoxide Poisoning

- blurred vision
- dizziness
- severe, persistent headaches
- nausea
- vomiting
- disorientation
- fainting
- loss of muscle control
- increased heart rate
- gradual disappearance of these symptoms once the individual has left the house (as opposed to flu symptoms, which would persist)

## Do's and Don'ts to Preventing Carbon Monoxide Poisoning

### *Do*

- have your furnace inspected annually.
- have a professional adjust the flame on your furnace or hot water heater when needed.
- make sure your chimney does not become clogged with a bird's nest during the summer.
- check the air intake vent at the bottom of your gas hot water heater to make sure it has not become plugged. (See the illustration on page 231.) If it has, simply pull off any paper, cobwebs, sawdust, and so on, that might have become lodged against the openings.
- have your chimney cleaned each summer.
- keep a close eye on an older gas or oil furnace; it's more likely to leak carbon monoxide fumes than a new model.
- install a carbon monoxide detector if your home has
  a. been sealed, weather-stripped, and overinsulated
  b. a wood-burning heater or fireplace
  c. an older gas or oil furnace
  d. a gas furnace or hot water heater near any bedrooms or living areas
  e. individuals exhibiting the warning signs of carbon monoxide poisoning

### *Don't*

- rely completely on your own furnace inspection.
- construct a tight enclosure around your furnace or hot water heater during a basement remodeling, unless you have provided an inspected and approved fresh air vent.
- use an unvented gas hot water heater.
- use a kerosene heater in your home; it is a notorious source of carbon monoxide.
- ignore other sources of carbon monoxide:
  a. letting a car or lawn mower idle in the garage
  b. using the barbecue grill in the basement or garage
  c. using the gas stove as a temporary source of heat
  d. kerosene heaters
  e. unvented space heaters

## Backdraft Test
## (for gas- and oil-burning furnaces and hot water heaters)

*Steps*                                    *Tools and Materials*

1. Securely close all windows, doors, and other exterior openings, including the damper in the fireplace.
2. Beginning in the attic, turn on every exhaust fan in your home, including any in the bathrooms, kitchen, and basement.
3. Start your clothes dryer (gas or electric).
4. Turn the thermostat up until the furnace burner ignites.
5. Turn the thermostat control on the gas hot water heater until you hear the burner ignite. (This step is not necessary on an electric hot water heater).
6. Allow 10 to 15 minutes for air currents to establish and stabilize.
7. Hold a lighted candle next to the                candle
   fresh air intake vent or draft hood on           matches
   the gas furnace.

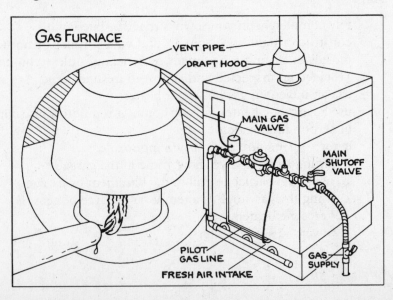

GAS FURNACE

VENT PIPE
DRAFT HOOD
MAIN GAS VALVE
MAIN SHUTOFF VALVE
PILOT GAS LINE
FRESH AIR INTAKE
GAS SUPPLY

*Steps*                                          *Tools and Materials*

8. Observe the direction the smoke from the flame travels.

9. If the smoke is drawn into the furnace, your home is drawing adequate air from outdoors. Repeat the test on the air intake vent on the hot water heater. If the smoke is drawn into the vent, your house has passed the test. You can return your house to normal.

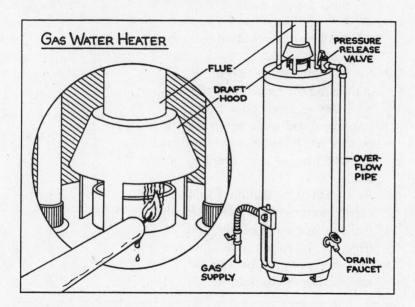

GAS WATER HEATER

FLUE

DRAFT HOOD

PRESSURE RELEASE VALVE

OVER-FLOW PIPE

GAS SUPPLY

DRAIN FAUCET

10. If the smoke is blown away from the intake vent, indicating that air is being drawn down the chimney, there is a dangerous backdraft. This prevents the carbon monoxide produced inside the furnace from escaping. Instead, it is entering the basement.

11. If backdrafting is occurring, turn the thermostat down until the furnace shuts off. Immediately open the window or door nearest the furnace.

*Steps*                                                    *Tools and Materials*

12. Wait 10 to 15 minutes, then restart the furnace by turning up the thermostat. Leave the window or door open.

13. Repeat steps 7 through 9 to make sure the airflow in the chimney has been reversed and is again traveling up the chimney. If backdrafting continues, turn off the furnace and call your gas company service department immediately. Leave the window or door open to supply fresh air.

14. Even if you have temporarily eliminated the backdraft, call your gas company to arrange for a furnace inspection and to determine how fresh air can best be supplied to the furnace, hot water heater, and fireplace, if you have one.

15. As a further precaution, install a carbon monoxide detector near the furnace, hot water heater, and fireplace. Keep in mind, however, that this is not a substitute for eliminating the backdraft.

> TIP: Never allow a gas furnace or hot water heater to be enclosed or installed in a small, tightly insulated space unless a direct vent to a fresh air source has also been provided.

# THE INTERIOR

When we talk about saving a house, most people immediately think about the roof, the exterior walls, or the foundation. These are critical areas and it is no accident that we covered them first in this book. But they're not the only parts of your home that deserve your attention. Just as a porch can deteriorate from the bottom up, a house can deteriorate from the inside out.

Granted, oversanding a hardwood floor is not going to bring your house crashing down around you, just as a squeaky step doesn't mean that the entire stairway is about to drop into the basement. Interior problems such as those affect the appearance and value of a home rather than its structural integrity. Others, however, such as cracks in the plaster or windows that don't work properly, can be warning signs of more serious problems that are attacking the basement beams or foundation.

So take a look at some of the problems you can avoid simply by taking a few steps to properly care for the inside of your house as well as the outside.

This chapter includes Home-Saving Guidelines 43 through 47.

# #43
# Foggy windows can mean serious condensation problems.

Nearly everyone, it seems, notices some condensation on their home's windows during the heating season, when warm, moist air comes in contact with much cooler windows. Generally, we just wipe off the water and go about our business.

But what should you do if you discover water not only running down the windows, but collecting on their sills? And not just in the bathroom after you've taken a shower, but in several rooms of the house, throughout the winter?

When condensation reaches this point, you have a problem. Standing water can damage the finish on the window frames and sills, then penetrate the wood. If this happens, it won't be long before you discover that the windowsill has some serious decay and the frame is about to fall apart at the joints. With that much water in the air, you're also going to notice some other disturbing developments, such as colonies of mold and mildew growing on the furniture, plasterboard beginning to crumble, and insulation that is losing its effectiveness.

Condensation requires certain elements and conditions before it can occur. First, quite naturally, is moisture in the form of vapors in the air, commonly referred to as "relative humidity." High humidity is more of a problem for most people in the winter, when homes are tightly sealed and the water vapors from showers, baths, and dishwashers have little means of escape. Summer breezes and open windows eliminate the moisture problem in the summer for all but those who live near the water and for whom high humidity can be a year-round battle.

Second, there must be a surface cooler than the moisture-laden air in the room. Since most of the objects in a room, such as furniture, silverware, and lamps, are completely surrounded by warm air, they don't provide the second element in the formula.

Glass windows, however, especially single-pane, uninsulated windows, are cooled by the outside air, often to several degrees lower than the interior of your home. When the warm, moist air collides with the cool windows, you won't hear the sound of shattering glass, but you will see a mist forming on each pane.

The amount of moisture that collects on the inside of the windows depends on (1) how much moisture is in the air and (2) the difference in temperature between the glass and the room. Therefore, to reduce the amount of condensation in your home, you have two recourses: lessen the amount of moisture in the air and/or raise the temperature of the glass.

Reducing the amount of moisture in the air isn't going to call for a drastic change in your lifestyle, for most daily chores, such as bathing, clothes washing, and doing the dishes, add an insignificant amount of moisture to the air. Cutting back on the number of showers you take makes less sense than installing an exhaust fan in the bathroom to remove the moisture-laden air.

The same theory applies to your kitchen. Rather than worry about whether you should boil potatoes or cook them in the microwave, install an exhaust fan that transfers the moisture outdoors. Water-reduction fanatics would have you throw out your houseplants, aquarium, pets, and dishwasher, but instead of nit-picking over these items, look for some serious sources of moisture, such as firewood stored inside your house or exposed ground in the basement or crawl space. When combined with exhaust fans in the bathrooms, laundry, kitchen, and basement, eliminating these major sources of moisture goes a long way toward drying out your house.

The second means of solving a condensation problem involves raising the temperature of the inside of each pane of glass. Many homeowners attack the problem from this angle, but installing storm windows or insulating film on the windows only reduces the amount of condensation, not the amount of moisture in the air. High levels of humidity trapped in a tightly sealed house with insufficient exhaust fans cause more serious long-term problems than just water on a windowsill.

Installing storm windows or an insulating film helps solve a condensation problem on the windows, but condensation also can occur on walls, especially exterior walls with little or no insulation. Since it is generally difficult to install insulation on walls and in closets, you need to identify and attack the moisture at its source. Only preventive measures, such as additional exhaust fans, increased air circulation, and crawl space covers, can significantly reduce the amount of moisture in your home.

## Warning Signs of Condensation

- mold and mildew
- water running down the windows
- water collecting on the windowsills
- paint or varnish peeling from the window frames or sills
- musty odors

## Do's and Don'ts to Eliminating Humidity and Condensation

### Do

- use kitchen and bathroom exhaust fans regularly.
- install exhaust fans where needed.
- install ceiling fans where exhaust fans cannot be installed. Moving air is better than still air.
- weather-strip your basement door and keep it closed.
- apply a plastic vapor barrier over the dirt crawl space beneath your house. (See #27 on page 143.)
- run the furnace fan even when the burner is not ignited. Doing so increases the circulation of warm, drier air.
- install a dehumidifier in any room that is a constant source of moisture, such as the basement.
- open windows and doors for a few minutes each day. You won't notice a change in your heating bill, but you will see a reduction in the humidity level.

### Don't

- confuse reducing condensation with reducing humidity. Simply insulating windows reduces condensation, but it won't affect the amount of humidity in the air. That requires attacking the source of the moisture (for example, a damp basement), plus providing an exit for the moisture that does accumulate (for example, a dehumidifier).
- stop using exhaust fans for fear of raising your heating bill. The damage caused by excessive moisture in your home costs far more than the few dollars you save on your heating bill.
- vent exhaust fans into the attic; you will simply be moving the problem, not solving it.

## How to Remove Damp Air from Your Home

*Steps*                               *Tools and Materials*

1. Begin by searching for sources of moisture in your basement, checking for and eliminating:
    uncovered crawl space (see # 27 on page 143)
    stacked firewood
    damp floors or walls (see # 23 on page 120)
    leaking pipes
    drafts around the basement door.    weather stripping
2. Install an exhaust fan (available    exhaust fan
   through home improvement centers)    drill and bits
   in the basement window. As a second    screwdriver
   choice, set up a household fan on the    household fan
   floor to circulate air.
3. Install exhaust fans in your    exhaust fan
   bathroom and kitchen.    drill and bits
      screwdriver

4. Eliminate persistent condensation problems with storm windows or insulating window film. The film can be easily measured and cut for individual panes.
5. When possible, open windows and doors to let in drier air.
6. Use household or ceiling fans to circulate drier air.
7. Install a dehumidifier in problem rooms,    dehumidifier
   such as a heavily used bathroom.

> TIP: Don't forget that the simplest way to quickly eliminate the moisture in a room, such as in a bath or laundry, is by opening a window.

# #44
# *Saving* doesn't always mean *sanding* your hardwood floors.

Many people assume there's only way to save a worn hardwood floor: use a menacing floor sander. In some cases, a sander is the best tool for removing an old finish, especially a thick layer of polyurethane, but many times you can avoid the expense, mess, and potential damage that can be caused by a floor sander by using some of the other options available to you.

Floors would be far easier to deal with if they would just wear more evenly. We could simply wait for all of the old finish to wear off, sand the floor lightly by hand, and brush on a new coat of finish. Unfortunately, things don't always work out the way we would like. Floor finishes would last indefinitely if it weren't for the bottoms of our shoes. Each time you walk across a floor without first cleaning off the grit, ground glass, and dirt partially imbedded in the soles of your shoes, you might as well be walking across with #40-grit sandpaper glued to the bottom of your feet. Add a few children, a dog, several regular guests, and an occasional plumber and it's easy to see why a floor develops traffic lanes where the finish wears off the fastest. What makes this even more frustrating is that only a few feet away, beneath a sideboard or dining room table, the finish looks as good as it did on its first day.

As I mentioned earlier, most people automatically assume that when traffic lanes begin appearing on a floor, the only solution is using a floor sander, which, if you haven't run one before, feels a lot like a garden tiller in hard ground. The 8-inch-wide sanding belts can cut a swath across a hardwood floor in the blink of an eye—and just as fast, can cut a channel deep enough to hold water. When used properly with a medium-grit (#100) sandpaper (beware, salespeople love to sell those dangerous #20-grit belts) a floor sander can remove a thick layer of finish faster than any other method. But used improperly, it can ruin a fine floor. The most common mistake people make is starting with a coarse-grit sanding belt, anything coarser than #100. To make matters worse, they invariably start in the middle of the floor. With a flick of the switch, the machine jumps to life and the whirling belt rips through the finish—and keeps on going.

Before exploring the alternatives, let's consider some basic tips for floor sanding. First, never sand when you don't have to, especially if the floor has been heavily sanded by a previous owner. The best way to determine whether or not it has is to inspect the corners of the room. If you can see or feel a groove left by the floor sander next to the baseboard, the floor has been machine sanded. Additional sanding, especially if much wood is removed, may uncover nail heads or expose the tongue-and-groove joints.

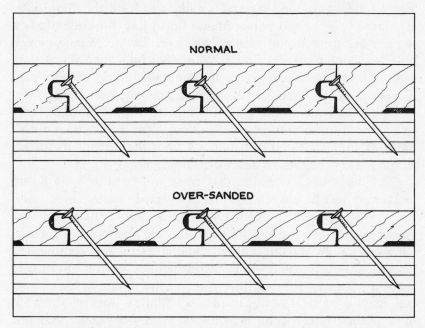

It is still possible to machine sand the floor, but do not use any sandpaper coarser than #100-grit, and be careful to stop sanding the moment the finish is removed. In addition, start out in an area you know is going to be covered by a piece of furniture or a rug. This way, any mistakes you make will be hidden from view.

Even more important is learning when to avoid sanding. The

most obvious choices for machine sanding are found in newer homes; a floor that has never been refinished but that has a worn-out coat of polyurethane on it is an ideal candidate for a careful machine sanding. However, floor sanders should never be used in historic homes, even if the floors have never been sanded before. The fine patina the floorboards have acquired over the years will be destroyed by the sander, and you will be left with floors that will never again match the woodwork or the historic character of your home. If you hope to retain or increase the value of an older home, a fine old floor must be treated like a fine old antique.

Although they should not be subjected to a floor sander, older floors, or those that have been subjected to heavy sanding in the past, can be refinished. While it's possible to sand off an old finish using a standard 3-inch belt sander or an orbital sander designed primarily for furniture projects, I don't recommend either. These sanders are too slow and are likely to leave the floor looking uneven. If the old polyurethane finish has to be removed, I suggest using paint and varnish remover. The technique differs little from that used to strip a tabletop. Set up a good ventilation system, brush on a heavy coat of a reputable brand of paint and varnish remover, scrape and scrub off the softened finish, then carefully sand the wood until it's smooth. (See "How to strip away an old finish" on page 243.) Now apply a fresh coat of the finish of your choice. The result is a floor that retains its prized patina while giving up its old, worn-out finish.

Finally, you must realize that what you think is a worn-out finish may just be a worn-out layer of wax. In many cases, once the wax is removed, the floor turns out to be in better condition than expected. To test the floor for old wax, simply use a rag and a liberal amount of paint thinner, mineral spirits, or a commercial floor cleaner to scrub a small, inconspicuous section of floor. If the rag becomes dirty and the spot on the floor brightens, you may just have a layer of wax to remove. While it does involve a lot of scrubbing (steel wool or synthetic steel wool will speed the process) and a small mountain of rags, it's still faster, easier, and less expensive than either stripping or sanding a floor. Afterward, you can leave the floor finish exposed or protect it with a fresh layer of floor wax.

Be sure to soak in water any rags you use in a floor finishing or refinishing project until you can safely hang them up to dry completely. Even then, always dispose of the dried rags in a metal container outdoors.

## Warning Signs of a Tired Floor Finish

* deep scratches in the finish
* exposed wood
* chipping or peeling finish
* water spots
* dirty, soft wax

## Do's and Don'ts to Refinishing a Floor

### Do

* try to save the existing finish before stripping it.
* set up a ventilation system using window fans.
* use plastic to seal off doorways leading to the rest of the house.
* read and follow all safety instructions of *all* machines or products you use.
* countersink all exposed nail heads deeply into the wood with a nail punch before starting the project. Before the final sanding, fill the holes with wood dough that matches the color of the boards.

### Don't

* think that an oak floor is different from an oak table when it comes to selecting sandpaper grits. Coarse grits remove finish material faster than medium grits, but at a price that is generally payable in pounds of sawdust and patina.
* start a floor finishing project with a pressing deadline staring you in the face. Allow extra time for drying, especially during periods of high humidity or cool temperatures.
* confuse "dry" with "cured." A finish that is dry to the touch may still need anywhere from two to seven days to completely harden. While you can carefully walk on it during this time, avoid placing heavy furniture on a freshly finished floor. Check the manufacturer's instructions for curing times.

## How to Restore an Old Finish

| *Steps* | *Tools and Materials* |
| --- | --- |
| 1. Countersink any exposed nail heads. | hammer<br>nail punch |
| 2. Set up a cross-ventilation system using fans and open windows. | fans<br>extension cords |
| 3. Conduct a test of the solvent on a portion of the floor that will be covered by a rug or furniture. | wax solvent (paint thinner, mineral spirits or a commercial floor cleaner)<br>medium (#0) steel wool or steel wool substitute<br>rags |
| 4. Brush a small amount of solvent on the test spot. Let stand for 3 to 5 minutes, then scrub off the softened wax with steel wool. | solvent<br>#0 steel wool |
| 5. Use a rag dampened with solvent to wipe up remaining wax, then wipe clean with a dry rag. | solvent<br>rags |
| 6. If successful, repeat over the entire floor, working in approximately 3-by-5-foot sections. | |
| 7. Let floor dry overnight. | |
| 8. Fill any countersunk nail holes with wood putty that is tinted to match the color of the floor. | tinted wood putty |
| 9. Touch up any scratches with a wood stain of the appropriate color. Let dry. | wood stain<br>rag |
| 10. For additional sheen and protection, apply a floor wax. | floor buffer<br>floor wax |

## How to Strip Away an Old Finish

*Steps*  *Tools and Materials*

1. Countersink any exposed nail heads.

hammer
nail punch

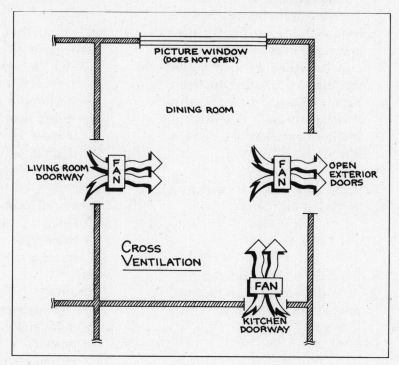

2. Set up a good cross-ventilation system.
3. Working on sections of floor approximately 3 by 5 feet, brush on a heavy layer of paint and varnish remover. Follow all manufacturer's instructions and precautions.

fans
extension cords
paint and varnish
  remover
brush
rubber gloves
old clothes and
  shoes
safety glasses
respirator

4. Allow 10 to 20 minutes for the remover to soften the finish.

| *Steps* | *Tools and Materials* |
|---|---|
| 5. Use a wide putty knife to carefully scrape up the softened finish. Deposit in a small cardboard box. Contact your local sanitation department for proper disposal. | putty knife<br>small cardboard box |
| 6. (optional) If some finish remains, immediately apply another coat of remover. Allow 10 to 20 minutes for the remover to soften the finish. Scrape off any softened finish with a wide putty knife, then scrub the wood with steel wool dipped in a solvent. | wide putty knife<br>rubber gloves<br>medium (#0) to coarse (#3) steel wool<br>denatured alcohol, lacquer thinner, or mineral spirits |
| 7. Rinse the wood clean with a rag dipped in the solvent. | rags<br>denatured alcohol, lacquer thinner, or mineral spirits |
| 8. Wipe dry with a clean rag. | rags |
| 9. After the wood has completely dried, sand it smooth. | dust mask<br>#120 sandpaper<br>hand sanding block or orbital sander |
| 10. Again countersink any nail heads. Fill the holes with wood dough using a small putty knife. Sand when dry. | hammer<br>nail punch<br>wood dough<br>small putty knife |
| 11. Vacuum to remove the dust. | vacuum with small brush attachment |
| 12. (optional) Apply a wood stain to adjust the color of the floor. Follow all instructions and precautions. | wood stain<br>brush<br>rags |
| 13. Apply the finish of your choice. (See "The best floor finish" on page 245.) | finish<br>brush<br>rags |

TIP: When it comes to applying a floor finish, leave the paint rollers for your next paint project and stick with a wide, high-quality brush. Rollers often leave bubbles in the finish, which dry as rough craters.

## *The Best Floor Finish*

What is the best floor finish?

That question is about as easy to answer as *What's the best wood?* or *What's the best style of home?* The answer can change with each circumstance.

For a brand new, never-been-finished floor in a modern home, I would recommend polyurethane, simply because it's tough, durable, and easy to apply. When it does wear out (which it will, like all finishes), it poses a problem, however, since it must be sanded or stripped off.

If a floor in a recently built (as opposed to historic) home is totally sanded rather than stripped, polyurethane would also be a top recommendation.

Chemically stripped floors pose a problem for polyurethane, since it has difficulty adhering to pores still filled with a previous finish. If a floor finish is stripped rather than machine sanded, a safer choice would be a wax finish. Wax will adhere to previously finished wood, but it's not as durable as polyurethane. It's best applied with a power buffer that drives the wax into the pores and heat hardens it. The weakness of wax is its low durability. If you opt for a wax finish, you can expect to need to buff it three or four times a year (depending on the amount of foot traffic) and to apply fresh wax once a year.

Other finish choices include shellac and a variety of oil finishes. Shellac adheres to previously finished wood and is often recommended for historic homes. Since shellac is susceptible to water and alcohol, I always recommend that the second coat be followed by an application of floor wax.

Oil finishes differ from all others in that they harden *in* the wood rather than forming a surface film on *top* of the wood. Oil finishes give a more natural, hand-rubbed effect, but they do require more maintenance in return. The oil finishes are easy to apply, but since they are so much thinner than surface finishes, such as varnish and shellac, more coats are required to build an attractive sheen. Since the wood is more exposed when finished with a penetrating oil, it's more likely to be scratched. When the oil does need to be replenished, however, the previous applications do not have to be removed. The new oil is applied directly over the old, given 15 to 20 minutes to be absorbed by the wood, and then the excess is wiped off.

So, what's the best finish?

That depends on the floor—and you.

# #45
# Stop squeaky floors and stairs.

While those of us who live in older homes have gradually grown accustomed to stairs that creak and floors that squeak, many new homeowners have not. And while a creaking staircase may only seem an inconvenience for a teenager hoping to slip in after midnight, it can signal more serious trouble. So even though you may elect to live with a squeaky floor, take a few minutes just to make sure that what you are hearing is no more than normal signs of age.

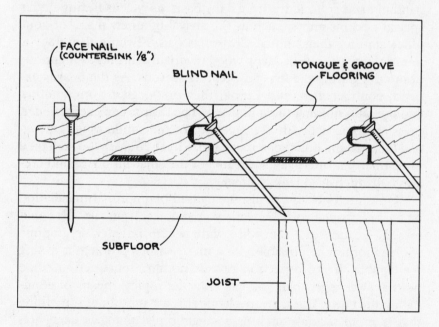

FACE NAIL
(COUNTERSINK ⅛")

BLIND NAIL

TONGUE & GROOVE
FLOORING

SUBFLOOR

JOIST

Squeaks are caused by two boards rubbing against one another or by one board moving ever so slightly against a nail. A typical hardwood or softwood floor consists of three layers, any of which can contribute to the squeaks you hear. The joists, generally 2 by 6 inch (or larger), or larger boards placed on edge 16 inches apart, support the subfloor, which may be either plywood, particleboard, or individual boards. The flooring, most often oak, maple, or pine, is nailed to the subfloor. For the past century, flooring boards have been manufactured with tongue-and-groove joints on all four sides for automatic alignment and increased resistance against warping.

Tongue-and-groove flooring is installed using a technique called blind nailing, in which the nails are driven at an angle through the protruding tongue of each board. The next board covers the heads of the nails, so the floor is free of any visible nails. The one exception is the final board, which must be face nailed. This technique calls for nailing directly through the top of the board, countersinking the nail head, then filling the hole with wood dough. Face nailing of an entire floor is most often found on pre-1860 homes.

Nearly every hardwood and softwood floor and staircase will eventually develop their own peculiar sets of squeaks and creaks. The floor in each room of your home is constantly moving, expanding, and contracting on a daily basis, as well as flexing under special circumstances, such as the arrival of a new piano or your office staff for their annual Christmas party. Even a new floor is not immune to squeaks; new wood invariably shrinks as it continues to dry during the first few heating seasons. As the boards expand, contract, flex, and shrink, they press against one another and the nails holding them in place. The boards can exert enough pressure to actually lift the nails out of the subflooring. Once a nail loosens, the board can move more freely. When you step on a loose board, it rubs against the nail or the adjacent board and creates a distinctive squeak or creak.

Unwanted noises can also be caused by improper installation or by a damaged joist beneath your floor or staircase. For that reason, treating just the noise with talcum powder or graphite while ignoring the possibility of a more serious problem is asking for trouble. If an inspection reveals nothing more serious than normal shrinkage, then you can consider topical means of eliminating the noise. But if a squeaky floor is a symptom of something that is more serious, such as a sagging joist that has been hollowed out by termites, then silencing the squeak is only going to allow the problem to escalate into an expensive proposition.

Squeaks on the ground floor are the easiest to locate and correct, provided the joists in your basement have not been covered. Second-floor squeaks are difficult to correct without drastic measures, since you simply have no way to reach the joists or sub-flooring without removing the finished flooring. Most people agree that removing the flooring just to eliminate a squeak is rather preposterous. Unless you have good reason to suspect a structural problem, including corroborating evidence, such as severely cracked plaster, doors that no longer close properly, or adjacent termite damage, you would be well advised to learn to live with a squeak or two upstairs. Where the joists are no longer visible, for example, in sealed staircases, your remedies are restricted to face nailing and lubricants.

The best way to eliminate ground floor noises begins with pinpointing the exact location of each squeak. If possible, have a partner methodically pace the floor, while you track his movements in the basement. When he hears a squeak, he should stop and repeat the motion, pressing down on the boards with his foot while you observe the joists and subflooring directly beneath him. Each of you should chalk the spot from which the noise is coming. If you have to work alone, start by identifying each squeak as you walk across the floor. Then, using a tape measure and a floor diagram, chart the location of each squeak. In the basement, find a common benchmark, such as an exterior wall or chimney, and locate each problem area using your floor plan and measurements.

While you're in the basement, note on your floor plan the location of the floor joists. This information is especially helpful if you're faced with a stubborn warped board, since a nail or screw will stay put if it penetrates both the subfloor and a joist. If a problem board falls next to or between two joists, you can nail an extra two-by-four to the nearest joist or between two joists (called bridging) to provide a deeper anchor for a nail or screw.

Any repairs requiring nails should be made with special ring-shanked flooring nails. These nails are a cross between a screw and a finishing nail, borrowing the threads of a screw for greater holding power and the head of a finishing nail for reduced visibility. Ring-shanked nails are less likely to work loose than conventional nails, yet they're easier to install than screws. Even though drilling is not mandatory, ring-shanked nails can split flooring boards. To be safe, drill a pilot hole for every nail you drive.

## Warning Signs of Needed Floor Repairs

- persistent squeaks

- cupped or warped floorboards
- exposed or raised nail heads
- soft or springy spots in the floor
- a gap between a joist and the subfloor

## Do's and Don'ts to Ending Floor Squeaks

### Do

- drill pilot holes before nailing to avoid splitting the wood flooring.
- check all diagonal braces between joists to make sure they are still intact and tight.
- use a caulking gun and a tube of construction adhesive to force a bead of glue between the top of each joist and the sub-floor. The glue will silence the squeaks by bonding the two boards together and by acting as a cushion when the subfloor flexes.

### Don't

- secure a loose floorboard by face nailing it if you can secure it from below the subfloor with a screw.
- remove diagonal bracing between joists when remodeling your basement or installing new pipes or ductwork. These braces help prevent joists from working loose from the sub-flooring.
- use wood dough or putty to fill gaps between floorboards. When the boards expand and contract with changes in the humidity, they will grind the wood dough into dust.

## How to End Floor Squeaks and Creaks Forever

| *Steps* | *Tools and Materials* |
|---|---|
| 1. Identify the source of each squeak. | chalk<br>flashlight<br>tape measure<br>room diagram |
| 2. Drive in any nails that have worked loose. | hammer<br>nail punch |
| 3. Fill the holes with tinted wood putty. | wood putty<br>rag |

*Steps*                                    *Tools and Materials*

4.  In the basement, check for any gaps          flashlight
    between the joists and the subflooring.
5.  If there's a short gap, fill it by tapping   glue
    in a wedge-shaped shim. Inject glue          shim or wooden
    into the gap before driving in the shim.         shingle
                                                 hammer

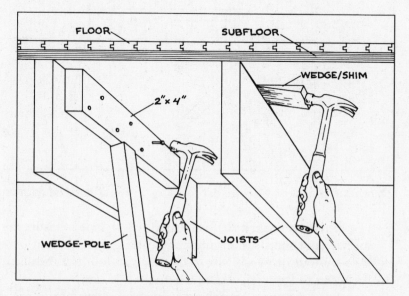

6.  If there's a long gap, glue and nail a       two-by-four
    two-by-four that spans the length of         wedge pole
    the gap to the joist. Before nailing,        glue
    force the new board firmly against           hammer
    the subflooring using a long board           nails
    (approximately 8 feet, or long enough
    to reach the floor) as a wedge pole.
    Kick the bottom of the wedge pole to
    apply pressure against the new board.

> TIP: A severe gap in one or more joists may indicate that
> an additional post is needed to support the weight of the
> floor.

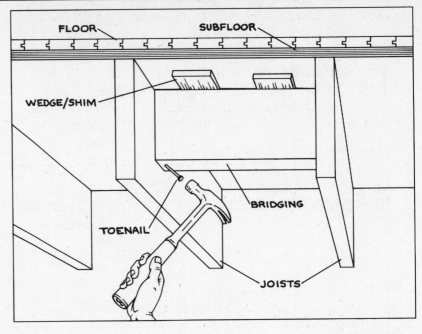

*Steps*                                    *Tools and Materials*

7.  To remedy a squeak that is located          tape measure
    between two joists, measure and cut a       two-by-four or
    two-by-four or two-by-six to fit snugly         two-by-six
    between the two joists (this technique      saw
    is called bridging). Nail the new board     hammer
    in place, then drive shims between the      nails
    board and the subfloor (see step 5).        shims
                                                glue (See follow-
                                                    ing Tip)

TIP: Sometimes a small squeak can be corrected by using an eyedropper or syringe to inject glue into the offending joint. Thin a standard woodworker's glue with water until it is runny. It is crucial that the watery glue penetrate into and past the joint. After a liberal application, do not walk over the treated area for 12 hours while the glue dries.

## How to Secure a Loose Floorboard

*Steps*                              *Tools and Materials*

1. Determine the thickness of the        tape measure
   flooring and subflooring by inspecting   flashlight
   openings cut for pipes or ductwork.

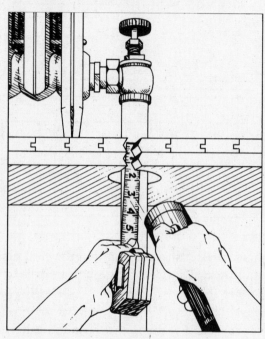

2. Select a number of #12 roundhead      #12 roundhead
   screws long enough to pass completely     screws
   through the subfloor, but only halfway
   through the flooring.
3. Working in the basement, drill a series   stepladder
   of holes the same diameter as the      drill
   screw's shank (nonthreaded portion)    bit
   *through the subfloor only*. Space the
   holes 2 inches apart to cover the area
   beneath the loose floorboard.

*Steps*                                              *Tools and Materials*

4. Switch to a smaller bit and drill pilot holes for the threaded portion of the screw into (but not through) the flooring.

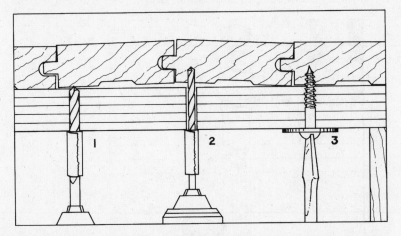

TIP: Wrap masking or electrical tape around the drill bit to act as a stop indicator. This prevents you from drilling through the flooring.

5. Slip a washer over each screw, then push the screw into one of the holes drilled in the subfloor. Turn the screw just until the washer touches the subfloor.              1-inch washers
screw
screwdriver

6. To pull the loose floorboard back into place, begin tightening the screws, giving each one only one or two turns at a time. Repeat this until each screw has been turned as tightly as possible by hand.              screwdriver

*Steps*

*Tools and Materials*

7. To secure a loose board that is over closed joists, such as a staircase or second floor, face nail the board using special ring-shanked flooring nails. Predrill each hole, nail the board in place, then countersink each nail with a nail punch and fill with wood putty.

drill
bit
flooring nails
hammer
nail punch
wood putty

TIP: For better holding power, drive each nail at a 70- to 80-degree angle. For stubborn boards, install two nails at opposite angles to form the letter *V*. This will help prevent the board from working loose.

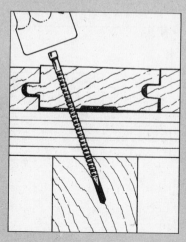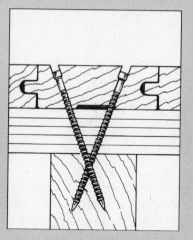

*Steps*                                        *Tools and Materials*

8. To secure a badly warped board,           drill
   drill a ½-inch hole halfway through       ½-inch bit
   the warped flooring.

9. Using a bit slightly smaller than the     drill
   diameter of the screw you plan to         bit
   use, drill a pilot hole through the
   remainder of the floorboard.

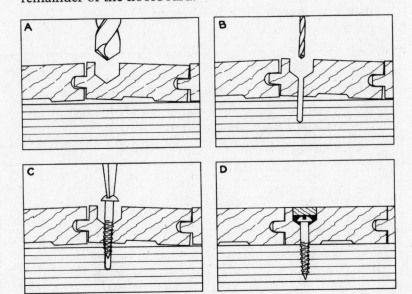

10. (optional) For extra pull, install a
    bridge between the two joists where
    the pilot hole emerged. (See "How to
    end floor squeaks and creaks forever"
    on page 252, step 7).

11. Select a screw that will pass through    #12 roundhead
    the flooring and into the subfloor           screw
    and/or bridge.

12. Pull the floorboard into place by        screwdriver
    tightening the screw. If necessary,
    repeat steps 8 through 11 for ad-
    ditional pull.

*Steps*                                    *Tools and Materials*

13. Fill the hole with a ¹/₂-inch plug of the       ¹/₂-inch plug
    same type of wood. Sand and stain the          #120 sandpaper
    end of the plug before installing it to        stain
    avoid damaging the surrounding floor           glue
    finish. Apply a finish with a fine brush.      finish
    Let it dry, then glue the plug in place.       artist's brush

TIP: The more time you spend selecting a plug of the same grain pattern, the less noticeable your repair will be. For a near-perfect patch, use a plug cutter attachment on an electric drill to cut a plug. The best donor boards can be found in the back of a closet or behind a radiator in the same room as your repair. Use the "old" plug taken from the same floor to fill the screw hole, then use a plug cut from a new board to plug the hole you left in the donor board.

## Lubricants

Do lubricants work? Temporarily.

But in many cases it's still easier to apply a lubricant two or three times a year than it is to tear up the entire second floor or an enclosed staircase.

If the problem is no more serious than two boards rubbing against one another or one board rubbing against a nail, then a lubricant may well be the least expensive, least intrusive means of silencing the squeak. There are any number of lubricants that may work, depending on the situation.

The two most popular granular lubricants are graphite and talcum powder. Application is as simple as shaking the powder onto the problem area, working it into the joints with your hand or a dry cloth, and wiping up the excess with a damp rag.

Granular lubricants, though, don't penetrate deep into the joints. While they can silence a surface squeak, the underside of a tongue-and-groove joint or a loose nail may never feel the effects of the powder. Three of the best alternatives are liquid soap, a lightweight oil, and spray silicone. Unlike a granular lubricant, each of these is absorbed by the wood and drawn by gravity toward the subfloor. If you suspect that the problem is a nail that keeps working its way to the surface, you can countersink the nail, then add drops of a liquid lubricant to the hole. The lubricant will slowly work its way along the shaft of the nail, eliminating any squeaks caused by the wood rubbing on the nail.

Aerosol cans of oil or silicone are handy when you're attempting to silence a squeak coming from between a joist and the subfloor. Make sure, however, that if you are spraying the lubricant over your head, you keep your eyes and lungs well protected.

# #46
# Keep an eye—and a ruler—on those cracks in the walls.

Like floors that squeak and stairs that creak, old houses—and, to the dismay of homeowners, many new houses—have collections of cracks in their walls. Most cracks are superficial annoyances, but some may represent significant problems.

Cracks occur when a house moves. The questions that the sudden appearance of a crack poses is *Was this caused by a normal one-time settling?* or *Is there something seriously amiss with the foundation?*

While some people will blame even the most disturbing of cracks on "normal settling," that may not always be the case. True, all houses do settle, but other problems can cause cracks to appear, including a deteriorating foundation, a weakened joist, and a sagging beam. Given the amount of weight that the roof, walls, joists, furniture, and appliances place on the foundation of a home, some settling has to be expected. Cracks appear also because different parts of a house settle at different times, rates, and distances. Wings, porches, additions, and other projections don't settle at the same rate, due to differences in weight, soil, or depth of footings. The stress these varying movements place on the internal skin of your home—that is, the plaster—is the primary cause for most cracks. While a stud or floor may flex under the stress when one side of the house settles at a faster rate than the other, the brittle plaster shell covering the walls cannot. Wood bends, plaster cracks.

So how do you distinguish between a settling crack and one that may be the harbinger of bad news? At a glance, you can't, since most cracks appear the same to an untrained eye. The difference is that, with the exception of a brand new home, a settling crack can be expected to remain stationary. As soon as the house has settled into its permanent position, the crack grows neither longer nor wider. A crack caused by a structural problem, however, continues to grow as the problem beneath it worsens. To complicate matters, a third type of crack—a seasonal crack—expands and contracts as the relative humidity and air temperature fluctuate throughout the year. Upon closer examination, though, a seasonal crack generally does not grow larger, but simply opens and closes to the same extent each year.

Old plaster develops surface cracks not unlike the alligatoring you often find in old paint and antique furniture finishes. Fifty-year-old plaster is also more apt to crack along a wall stud or ceiling joist as it ages and becomes brittle. It then can no longer bend with the seasonal expansion and contraction a house experiences. Just because it does not stem from a looming structural problem, though, alligatored plaster should not be ignored. Those tiny cracks can eventually develop into larger cracks, but unlike a furniture finish that simply flakes off, chunks of plaster dropping from your ceiling can make your friends and family just a little nervous.

The same is true for cracks that develop when water seeps between the plaster and the wood lath. The resulting crack and distinctive discolored, bulging plaster is not indicative of a crumbling foundation, but it is trying to let you know that there's a leak in your roof, a problem with your plumbing, or serious condensation in your attic. If you ignore it or simply patch it each year, the moisture has the opportunity to damage the wood behind the plaster.

Cracks also reveal something about themselves in the direction that they travel. A diagonal crack is usually caused by a structural problem, such as a rotted joist or a crumbling foundation, while a vertical or horizontal crack generally is indicative of a problem between the plaster and the framework behind it. While such cracks must be dealt with, since they could signal encroaching water or aging plaster, they shouldn't send you racing to the basement expecting to see the walls caving in. Unless, of course, they're spreading throughout the house.

A small diagonal crack is no cause for alarm either, provided it's an isolated development that is not increasing in size. Since cracks seldom change drastically, you cannot depend on a casual visual inspection to determine whether or not a crack is moving. The change can be so gradual you might not even realize it's happening. For that reason, it's a good idea to measure and chart any progress of a new crack. Those that stabilize before they exceed $1/16$ of an inch should be no cause for alarm; they're probably due to minor settling of the house, the age of the plaster, or seasonal movements.

If, however, a diagonal crack shows signs of increasing beyond $1/16$ of an inch in width, you should look for corroborating evidence, such as nearby doors and windows that no longer operate properly or gaps between the shoe molding and the floor. If you discover additional signs of abnormal settling, call in an architect or engineer for advice on the situation. Your home's foundation may have been eroded by underground water or deteriorating timbers, causing the walls to drop and the plaster to crack. Other reasons for cracks to suddenly appear, reappear, or grow larger can be changes made during a renovation, additions or demolitions that altered the existing stress pattern on beams and joists, or simply the vibrations set off by sledgehammers and hammerdrills.

So find those cracks—and what caused them.

### Warning Signs of Structural Problems

- reappearance of cracks that had been repaired
- cracks that are increasing in length or width
- appearance of new cracks near existing ones
- floors that have begun to tilt
- doors and windows that no longer operate properly
- bulging foundation or exterior wall

### Do's and Don'ts to Inspecting Cracks

**Do**

- measure and chart the progress of any cracks in your walls.
- search for the cause of any crack.
- check for corresponding cracks on the exterior side of a wall.

**Don't**

- be as concerned with an older, stable crack as with the appearance of a new crack.
- treat the symptom and ignore the disease. Find the cause of the crack before you worry about patching it.
- be as concerned with cracks that open and close with changes in the humidity and temperature; they're not a sign of a structural problem.

## How to Interpret Cracks

| *Steps* | *Tools and Materials* |
|---|---|
| 1. In your home notebook, make a room-by-room inventory of any cracks you find, noting their location, size, and direction (vertical, horizontal, diagonal). Don't overlook closets. | notebook<br>pen<br>tape measure |
| 2. Study your findings, searching for any pattern that would indicate a structural problem in the foundation or exterior walls. | |
| 3. Check for other indications of structural problems, including leaning walls, sloping floors, uneven windows and doors, and a sagging ceiling. Look for patterns in the changes that have occurred since the house was completed that point toward the source of the problem. Note your observations in your house notebook and make the necessary repairs. | level<br>notebook<br>pen |
| 4. To measure the rate at which a crack is increasing, use a quality ruler to make two marks exactly 1 inch apart, one on either side of the crack. | ruler<br>pencil |
| 5. Every month, measure the distance between the two marks to determine if the crack has widened. Record your findings in your home notebook. | ruler<br>notebook<br>pencil |
| 6. As another option, simply patch the crack with spackling compound, then check to see if the crack reappears. If it does, follow steps 4 and 5. | spackling<br> compound<br>putty knife<br>rag |
| 7. If you discover a number of cracks or even one crack that continues to increase in size, find the cause of the problem in the basement or foundation. If necessary, consult an engineer, architect, or contractor. | |

TIP: When marking a crack, always measure at the widest point. This indicates where the greatest stress is being released and where any movement is the most obvious.

# #47
# Keep your windows and doors operating smoothly.

Those of you living in newer homes probably aren't experiencing any serious problems with your windows or doors, and shouldn't expect any for several years. But like any movable part, windows and doors do eventually develop problems, especially after they've been opened and closed several thousand times. Add a few bone-jarring slams, plus beatings from several hundred thunderstorms, and you may wonder how it is that your doors and windows have operated so efficiently for all these years.

A well-made and properly maintained door or window can last for decades. A cheap door or window, however, can begin to fall apart even before your children have an opportunity to knock a base-ball through it. You probably won't be able to stop a baseball, but if you pay attention to the little problems that begin to develop, you can avoid the high cost of a replacement window or door.

The most popular type of window is the double-hung variety. Adaptable to many architectural styles, the double-hung window is actually two windows (called sashes) that work in tandem: The upper (outside) sash can be lowered, while the lower (inside) sash can be raised. When they're in the closed position, they can be latched where they overlap.

Older (pre-1950) double-hung windows feature a weight-and-pulley system. Weights in the jamb are attached to a rope or chain. The rope or chain emerges at the top of the jamb over a pulley and extends down the parting strip to each sash. The weights originally were intended to reduce the amount of effort needed to raise or

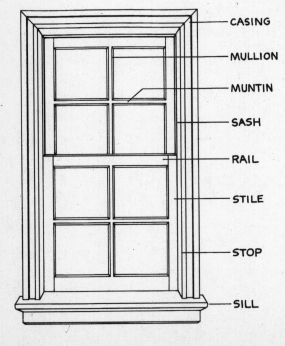

CASING

MULLION

MUNTIN

SASH

RAIL

STILE

STOP

SILL

lower the window and to hold the sash in any position. Over the years, however, the ropes can become brittle and break, dropping the weights to the bottom of the jamb cavity. Replacing a sash cord or chain is a complicated procedure that requires disassembling part of the jamb and removing the windows. If you want to undertake this project, you would be well advised to refer to a detailed home repair book or home improvement magazine, such as *Old House Journal*.

You don't have to replace a broken sash cord to use a double-hung window. Without the weights, you simply have to exert more strength to raise or lower each sash. If the parting strip is well lubricated and not encumbered by layers of old paint, the windows may slide quite easily even without the weights. Newer double-hung windows, in fact, have been designed without weights, relying instead on springs or a more efficient parting strip material to aid in raising or lowering each sash.

Remember, though, that sash weights were designed to prevent a raised sash from slamming down on unsuspecting fingers. If you decide not to repair a broken sash cord, you may need to custom-cut a length of dowel to hold a well-lubricated sash in the open position. Even so, this could prove dangerous to a young child who decides to pull the dowel out from beneath a raised window. To prevent accidents, take the necessary precautions. Among your choices are friction-fit parting strip liners; a device called a sash balance, which serves the same function, but without bulky weights; or a foolproof means of holding the window in an open position.

There are several problems you can solve without dismantling the entire window or door; these are listed below. Some are bound to be found in your home, while others can be avoided simply with a little preventive maintenance. In either case, making sure that your windows and doors operate smoothly and efficiently not only makes your life safer and easier, but extends their life as well.

## Windows

### Sticking Sash

Minor sticking may be cured by cleaning away excess paint in the parting strip and lubricating it with wax. But if the window has been painted numerous times, the problem may be too much paint. Scrape or strip off the layers of paint from inside the parting strip. If necessary, repaint the parting strip with a thin coat of paint.

The bottom layers in the window's parting strip may well be lead paint. Be sure to read the cautions detailed in #4, "Recognize the hazards of lead paint," on page 20, before scraping or stripping paint which could contain lead.

When repainting a window, come back every 15 minutes while the paint is drying to move the window slightly. This prevents the paint from sealing the window to the parting strip. After it dries, lubricate with furniture wax.

### Window That Has Been Painted Shut

With several strokes of a utility or pocketknife, carefully cut through the paint over the joint of the sash stile or rail and the parting strip or sill. With each pass, press the knife deeper into the joint. Gently tap the window stile with a padded hammer or rubber mallet to break any paint bond beyond the reach of the knife, but take care not to crack the glass. You can use a wide-blade putty knife to separate the frame from the sill, but don't use a pry bar, which can place too much uneven stress on the glass. Similarly, never use a screwdriver to pry open a window, since the blade can splinter the wood. If the window refuses to open, check for nails that may have been countersunk and painted. A previous owner may have nailed the window shut for security.

Don't give up on a window that's nailed shut; it could eliminate a route to safety in the event of a fire. On a more comforting note, windows provide critical ventilation for your home. In short, no window should be allowed to remain nailed or painted shut.

### Swollen Window

If the sash stile has absorbed moisture and the window has swollen shut, carefully pry off the inside molding and renail it slightly farther away from the sash stile. If the molding breaks, as it often does, use an inexpensive replacement available at a lumberyard or home improvement center.

*Note:* Check to determine why the sash stile has swollen. Has the paint peeled from either side? Has the glazing around the glass loosened or broken off? Is moisture leaking inside the window?

### Rattling Window

A window rattles if the sash stile has shrunk or the molding has been removed. If this is the case, carefully pry off the inside molding and renail it closer to the sash stile. If the molding breaks, use an inexpensive replacement available at a lumberyard or home improvement center.

Make sure the shrunken sash is not simply the result of several weeks of dry weather. If you move the molding closer and the sash swells when the humidity returns, the window may not open. Check that the window is not losing and absorbing moisture through portions of bare wood. If so, seal with paint, varnish, or the appropriate finish.

### Missing, Broken, or Loose Latches

New, more security-conscious latches are available at hardware stores. Historically accurate latches are also available. Loose screws can be replaced with longer screws, or you can plug a hole with a short length of dowel (glued in, of course) and redrill the pilot hole.

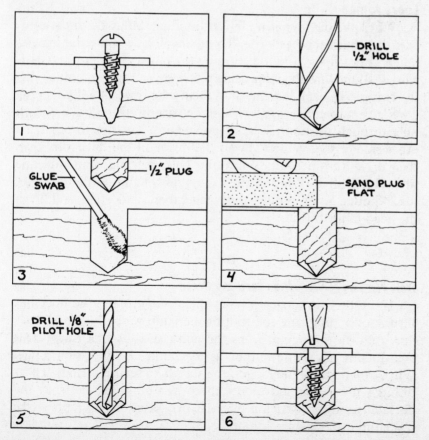

A properly aligned latch does more than lock the two sashes together. A good latch also pulls the two sashes snugly together, preventing cold air from infiltrating the room.

### Inoperable Sash Pulley

A sash pulley usually freezes when rust or paint gets in the axle. The pulley is generally held in place by two nails or screws. To repair, remove them and pull the pulley out of the parting strip. If you want to remove the rope or chain from the pulley so you can soak the pulley in paint stripper or a rust remover, unhook it from the sash and tie it to a dowel, ring, or anything that prevents it from being pulled by the weights into the jamb cavity. If possible, leave the pulley on the chain or rope and brush on a coat of stripper or rust remover, then wrap it in plastic or aluminum foil until the paint or rust has been softened. Remove the paint or rust with a toothbrush, then rinse, lubricate, and reinstall.

### Loose Joint

When the old glue is no longer bonding the tenon to the mortise, the joint becomes loose. To repair, first separate the joint as much as possible without disturbing the other joints. Inject woodworker's glue into the joint using a syringe or squeeze bottle. Pull the two pieces back together into their proper position by tapping a wedge between the sash stile and the parting strip. Drill a $3/8$-inch hole through the mortise and tenon joint, but not through the other side of the window. Swab the inside of the hole with glue, then drive a $3/8$-inch dowel into the hole, pinning the tenon and mortise together. Trim off the excess dowel and let the joint dry for 24 hours. Later, remove the wedge, then sand, stain, and finish the head of the dowel.

## Doors

### Bolt No Longer Reaches Striking Plate

If the bolt no longer reaches the striking plate, the door has shrunk over time and does not fit the jamb properly. To remedy this, remove the hinges from the jamb and insert a thick cardboard shim (the same outline as the hinge) behind each hinge. When you reinstall the hinges, the screws to secure them will pass through the shims and secure them as well. This will shift the door closer to the striking plate. If necessary, remove the strike plate and insert a shim behind it.

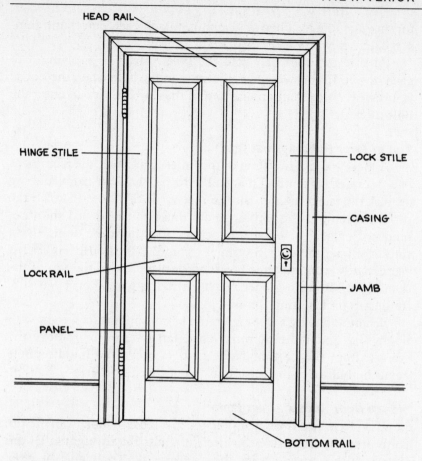

HEAD RAIL

HINGE STILE

LOCK STILE

CASING

LOCK RAIL

JAMB

PANEL

BOTTOM RAIL

## Bolt and Strike Plate No Longer Line Up

Loose hinges or settling of the house can affect how the door's bolt and strike plate line up. First tighten all the screws. If that doesn't work, see if you can adjust the position of the strike plate. As an alternative to moving the strike plate and drilling new holes, enlarge the opening in the strike plate with a file.

## Loose Hinges

Daily stress on a door can pull hinge screws out of their holes. Simply switching to longer screws does not provide enough bite for the threads. You need to remove the screws from the hinges, inject some glue, then drive in a hardwood dowel. Cut or chisel the dowel flush with the surface of the door and allow 12 hours for the glue to dry. Then drill a pilot hole in each dowel and reinsert each screw.

Be sure to squirt glue into the hole instead of applying it to each dowel. In this way, the glue stays in the hole when the dowel is inserted. Also, sharpen one end of the dowel so it can enter the hole more easily.

### Top of Door Rubs Against Jamb

A loose hinge or settling of the house can affect the alignment of a door and its jamb. To keep the top of the door from rubbing against the jamb, tighten all the screws. If this doesn't solve the problem, remove the top hinge and insert a cardboard shim behind it. Replace the hinge and screws and check the door. Use a thicker shim if the door continues to bind. If the house has settled significantly, you may need to sand or plane down the top of the door. (See "Bolt no longer reaches striking plate," on page 268, for details on inserting shims.)

When removing a door from the jamb, support its weight with books slid under the bottom. Then tap the pin, or remove the screws, from the bottom hinge first. Remove the middle hinge next, then finish at the top. Reinstall in reverse order.

### Side of Door Rubs Against Jamb

If a door swells or if its hinges are loose, it may not fit the jamb properly from side to side. To adjust the fit, tighten all the screws. If this doesn't solve the problem, sand or plane the edge of the door until it closes freely. If the entire length of the door rubs on the jamb, you may need to sand or plane the hinged edge, not the latch edge.

If a door sticks only during periods of high humidity, hold off on the sanding or planing. Wait until the humidity drops and the door shrinks back to its normal size. Then apply an additional coat of finish to prevent the wood from absorbing moisture in the air. Be sure to coat all surfaces, including the edges.

### Bottom of Door Rubs on Floor

A loose hinge or settling of the house can affect how a door hangs. To keep a door plumb and prevent it from rubbing on the floor, tighten all the screws. If this doesn't solve the problem, remove the bottom hinge and insert a cardboard shim behind it. Replace the hinge and screws and check the door. Use a thicker shim if the door continues to bind. If the house has settled significantly, you may need to sand or plane down the bottom of the door.

### Loose Joint

When the old glue no longer bonds the tenon to the mortise, the joint becomes loose and eventually comes apart. To repair a loose joint, separate the joint as much as possible without disturbing the other joints. Inject woodworker's glue into the joint using a syringe or squeeze bottle. Pull the two boards back together into their proper position with a bar clamp or an improvised tourniquet (a length of rope and a dowel). Drill a 3/8-inch hole through the mortise and tenon joint, but not through the other side of the door. Swab the inside of the hole with glue, then drive a 3/8-inch dowel into the hole, pinning the tenon and mortise together. Trim off the excess dowel and let it dry for 24 hours. Later, sand, stain, and finish the head of the dowel.

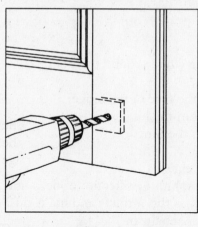
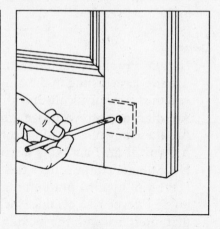

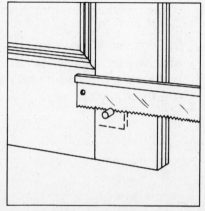

## Maintenance Checklist for Windows and Doors

### Windows
__ Is the exterior glazing around the glass intact?
__ Is water seeping between the glass and the wood?
__ Is the paint or finish peeling?
__ Is there any sign of deteriorating wood?
__ Is the sash cord in good condition?
__ Does the sash pulley need to be oiled?
__ Does the parting strip need to be lubricated?
__ Does the latch work?
__ Is the screen strong enough to prevent a child or pet from falling through it?
__ Is the weather stripping interfering with the operation of the window?
__ Is paint buildup interfering with the operation of the window?
__ Have you lubricated the mechanism in any casement windows in the past year?

### Doors
__ Is there any sign of deteriorating wood around the door?
__ Are the screws snug in the hinges?
__ Are the screw heads flush with the face of the hinge?
__ Are there any screws missing from the hinges?
__ Are there any pins missing from the hinges?
__ Are any of the pins badly worn?
__ Have you oiled the hinges this year?
__ Have you applied powdered graphite or silicone to locks and bolts? (Never oil a cylinder lock, as this attracts and holds dust that interferes with the locking mechanism.)
__ Is the weather stripping interfering with the latching mechanism?
__ Are there any loose joints in the door?
__ Are there any cracked panes of glass that need to be replaced?
__ Is the paint or varnish peeling?
__ Are there any raw edges that need to be finished?

## Are Old-fashioned Storm Windows Really Necessary?

In my boyhood home back in Illinois, we judged the approach of winter not by flying geese or woolly caterpillars, but by the sight of my father lugging stacks of black-framed storm windows out of the small barn in the back of our property. Since the annual rite involved large panes of old glass and trips up and down a shaky wooden ladder, my brother and I were assigned seats in the grass from which we could safely watch my parents. My mother would wash and carefully dry both sides of a window, then my father would study it carefully, attempting to confirm that it, indeed, did fit the second-story window he was about to climb to. He obviously had learned that each window in our 1911 home varied slightly, for most of the similar-looking windows had been labeled according to their location. Despite the often-gusty days that accompany November on the rolling plains of the Midwest, I don't recall that my father ever dropped one of the storm windows from atop his ladder. However, each year he did swear that next spring he was going to buy aluminum combination storm-and-screen windows for the house.

Now I'm struggling to cut my own heating bills in a house built just a few years after my parents'. The old wooden storm windows that my house probably had when it was built have long since disappeared and I'm faced with a dilemma: Do I have storm windows custom-made for my house? Or do I concentrate instead on caulking and weather-stripping the windows?

Storm windows present one of those good news, bad news scenarios. The good news is that storm windows do reduce the amount of cold air infiltration through the primary windows. The bad news is that they don't reduce it by much. When the cost of a new storm window (especially custom-made storms for odd-sized windows) is compared to the savings generated by that window, you suddenly realize that you would have to live in your house for a long, long time to pay for it in savings.

Caulking, weather-stripping, and other means of reducing cold air infiltration around and through the windows, however, are much cheaper than storm windows. And they don't take up any space from April through October.

So what should you do, provided, of course, that you live where the cold air howls for several months each winter?

First, caulk and weather-strip the primary windows.

Second, keep any storm windows you have in good working order.

Third, if you plan to live in your house for several years, invest in storm windows, but only if it does *not* mean that you will have to delay other, more effective energy-saving projects.

As for me, I'm going to call my father and see what he did with all those old storm windows.

# WRAPPING THINGS UP

The last three Home-Saving Guidelines may seem at first to have little to do with the main topic of this book. And yet the advice they provide can very much help you save your house.

Hint #48, for instance, deals with preventing fires. One of the most common causes of house fires is spontaneous combustion of flammable materials. Those who become careless with refinishing rags and other such hazardous products can suddenly discover that spontaneous combustion translates into one simple, frightening word: fire.

The last two guidelines go beyond home safety and maintenance. As a homeowner, you should realize that other people can have as much of an impact on your home as you and your family. Knowing how to keep a burglar—and the wrong contractor—out of your house is terribly important. One scoundrel or ignorant contractor can do more harm to your home in a matter of hours than a normal family could in a decade. Know what safety precautions are needed to secure your property. Also, take your time when selecting contractors or craftspersons. Check their references, and make sure that the lines of communication are never down. In other words, be a bit of a pest. Hired workers may mumble about you under their breath or over a beer after work, but consider the alternative: They're happy because they finished the job in record time, but you're miserable because they didn't do what you wanted.

So don't stop now. These last three Home-Saving Guidelines could be the most important in the book.

# #48
# Don't burn down what you just fixed up.

Across the United States today, there will be approximately 1,000 house fires. The same thing will happen tomorrow, and the day after, and the day after that. During the course of this year, more than 3,000 people will die in residential fires. An additional 15,000 will be injured.

Why?

Researchers have identified the primary causes of house fires as being:

1. careless smoking
2. faulty electrical systems
3. heating and cooking appliances
4. children playing with matches and lighters
5. open flames
6. flammable liquids
7. arson
8. faulty chimneys
9. lightning
10. spontaneous combustion

Perhaps the least understood and most underestimated cause on this list is spontaneous combustion. Years ago, when you could find a can of linseed oil in nearly every home across the country, spontaneous combustion was near the top of this list. The number of fires caused by spontaneous combustion has declined as linseed oil has dropped from the ranks of the most popular furniture finishes. Nevertheless, linseed oil remains a major ingredient in several furniture finishes. Many manufacturers, however, don't list the ingredients (including raw or boiled linseed oil) of their product on the label, and this has lulled most people into believing that spontaneous combustion is no longer a threat.

One of the characteristics of a furniture finish is its ability to transform from a liquid state to a solid once it has been applied. Most oils, such as linseed, remain in a liquid state until they come in contact with oxygen, at which time a chemical reaction takes place. During the oxidation process heat is generated but, in most instances, dissipates harmlessly into the air. But if the heat is trapped inside a wadded refinishing rag, for example, it can burst into flames which immediately feed on the oil-soaked fibers of the cloth.

The amount of time required for the heat to build up to the combustion point varies according to conditions, but spontaneous combustion can occur in a matter of hours. Since you seldom know the exact ingredients of any refinishing products, you should always treat all refinishing products as if they could cause a fire if handled improperly. In that way, you can never make a mistake that would destroy all you have worked so hard for.

### Fire Danger Warning Signs

- cans of tung oil, Danish oils, and other furniture finishes, especially those applied with a rag
- rags tossed carelessly around a work area
- a full trash can in your workshop
- a cluttered basement or garage

### Do's and Don'ts to Preventing Spontaneous Combustion

#### Do

- assume that all wood finishing, refinishing, and polishing products are potential fire hazards.
- properly dispose of every wood finishing, refinishing, and polishing rag immediately.
- keep a bucket of water nearby to soak all used rags in water as soon as you are finished with them.

#### Don't

- think that only rags can catch on fire. Steel wool, foam brushes, and paper towels are also potential sources of spontaneous combustion.
- put wood finishing materials in a plastic garbage bag. It will inhibit air circulation that deters spontaneous combustion.
- delay. Start the proper disposal treatment the moment you lay down a rag, paper towel, or pad of steel wool.

## How to Dispose of Finishing Materials

| *Steps* | *Tools and Materials* |
| --- | --- |

1. Spread out all materials—such as rags, brushes, and steel wool pads—completely flat in a well-ventilated area, preferably outdoors away from children and pets.
2. Allow them to dry completely.
3. Dispose of the *dried* materials in a     metal garbage can metal garbage can away from all buildings, children, and pets. Keep the dried rags and other materials at the top of the can and allow plenty of air circulation.

**or**

1. Place all materials in a water-filled container.     old paint or varnish can
2. Seal tightly.     lid
3. Contact your local sanitation department for proper disposal procedure for the water-filled can.

> TIP: Stretch a short length of clothesline in a safe area and use clothespins to hang oil-soaked materials until they are completely dry and safe to dispose.

### *Fifteen Ways* Not *to Burn Down Your House*

1. A wood shingle roof (as well as dried leaves in a rain gutter) can be set ablaze by sparks from a wood-burning fireplace or stove. Avoid burning paper that can be sucked up the chimney and dropped on your roof.
2. Install a screen in your chimney to catch burning papers and sparks.
3. Chimney fires are fed by excessive creosote in the chimney. Avoid creosote buildup by burning seasoned

soned hardwoods, such as oak or ash, rather than soft-woods, such as pine or fir.

4. Burn a hot fire using dry hardwoods at least once a week to reduce the amount of creosote in your chimney.

5. Clean your chimney at the end of each heating season. The creosote continues to harden during the summer.

6. Make sure your chimney has no old, unsealed openings left from a former woodstove or oil heater.

7. Make sure your chimney was properly installed.

8. If your house is more than 50 years old, have the wiring, not just the breaker box, inspected.

9. Keep any room in which you use paint and varnish remover or any wood-finishing products well ventilated to prevent the buildup of fumes.

10. Don't use propane torches or heat guns to strip paint from the siding on your house. Dust, bird and rodent nests, and other remnants can ignite in the walls from the heat these tools generate.

11. Don't let sawdust accumulate in your work area—fine, swirling dust can be ignited by a spark.

12. Keep all matches and lighters stored in a locked drawer or one that is out of the reach of your children.

13. Have your furnace inspected annually.

14. Discourage family members and guests from smoking in your house.

15. Install smoke detectors in your home.

# #49
# Think like a burglar.

Like other homeowners, you probably have followed one or two strategies to home security: Either you've taken only minimal steps toward securing your home, believing that your neighborhood is relatively safe, or you've hired a professional to install a burglar alarm system. In either case, you've left yourself, your home, your family, and your possessions vulnerable to burglars.

Homeowners with alarm systems often become terribly careless about maintaining strong, secure locks on their doors and windows. They take comfort in believing that if someone does pry open a window or force in a door, the alarm system will drive the burglar away and bring police cars howling down the street. With any luck, that's exactly what will happen, but if you have an alarm system in your home, you have to realize that it's not infallible. Here are three common scenarios:

1. The alarm fails to go off because the owner forgot to arm it, the system broke down, or the thief knew how to circumvent it.
2. The alarm goes off, but the police do not respond or respond slowly because of the high number of false alarms caused by faulty systems and careless owners.
3. The burglar breaks open a door or window, purposely setting off the alarm. He then retreats to watch what happens. If no one responds and the alarm automatically shuts off after a predetermined length of time, the burglar then approaches the house and enters undetected.

An alarm system is a valuable crime deterrent, but it should not be your only line of defense. In fact, it should be your third or fourth. The other proven means of preventing theft, in order of contact with a potential burglar, are:

1. perimeter lighting
2. a barking dog

3. proper door and window locks
4. an alarm system

As you can see from the list, it is only when a thief has crossed your property undetected and has actually opened a door or window that the alarm system is called upon. If the system fails, the thief has easy access to your house. So rather than relying solely on an alarm system, take the necessary steps to make sure that a thief never has the opportunity to test the alarm. Besides, a home that appears well kept is less likely to be struck by mischief makers and thieves. And if you don't feel that an alarm system is required in your neighborhood, you should take the same steps to make sure you never regret that decision.

## How to Determine the Security of Your Home

1. Walk the street(s) adjacent to your property both during the daytime and at night. Try to think like a burglar and note the most obvious entry points to your property. Also note how well lit your property is at night.
2. Walk around your house both during the daytime and at night, looking for potential entry points. Don't forget the second floor. Working with a partner or a ladder, a burglar can easily reach a second-floor roof, deck, or window.
3. Make sure any trees next to your house don't serve as ladders for a burglar.
4. Don't store a ladder in an unlocked garage or, worse yet, next to the foundation.
5. Don't leave any tools in the open or in an unlocked garage. Most burglars travel without tools, hoping to find them on the property.
6. Don't overlook cellar doors, rooftop hatches, skylights, decks, and basement windows beneath a porch as potential entry points.
7. Trim back shrubbery that would disguise a burglar working on a door or window. If you want to plant shrubs beneath the windows, select thorny varieties, such as holly.
8. Keep your yard well maintained. Present the appearance of an occupied, closely monitored property.

## Daily Precautions

- Install yard lights to illuminate the driveway, garage, doors, and other key areas. If your bedroom is on the second floor, check with an electrician on having an additional switch installed so you can operate the yard lights from upstairs.
- Consider getting a dog for a pet. A barking dog is a major deterrent to a thief. But don't make the mistake of saying to every worker or visitor, "Don't worry. He won't bite." Word can spread through casual conversations in bars or at parties that your mean-looking German shepherd is just a big pussycat.
- Change any locks for which you cannot account for all of the keys, especially if you've given copies to a former babysitter, worker, or contractor.
- Lock the outer screen or storm door at night to delay access to the lock on the primary door.
- If you've just moved into an area, check to see how many of your neighbors have installed alarm systems.
- If necessary, have an alarm system installed.
- Clearly display alarm system warning stickers on doors and windows that would be targeted by a burglar.
- Establish a neighborhood watch system. Your local police force has detailed information and suggestions.
- Keep an eye on your neighbors' homes and yards. Call them if you see something suspicious. They will be more likely to do the same for you.
- Don't let an attached garage serve as an entry for a burglar. Once inside, he can work on the house door undetected, perhaps even using your tools.

## When You're Away

- When leaving for the evening, vary the lights you turn on. Don't use a solitary porch light as a signal that no one is home. Combine it with other lights to create the effect that you are home waiting for someone else to arrive.
- When going on vacation, have your newspaper and mail held, or have them picked up daily by a neighbor.
- Consider hiring a guard dog service while you're away on vacation.

- Hire a house sitter.
- Alert a trusted neighbor who can watch for suspicious persons, lights, cars, or activities.
- Have a neighbor park his car in your driveway.
- Call the police. Tell them how long you will be gone, and give them the name and phone number of the person who will be looking after your house.
- Have someone keep the lawn mowed.
- Use timers to turn lights on and off to imitate activity.
- Be creative when you hide cherished valuables, avoiding such obvious places as in a closet or under the bed. Leave enough cash and inexpensive jewelry accessible so thieves won't rip your house apart looking for your hiding place. Locking a closet or bedroom door only guarantees that a thief is going to smash it open.

## Doors: A Primary Entry

Most people put far too much trust in the locks on their doors. What they fail to realize is that locks don't stop a burglar; screws and door frames do. If the screws attaching the strike plate, latch, or lock to the door or door frame can't stand the abuse a burglar can dish out, then it doesn't matter how much you paid for the lock.

Take a moment to remove one of the screws from the most important lock in your home. How long is it? If a screw from the door frame facing is less than 2 inches long—most are less than 1 inch—even a puny thief could kick the door open swiftly and quietly.

Most door frame facings are simply $3/4$-inch boards held on with finish nails. Attaching one end of a dead bolt or a chain to the door facing with even four small screws that are less than an inch long is a waste of money. To be effective, the screws must pass through the facing and penetrate the wall framing behind it. And don't confuse the plasterboard with the real framing. In a typical house a $3/4$-inch-thick facing board is backed by a $1/2$ inch of plaster or plasterboard. You need a 2- to 3-inch-long screw to penetrate the facing board, the plasterboard, and the wall studs. By predrilling each screw hole, you can judge the strength of the material you encounter by the resistance it mounts. A drill bit glides through plasterboard, but it slows down when it comes in contact with the stud. Watch the dust, too. White dust is simply plaster, but sawdust indicates that you've reached real wood. The deeper the screw penetrates, the stronger the lock will be.

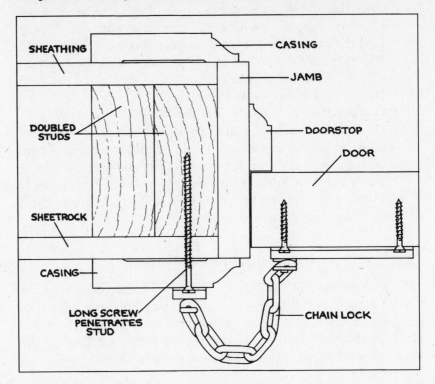

Locks must also be easy to operate. If they aren't, your family could be trapped in your home during a fire. Run a test to see if everyone (except very young children) can unlock each door in the dark. If they can't, you'll need to make some changes. For that same reason, never use a padlock on an exit door, for you may not be able to find the key or read the combination in a dark, smoke-filled room.

Instead, install sliding bolts on the inside of your doors. If a thief could reach an existing sliding bolt by breaking a pane of glass, reposition the bolt or add a second sliding bolt beyond anyone's reach from the outside. By mounting a sliding bolt near the bottom of the door, you (1) keep it out of reach of a burglar, (2) make it accessible for children or adults crawling along the floor during a fire, and (3) provide additional strength at the point where a burglar is most likely to kick. Sliding bolts attached at the top of a door are less effective against burglars and more dangerous to the occupants, who might not be able to reach them.

Doors with large windows are particularly vulnerable and should have their standard glass replaced with highly resistant safety glass.

## Windows: Another Entry Point

Window latches, such as the kind found on standard double-hung windows, provide very little resistance to an experienced burglar, who can pry them easily and quietly out of soft, narrow wood. Nevertheless, you should keep the latches in good working order, as they cut down on cold air infiltration and may foil an amateur burglar. At the same time, you should devise a stronger lock for any vulnerable window. In this case, the best means is also the least expensive and can be accomplished in just a few minutes on a wooden window.

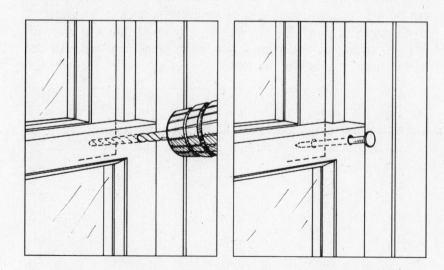

Begin by closing and latching the window. Then, drill a ¼-inch-diameter hole at a downward angle through each corner in the top of the lower sash and halfway into the bottom board in the upper sash. Simply by slipping a 10d common nail into each hole, you can effectively pin the two sashes together, making it impossible for a burglar to raise or lower either. By drilling each hole slightly shorter than the length of the nail, you can remove the nail by grasping the protruding head. And if the curtains don't cover the nail heads, paint them the same color as the window.

If you want to keep a window open at night for ventilation but still pinned for protection, raise the lower sash approximately 5 inches. Using each hole in the lower sash as a guide, drill a second hole in the stationary upper sash. This way, you can open the window at night and still sleep soundly with the two sashes pinned securely.

No one likes to think that bars on the windows are necessary, but in some neighborhoods the sound of breaking glass may not arouse anyone. Bars should be considered as a last resort, since they can turn a room into a locked cell during a fire. Many communities have fire laws regulating the installation of bars on windows, so your first step should be to contact the local building permits department.

If you must take this extra precaution and have received permission, consider having grilles custom-made to match the style of your home. Basement windows that are not readily visible can be secured by iron bars aligned with the window muntins. If there are no muntins, the bars can be installed to create the effect of small panes of glass. As always, bear in mind that the bars are only as strong as the screws that hold them in place and the frames on which they're mounted.

TIP: Storm windows may discourage amateur burglars, who are less inclined to break two panes of glass.

# #50
# Learn how to choose
# a contractor.

While we would all like to think that every home improvement project is within the scope of our abilities, the simple fact is that even if we did have all the necessary skills, most of us do not have the time to undertake and complete each and every project. Failing to recognize this can mean that our houses—and our relationships with the other people living in them—can suffer the consequences.

Delaying important gutter work, for instance, could mean that when you do finally rent an extension ladder and make it to the roof, you discover that what could have been a simple cleaning last year has turned into an extensive soffit repair and replacement project this year. Some projects simply cannot wait another year or even another week. As a homeowner, you have to recognize which projects need immediate attention and which can wait a few more weeks or months. Those that can't wait have to be placed at the top of your priority list. And if your job or your family commitments are going to prohibit you from solving those problems right away, you had better start thinking about hiring help.

Before heading for the Yellow Pages, however, consider one of the most underutilized work forces in America: college students. If you have access to college students, you have access to bright, energetic, intelligent, strong, and *hungry* workers. A simple note tacked to the bulletin board in the student center can bring dozens of calls.

> Wanted: Energetic, self-directed student to help with lawn work, gutter cleaning, and exterior scraping and painting. Flexible hours. Must have own transportation. $6 hour. 555-1111.

Unlike a contractor or a professional craftsperson, a college student must be supervised. Depending on the project, this may mean that you drop by the house on your lunch hour or that the two of you work side by side on your day off. It also requires that you or the student knows what needs to be done. College students learn quickly. A few minutes of instruction on removing wallpaper, painting a ceiling, or buffing a floor may keep them busy the remainder of the day. Stopping by or calling every hour or so to make sure that they understand your directions and to provide a few tips to improve their efficiency ensures the success of the project.

When a project looms larger than your skills and those of the entire student body, though, it's time to call in a professional.

## Contractor or Craftsperson?

A contractor is an individual who organizes, arranges, and sees to it that the work you need to have done is done. On a small project, the contractor or the crew may handle all the work themselves. On a large project, such as a kitchen remodeling or an addition to your home, the contractor hires other specialized firms or craftspersons, such as electricians, plumbers, and carpenters, to complete each phase of the project at the proper time and in the proper order. At this level, a contractor may never pick up a hammer or lift a sheet of plasterboard. Instead, he or she spends his time making sure that each subcontractor arrives on the appointed day, does the required work properly, and completes that work on schedule. In addition, he orders materials, arranges for required permits and inspections, pays the bills, and in short, sees to it that your plans are completed.

A craftsperson generally specializes in one particular line of work, such as plastering, carpentry, painting, or plumbing. He or she often works both for contractors and homeowners who elect not to hire the services of a contractor.

No law requires that you hire a contractor. Most of us have actually worked as contractors, albeit on a small scale, such as directing and supervising yard work. Since contractors charge for their services, you can save yourself thousands of dollars by acting as your own contractor. But this savings does not come free of charge. Being a contractor requires that you

1. remain extremely well organized through every stage of the project.

2. devote a good deal of time interviewing craftspersons and subcontractors, checking references, obtaining bids, and comparing quotes.

3. devote time to making sure that each craftsperson is scheduled in the proper order. Having the plasterboard crew cover the walls before the electrician has run a new line to the built-in oven is going to result in flared tempers and a sagging budget.

4. get craftspersons to start and finish their work on time. Keeping everyone on schedule—and rearranging schedules when someone falls behind—is the toughest aspect of supervising.

5. inspect the work yourself and arrange for the required local permits and inspections at the appropriate times. Generally, inspectors are tough on do-it-yourselfers, who may not be familiar with the appropriate building codes. If you let that insistent plasterboard crew cover up those walls before the new wiring has been approved, you can expect to hear the inspector bellow, "Tear it down and let me see it!"

The list goes on and on. If you work at home, you have taken the first step toward being your own contractor—the easiest step. The rest gets tougher. If you don't work at home but want to act as your own contractor on a large project, such as a kitchen remodeling, you won't be courting disaster, you'll be marrying it. Play it safe. Hire a contractor for major projects. A good one can actually save you time, money, and your relationship with your family.

### Scam Artists

Scam artists prey on homeowners who don't have the skills to undertake their own home improvement projects, the money to pay a qualified professional, or the time to do it themselves. These fly-by-night operators literally cruise the streets searching for the perfect house and homeowner to swoop down upon. When they do, they rely on impulse buying, hoping that you can be lured into making a quick decision without checking their references, asking for a second opinion, or getting additional bids.

Among the repairs and improvements that lend themselves well to unscrupulous contractors are driveway coatings, radon testing, insulating, waterproofing, tree trimming, and painting. But there is no field scam artists won't try and no sales technique too treacherous for them to attempt. An astute homeowner can easily spot fly-by-night contractors simply by asking a few key questions and watching for telltale clues.

Scam artists generally show up on your doorstep unannounced, often with the line "We just finished a job in your neighborhood and have some extra time (or material). We can save you a lot of money if we can use it on your (fill in the blank)." This may be true, so simply ask for the name and address of the homeowners they've been working for, and if they would mind waiting while you call them. Scam artists immediately get nervous and may bolt, while honest operators are pleased to provide you with that information. If they do, and if you're interested, make the call. They may be bluffing, hoping that you won't realize they gave you a bogus name.

Never be swayed by a sales pitch emphasizing how much money you can save. You can only save money if the work is necessary and if it's done properly. Ask for a free, written estimate, which you can then study for a few days. Then ask for their phone number, stating that you will call if you decide to have the work done. Don't volunteer any information, such as your phone number, when you're home, or any other facts that could prove valuable to someone who decides to burglarize your home. And never invite strangers who show up unannounced into your home to make an estimate.

If the so-called sales representatives or contractors ask for an advance, end the conversation. No money should ever be paid until the work is completed to your satisfaction. Even then, the payment should be by check, not cash. Many scam artists offer a discount with a cash advance, never planning to show up with a crew once the advance has been pocketed.

### The Selection Process

1. Decide what work needs to be done.

Despite what some high-pressure sales representatives may say, you know your house better than anyone else. Don't be intimidated into having work done that you had not planned. While you should be flexible in the event a worker discovers hidden damage, don't be talked into a new roof or a fresh coat of asphalt just because someone at your door has it to offer.

Your first step toward selecting a dependable contractor is to make a detailed list of the work you want to have done.

2. Turn to the Yellow Pages.

Any firm that has been in business for more than a year has had the opportunity to place an advertisement in the Yellow Pages. While some fine, individual craftspersons may not advertise, relying instead on word of mouth, their numbers are dwindling. Without a personal recommendation from a friend of yours or one of their customers, it is difficult to distinguish an experienced craftsperson from an inexperienced one.

A Yellow Pages ad doesn't automatically signify quality work, but it can tell you how long a firm has been in business, its location, the names of its owners, professional organizations to which they belong, and whether or not they're licensed and insured.

But just as you've learned not to judge a book by its cover, don't pick or reject a contractor or craftsperson by the size of an ad.

3. Ask friends, business associates, and neighbors for recommendations.

Most homeowners face projects that often require professional assistance: roofing, painting, electrical upgrading, plumbing repairs, and so on. If you spread the word around your office or neighborhood that you're looking for a reliable plumber or roofer, recommendations and warnings will soon be coming in. Homeowners like to look out for one another and gladly share names, phone numbers, and personal experiences. The biggest mistake most homeowners make is *not asking*.

4. Begin calling contractors or craftspersons to set up appointments.

At this stage, you should have the names of a half dozen or so contractors or craftspersons who have been recommended to you. The Yellow Pages ads may have added a few more to your list. To begin paring down your list to a more manageable number, call each firm and, after explaining the work you want to have done, ask

- if they're interested in your project.
- where on their calendar it would fall.
- if they can provide three references for whom they have done similar work.
- the type of insurance they carry and who their agent is.
- if they would be willing to come to your home to prepare either an estimate (an approximate cost) or a bid (a firm quote).

Whether you receive estimates or bids from contractors or craftspersons is going to depend on the nature of the work and how specific you've been in your list. If you're vague or indecisive ("We think we might want something done with our cabinets."), you can expect to receive only an estimate or an approximate cost. If you're specific ("We want the wallpaper in the dining room removed, the holes and cracks repaired, and this particular wallpaper hung"), you will be more likely to get a firm bid to which the contractor or craftsperson will abide, provided you don't change your mind later.

At this point, the contractors or craftspersons cannot tell you how long the project will take or how much it will cost, so don't bother asking. Listen as much to their tone of voice as you do to their answers. If you find them impolite, uninterested, pushy, or rude, simply close the conversation by stating that you will call them back if you decide to set up an appointment. If two or three firms respond to you in the same manner, you had better reevaluate your own manner. Continue calling until you've set up appointments for estimates with at least three different firms.

5. Check each firm's references.

Rather than wait until after the contractors or craftspersons have arrived, begin calling the references they provided over the phone. In talking to one former customer, a friend of mine discovered that the family was pleased with the work, but annoyed that the crew smoked the entire time, filling their house with cigarette smoke. In addition, the crew did not clean up when they were finished. When the contractor arrived for the appointment, my friend was prepared to stipulate that the crew not smoke in her home and that complete cleanup be included in the work. The contractor had no problem with her requests.

You also should contact the regional Better Business Bureau

to inquire whether or not anyone has lodged complaints against the firms you are considering. Also check with local permits or inspections departments to learn of any licenses, bonds, or insurance required of contractors or craftspersons. Ask about the firm's insurance status. If the contractor is not insured, you may be liable for any injuries that occur on your property.

6. Meet with each contractor or craftsperson and review your project plan.

It helps if you type a copy of your project plan to give to each contractor or craftsperson before you begin your tour. Explain what you would like to have done, but don't dominate the conversation. Listen closely to any suggestions and take good notes. If you have any questions about materials ("What thickness of plasterboard do you use?") or techniques ("How are you going to remove the old bathtub?"), ask them.

Depending on the complexity of your project, the contractor or craftsperson may be able to provide you with an estimate or bid while in your house. If not, ask when it will be mailed. As a professional courtesy, set a date by which you will let them know whether or not you have selected them to do your work. Don't simply call the firm that you choose, hoping that the other two will soon figure out that they finished second and third. You can quickly earn a reputation among contractors and craftspersons as being someone who asks for estimates, but never bothers to call back with your decision. Before long, you'll be the one being stood up.

7. Draw up a simple contract.

No one likes contracts. No one, that is, except people who have been burned by verbal agreements, miscommunication, delayed completions, and shoddy workmanship.

You don't need an attorney to draw up a simple, but effective agreement between you and your contractor. Most contractors, in fact, have a form that they use, since they can be burned as easily as homeowners. Obviously, the larger the project, the more pressing the need is for a contract that spells out each party's responsibilities.

Most contracts between homeowners and contractors include the following:

- a specific description of the work to be performed
- a materials list, including, if pertinent, types of wood, color of paint, brand of appliance, suppliers, and so on
- the cost of the project, including the contractor's fee, building permits, and so on
- a payment schedule
- permits required by law
- responsibility for cleanup
- insurance, licenses, or bonds
- starting date
- completion date
- any work that the homeowner is going to undertake
- a change order clause, prohibiting changes in the contract by either party unless approved in writing by both parties.

Most contractors remain in business by being honest and dependable, so don't be left feeling like a lamb amid the wolves. By planning your work, doing your research, and keeping the lines of communication open, you can expect nothing but satisfaction with your project and your contractor.

# GLOSSARY

**alligatoring**—a sign of deterioration in paint or varnish, characterized by scores of cracks that penetrate to the wood.

**backsaw**—a short, stiff saw with fine teeth, often used in a miter box to cut trim.

**baluster**—the spindles, round or square, in a railing.

**bridging**—a board installed between two joists to provide additional stabilization.

**bungalow siding**—a beveled board used for siding, generally wider than 8 inches and thicker than clapboards.

**capital**—the cap, usually square, on a column. It is designed to protect the end grain of the column and to distribute the force over a larger area than the column alone could cover.

**carriage**—the enclosed, nonvisible, weight-bearing boards in stairway construction.

**casing**—the visible framework around a window or door.

**cat's paw**—carpenter's tool for removing nails.

**checking**—see *crazing*.

**circuit breaker**—a toggle switch installed on an electrical line in a panel box, designed to open ("trip") if the wires attempt to carry more power than they are capable of handling without overheating.

**clapboard**—a beveled board used for siding, generally less than 8 inches wide.

**colonial siding**—a beveled board used for siding, generally wider than 8 inches and thicker than clapboards.

**consolidant**—a wood hardener.

**cornice**—the overhang beneath the roof consisting of a fascia board and soffit.

**crawl space**—the unfinished area under a house, usually a dirt floor.

**crazing**—hundreds of tiny cracks in the surface of a finish (also called *checking*).

**double-hung window**—a window with two movable sashes.

**drop siding**—see *novelty siding*.

**drying oil**—an oil that dries when it comes in contact with oxygen. Most common examples are linseed oil and tung oil. See also *spontaneous combustion.*

**dry rot**—a misleading term for decay caused by moisture. Only in its final stage of decay is the wood dry; the cause of the decay is moisture, not dry air.

**dutchman**—a wooden patch carefully hand-cut, shaped, and sanded to fit the damaged area.

**efflorescence**—salts that are dissolved by water, transported into or through the brick, then deposited either in the brick or on the outside of the brick when the water evaporates. Efflorescence on the outside of a brick wall is not harmful, but it does signal the presence of water behind or within the wall.

**fascia**—a flat board on the outside of the cornice.

**flashing**—the material, often metal, asphalt, or rubber, that bridges the gap between the roofing material and protrusions on the roof, such as a chimney, vent pipe, or dormer.

**frass**—a fine sawdust created by wood-boring insects.

**fungus (plural: fungi)**—airborne organism that feeds on dead or living matter; includes mold and mildew.

**fuse**—an inexpensive electrical device located inside a panel box and designed to fail ("blow") when the wires are overloaded and in danger of overheating.

**galvanized**—coated with zinc to prevent rusting.

**joist**—a large board, often 2 by 10 inches, placed on edge and generally spaced 16 inches apart across beams to support the flooring.

**lap siding**—another term for clapboards.

**membrane, asphalt**—an asphalt-coated mesh available on rolls and used in conjunction with roof patching material to repair holes and cracks in flashing or roofing.

**mullion**—a vertical divider in a door or window.

**novelty siding**—clapboards with special patterns, including *rustic, cove rustic,* and *drop.* Generally nonbeveled and often applied directly to the studs in garage and outbuilding construction.

**oakum**—a ropelike material that is saturated with tar to form a packing material for large gaps and seams.

**oxidation**—in wood finishing, the process of drying by combining with oxygen, as opposed to evaporation. Oxidation produces heat that, if not released, can cause a fire through spontaneous combustion.

**pitch**—the slope of a roof or floor.

**plinth**—the base, generally square, beneath a column. It is intended to distribute the weight transferred from a load through the column to a larger area than the column alone could cover.

**repoint, repointing**—to repair a mortar joint by the addition of new mortar (also called *tuck-pointing*).

**riser**—the vertical component of a set of stairs, set against the stringer at a right angle to the tread. The riser is often omitted in rough construction, such as found in basements and outbuildings.

**rising damp**—the invasion of moisture into a home through the foundation or floor of the basement.

**sash**—a single window frame containing one or several panes.

**shake**—a thick wooden shingle.

**sheathing**—boards or sheets of plywood or particleboard nailed to the studs of a structure to provide a surface for the siding.

**sister**—a board attached to a joist, post, or beam to provide additional strength.

**soffit**—the underside of a cornice.

**spontaneous combustion**—a fire started in a confined area where the heat produced by the oxidation of a drying oil cannot dissipate, but instead builds up until the article bursts into flame.

**stringer**—generally a 2-by-12-inch or similar-sized board notched to accommodate the treads and risers in stair construction.

**studs**—a common name for the vertical framing of a wall; usually two-by-fours or two-by-sixes.

**trap**—a special plumbing fitting, often shaped like the letter *U*, beneath a sink, tub, or shower that holds water to prevent dangerous sewer gases from entering the room.

**tread**—the horizontal component of a set of stairs; the actual step.

**trisodium phosphate**—a powdery chemical detergent dissolved in water. Heavy concentrations can remove certain paints and clear finishes.

**tuck-point, tuck-pointing**—the process in which loose mortar between bricks, concrete blocks, or stones is removed and replaced with fresh mortar (also called *repointing*).

**vapor barrier**—a sheet of plastic laid on the ground or attached to the wall framing to inhibit the passage of moisture.

**water preservative**—any solution that, when absorbed by wood, repels water. Often contains toxic chemicals.

**water repellent**—any solution that, when absorbed by wood, repels water. Usually includes a liquid wax.

**weatherboard**—similar to clapboards, but often nonbeveled.

# INDEX

## ABOUT THE AUTHOR

Bruce Johnson and his wife, Lydia Jeffries, live with their two sons, Eric and Blake, in a 1914 Arts and Crafts home in Asheville, North Carolina. Johnson is the author of *The Weekend Refinisher* and *The Wood Finisher*. He is also a contributing editor and columnist for *Country Living* magazine. His newspaper column, "Knock On Wood," has appeared since 1979. In addition to his writing, Johnson hosts the national Arts and Crafts Conference and Antiques Show each February at the historic Grove Park Inn overlooking Asheville.